The Barilla Collection
of Modern Art

Fondazione Magnani Rocca
Corte di Mamiano
Traversetolo, Parma
18 April - 28 November 1993
Open 10 am to 5 pm
Tuesday through Sunday

Graphic design by
Pierluigi Cerri
and Ginette Caron

Translation by
Pamela Cowdery

Photographs by
Giovanni Amoretti, Parma.
For the painting by Paolo Vallorz
Stefano Zardini, Cortina d'Ampezzo

Front cover:
Umberto Boccioni,
Il romanzo di una cucitrice
1908

Back cover:
Giacomo Manzù
San Giorgio
1964

Works by:
Marc Chagall, Leonardo Cremonini,
Giorgio de Chirico, Filippo de Pisis,
Nicolas de Staël, Jean Dubuffet,
James Ensor, Max Ernst, Sam Francis,
Franco Gentilini, Fernand Léger,
Mino Maccari, René Magritte,
Marino Marini, Giorgio Morandi,
Zoran Music, Constant Permeke,
Pablo Picasso, Jean-Paul Riopelle,
Alberto Savinio, Ruggero Savinio,
Chaïm Soutine, Graham Sutherland

The Barilla Collection
of Modern Art

The Barilla Family

Roberto Tassi, curator
with the collaboration of
Simona Pizzetti and
Giorgio Soavi

Organizing Committee:

Attilio Bertolucci
Enzo Biagi
Giorgio Cusatelli
Antonio Marchi
Indro Montanelli
Riccardo Muti
Giorgio Soavi
Roberto Tassi

Contributing authors:

Maria Teresa Benedetti
Ester Coen
Leonardo Cremonini
Maurizio Fagiolo dell'Arco
Piero Guccione
Simona Pizzetti
Eugenio Riccòmini
Ruggero Savinio
Roberto Tassi
Paolo Vallorz
Pia Vivarelli
Claudio Zambianchi

Fondazione Magnani Rocca
Alberto Galaverni, President

We would like to thank the following
individuals for their help and collaboration:

Fulvio Abbate, Rome;
Archivio Arte Contemporanea, Associazione
Crispolti, Rome, in particular Enrico
Crispolti, Carlo Alberto Bucci, Manuela
Crescentini, Piero Valducci;
Archivio Lucio Fontana, Milan;
Mario Ceroli, Rome;
Elisabetta Cristallini, Rome;
Giuliano de Marsanich, Rome;
Barbara Drudi, Archivio Afro, Rome;
Paola Forni, Bologna;
Galerie Bayeler, Basel;
Galleria Contini, Venice-Cortina d'Ampezzo;
Galleria de Foscherari, Bologna;
Augusto Garau, Milan;
Annie Gnoli de Garrou, Rome;
Carlo Guarienti, Rome;
Marta Melotti, Milan;
Ines Millesimi, Rome;
Franco Paglia, Parma;
Lorenza Trucchi, Rome;
Paolo Vallorz, Paris;
Livia Velani, Galleria Nazionale d'Arte
Moderna, Rome;
Roberta Visco, Rome;
Klaus Wolbert, Director, Institut
Mathildenhohe, Darmstadt

Public Relations Office
Giovanna Pesci for
Coop. Eclisse, Bologna

Organizational Secretary
Stefano Roffi

Table of Contents

Having reached the age of eighty,
I asked myself whom I should say «thank
you» to. My lucky star, of course,
and heaven; my family, the people
with whom I spent a happy youth and
my city where I have worked for such
a long time, overcoming difficult periods
but always in an atmosphere of respect
and civility.
This exhibition offers the collection of
works that has brightened almost forty
years of my life, and which today
I would like to be a token of thanks to
the people of this city, my beloved Parma.

Pietro Barilla

Giorgio Soavi

I would not say that it was only his *joie de vivre* that led to his wealth and success. But his sense of adventure, yes. Pietro Barilla has always been so ready to live, to even throw himself into the breach with enthusiasm, that he had to accomplish something special. Like when he realized he could not continue without the family business which, in a moment of fear, he had given up. In those months he discovered he was living in a different physiological state, like an organism with incompatible cells: he was no longer himself and, to get back his sense of self, he engaged in a strenuous battle to buy back what he had sold to the Americans.

I met him by chance in Basel, all alone, and, at the bar of the International Art Fair, surrounded by endless lists of paintings, drawings and sculptures which nonetheless remain at the top of his list of major passions, he related what had happened to him recently. A drama. He was going through the most atrocious and intense moments of his existence. The most difficult. He told me he was about to buy back something that bore his name. Would he succeed? Perhaps he was already close, but he did not say very much for fear of overstating things. He, who by nature uses overstatement, or enthusiasm, as a benevolent and necessary medicine.

I remember that the first Christmas presents I saw appear before the eyes of Pietro and his wife, Marilena, were a small painting by Magritte and another by Max Ernst. Seeing them again today, tidy and lined up by Roberto Tassi for this exhibition at the Magnani Rocca Foundation, I realize almost twenty years have passed since they were acquired and I also see that, creativity and poetics aside, the color blue, the color of the sky, dominates in the two paintings. In the former as well as in the latter there is a transparent light that later was swept away by quite different masters with equally different strengths. But that light and luminous color at the beginning of the adventure remains the symbol that offers me today a way to remember an extraordinary man who had those paintings in Turin.

We had gone to Turin to look at paintings and the man who sold them was Mario Tazzoli. He only handled modern art and I am convinced that his choices were, unquestionably, something more than the selections of a man who was avid for refinement as well as extremely demanding, but rather those destined to make up, in an ideal way, an extraordinary small museum of contemporary art. In recalling the paintings gathered by Mario Tazzoli, the perfection of the Oscar Reinhardt Collection at Winterthur comes to mind. I do not know why at that time Pietro Barilla and I myself, there to give him a hand, did not grasp that all we would have had to have done in order to build up a formidable collection of works of art of our own day, was to have said to Tazzoli, «Fine, my friend. I'll take everything immediately.» This decision was not made and perhaps never even dreamed of. But of that period I also recall that when I spoke to Alberto Giacometti about one of his Turin shows of drawings, paintings and sculpture which Tazzoli himself, aided by the extraordinary and unforgettable Luigi Carluccio, put together in his Galleria Galatea, Giacometti confessed, dumbfounded, that no private individual, with the exception of Pierre Matisse, had ever succeeded in bringing together so many works of such high quality.

But the job of being a wealthy man is also a difficult one. And something should be said right off: not everyone likes rich people. It can also happen that wealthy people themselves find each other detestable. But the wealthy exist and the fact remains that they are almost certainly self-absorbed, or better: rich. Not lovable.

Except one. I can say it calmly and serenely because I have known my man for at least thirty years. With him I have skied, gone up and down hills and valleys at the sea and in the mountains, wolfed down chunks of bread and cake or bars of chocolate and seen arrive at his home entire truckloads of supplies for his larders. But I have also seen him sick many times, sick and operated on in many clinics and I have always come away from those little torture chambers more heartened than when I had entered and seated myself on the edge of a chair to ask him, in a subdued tone: «How's it going?» How should it have been going? Do you ask an oak tree how things are going? Of course. Because the oak has seen and lived through many battles, has absorbed extremely hard blows and finally, records events in the proper way: accepting storms of rain and lightning while waiting to dry its leaves and branches, ready and grand, or better, grandiose, primed for adventure as always. Of course one might also happen to be present at those times in which the emotion of staying with a sick person offers moments of terror and raises chills up and down your spine. But the oak, when it understood you were worried about it, was there ready to reassure you. And when I left I was more tranquil, perhaps more so than he, because if a sick person is like this, you understand that the oak has divulged something extraordinary and has given you courage since you, healthy, had less of it. Good, I thought on my way home, now I know what I must do: I must have faith in my profession, work with all my strength, choose the best people and work with them. I have no doubts.

When Pietro has five minutes free he buys a painting. One, or even two, because his human tissue is run through by an electric current called painting. Not bread and butter or bread and chocolate, but bread and paintings. He pursues them and they are his.

But this little profile would not be complete if I did not tell about his meeting with the sculptor, Manzù. It was clear that he liked his sculptures very much and would buy them at the agreed price. But that first time Pietro did something which became famous and flooded with joy even the most self-centered and snobbish collectors. Having paid for the sculptures, he had shipped to the famous sculptor's address a number of cases of products, not just spaghetti and cookies, but prosciutto, culatello, coppa and salami and dried mushrooms from the Taro Valley because Pietro is an enthusiastic admirer of the resources and creations of his home territory. Then, to round things out, he added some Parmesan cheese, spicy preserved fruits, tins of anchovies and a strange tube of tomato-vegetable paste called «Ortolina». Ortolina seems like a name invented for a little girl living in a comic book or fairy tale invented by a writer who passes his life alongside the hearth of the Brothers Grimm, or perhaps the name of a little match girl who sells vegetables. For years, I myself encountered Ortolina in Christmas baskets, and all this was the accompaniment, and what accompanied, the works of art Pietro had taken it into his head to have. In the large room of his own house, and at a time of year completely bereft of holidays, the sculptor Manzù, awestruck by such bounty, watched his wife open with joy and a completely unexpected sense of greediness all those packages containing everything under the sun and which for them was a gift. Works of art are paid for, of course, while those crates were something more, a true gift.

For some years the eyes of our man have seen the world around him with some difficulty. For someone who loves paintings this is certainly not a nice present, but Pietro goes ahead undeterred as if he could perfectly intuit everything there was to see. And he comports himself not as a visionary, but as one who knows what he sees. I think he realizes how things are and, cognizant of the specks of light that whistle through people and objects around him, he perceives the quality and truth at the core of a piece of painted canvas as if auscultating a patient according to age-old remedies. He performs a careful examination of what he sees and explores the inner mysteries that exist between us and things. And in the meantime he retains his sense of enthusiasm. He has explained to me well what he can see. Starting from the ground he encounters a form — and therefore a stature — which immediately gives him a certain security. This form — person or painting — takes on consistency, color and, little by little, becomes more perceptible. With a large lens he approaches the canvas he likes and starts to explore the content of that wrapping that he, listening to his own intuition, is able to define. It is not much, but neither is it nothing. Plus, in addition to that oak-like strength of his, he has another that the ophthalmologists have given him, that is, that his eyesight will not get worse. For an optimist like him, this is sensational news. In fact, I am convinced that with this certainty in hand, he is able to graze over ideal perfection: possessing the paintings he likes. It seems a dream, but this is the way he has had almost all of them.

Introduction

Roberto Tassi

Towards the end of 1957, in the fourth issue of a magazine published in Parma called *Palatina*, Pietro Barilla saw a «still life» by Morandi beautifully reproduced in full-color. It had just recently been painted and had been chosen by the painter himself for the publication. It displayed the usual, yet brand-new, gathering of objects very different from each other, united only by the stupendous tonal patina that finished in light shadow on the delicate violet of the table, but revivified in this case by a brighter shine of colors on the unrecognizable objects in the background, boxes or whatever they were. Barilla was enchanted; I doubt if he asked himself why, but he wanted to have that painting. His friend, Valerio Zurlini, accompanied him to the Galleria del Milione owned by Gino Ghiringhelli. The painting was bought, along with a small «cardinal» by Manzù. Because, having seen that reduced-size, one could even say table-top, sculpture, and having been drawn to touch and caress it, for the first time he had the impression of also being very attracted to this other art form, companion to and the opposite of painting, usually less loved and less well-known and -understood.

The fact that sculpture must be touched, that it asks or draws one to touch it, is something that usually does not enter into a critical discourse and could almost seem «naive.» Instead it is a profound point which, if examined in depth (and this is not the right moment), could say much about its essence and its diversity from painting, the untouchable art, that instead requires a certain distance and motionless contemplation. This double acquisition was the first act in the story leading to this exhibition I am about to relate. Its two-fold nature is its first distinguishing feature. In fact, among those who surround themselves with works of art, it is rare to find a similar love for painting and sculpture. It is not easy, consequently, to encounter a collection in which, as in this one, sculpture plays such an important role.

Another feature I would like to clarify here so that it may be understood in its deepest implications, is that the first work, the one which began the collection, came from the pages of *Palatina*. Something must be pointed out about this magazine, a modest claim made since during its life-time, from 1957 to 1966, it was accused of being formal, superficial and, above all, of representing a type of «right-wing» culture enclosed between the «Quaderni piacentini» on one side and that movement which went by the name of «Gruppo 63» on the other. There is certainly no need to rekindle this old debate, but I just want to draw attention to the authors the magazine firmly believed in and thus published — Carlo Emilio Gadda, Attilio Bertolucci, Pier Paolo Pasolini, Alberto Arbasino, Beppe Fenoglio, Antonio Delfini, Silvio D'Arzo, Giovanni Testori, Fellini of the *Dolce Vita* — and note how today they have all been appraised and reappraised to the point of being included among the best. It must be recognized that if the choice of these authors was completely based, as they say, on quality, i.e., on poetry, for them and the others appearing in the pages of the magazine, it represented an editorial policy that did not take the avantgarde much into account. If anything it ran parallel with it. It did not negate it, but neither did it embrace it. It stayed still, watching. It was not «very new,» just new. As for the artistic aspect of the magazine, among others one can extract the names of Morandi, Soutine, Morlotti, Burri, Pollock and Wols: here the avantgarde was welcomed. Could it be called, to use a somewhat bold oxymoron, a moderate avantgarde? To its editors it seemed the true avantgarde, after its early exponents, of that passage from the Fifties to the Sixties: the Informal.

My dwelling on the *Palatina* is not without purpose. The magazine was in fact financed by Pietro Barilla. It was a purely cultural act, diametrically opposed to today's so-called sponsorships since the rule was that the name Barilla should never appear nor be raised in conjunction with the magazine. It was love (for Parma), not business. But there was something more: the magazine did not just furnish the image from which the collection took its origin, but also almost formed, even if in a partial and indirect way, fertile terrain for it. It influenced the choices a bit from the sidelines and probably unconsciously. It embraced the same climate, the same writings, the same discussions, that took place in Parma in a culture that was somewhat closed, aristo-cratic, specific to its own tradition and history and therefore more easily assimilable for those on the inside. A good number of these artists we also find in this exhibition: Morandi, Soutine, Morlotti and Burri. But *Palatina*, with basically Longhian roots, paid little or no attention to sculpture.

Love of sculpture is something specifically personal to Pietro Barilla. It is part, a fairly rare detail, of his wider interest in the figurative arts to which he is attracted instinctively with good intuition, pleasure and an outlook both far-reaching and deeply-rooted. Added to this is his tremendous respect for artists whom he sees as the true aristocracy. He is very clear about the concept that great managers and business-men are as ephemeral as life itself. They do and create things destined to come to an end, be surpassed or change into something else. The artist, on the other hand, creates definitive, immutable works and wherever these works appear, the artist is remem-bered and honored. These are simple ideas, but they reveal a lack of personal conceit, a balance of judgment and modesty difficult to find in an industrialist. To give up one's superiority in favor of the true superiority of art is not a normal action, but remains something of great human value. Even more so if, as in this case, it is done with an absolute feeling of truth.

Pietro Barilla said something very beautiful I believe is basic to him, his relationship with others, his way of working and his passion for art: «If I step outside the truth, I am lost.» I believe this must have created many problems and caused him much pain, yet it is not the expression of a rule to live by, but rather the verification of a way of life. Like Ariadne's thread, not only has it guided him through the labyrinth of relationships and business dealings, but also through the labyrinth of the artistic field giving him a way to orient himself and make choices. In these choices he has had a number of advisors, above all Giorgio Soavi, but at base he has never forgotten this fundamental truth that has served as a beacon to accept or refuse by. With those advisors (always friends), and with artists as well as art dealers, Pietro has need of direct, human and sincere relationships. Of this last group, it is useful to name at least two since, above and beyond their role of dealer, they also played that of initiator, introducing him into the secrets and miracles of contemporary art, thus contributing to the creation of the collection's foundations: they are Mario Tazzoli and Romeo Toninelli, cultured, elect connoisseurs, the former practically infallible. With the artists, when admiration and respect bonded into friendship, enthusiasm was born. This happened with Marino, Manzù, Mattioli and Morlotti and explains the presence of large numbers of their works in the collection.

There is another profound aspect of Pietro Barilla's personality that should be mentioned in order to understand everything a bit better: the firm's structure, the art collection, the rapport between the firm and the works of art and his various acts of support for cultural initiatives. It is a subtle aspect, one that is also difficult to articulate and comprehend in all its hidden facets, and not easily accepted in its entirety by the almost always suspicious judgment of the vast majority. It is a deep-seated drive, innate and uncontrolled in its enthusiasm for other people: openness, trust, gratitude, a desire to do something, small or large depending on the occasion, something useful, favorable, demonstrative for others, for society in general and more particularly for his beloved city, Parma.

In an interview covering various themes, having arrived at a question concerning truth, Pietro Barilla recalled his wartime experience and the thought of death predominant in war: «Confronted by the end of life, I thought that the truth lay in good and evil,» and he stated that in the presence of these absolute alternatives, his tendency and his aspiration was to dedicate his life to the good of others. In moments when we are stripped bare, basic drives are uncovered, but then life undertakes to cover them up again, to confuse, complicate and even eliminate them. With the war over, returning to his job in industry, those tendencies disappeared and everything returned to normal, even if, at base, there remained a root which then nourished and influenced his actions, gestures, decisions and behavior. But industry was what had the upper hand in those difficult situations of innovation and post-war reconstruction; he poured all his strength, ideas and desires into it.

So that it not appear that we want to dwell too much on subjective considerations, we hasten to say how much of his life has been dedicated to the firm starting from that moment. The firm took on absolute pre-eminence. In the same interview cited above he also said: «Barilla is my story, it is my whole life; it is almost the blood that flows in my veins.» Total dedication to industry, development, truth and also the beauty of industry. For various personal as well as objective reasons, in 1971, a year that for Pietro Barilla remains ill-fated, the business was sold. Following enormous and very courageous efforts it was reacquired, and thinking back on this his comment is: «In 1979, regaining possession of the firm, my joy was unbounded.» Work and dedication to industry are also based on the idea of creativity: «To be the president of a large company requires love, passion and also a bit of poetry.» And always with the idea of respect for others and to accomplish something useful for all, as well as to create a relationship of mutual trust and mutual benefit with the city of Parma.

Pietro's declarations of love for Parma have been continual, always accompanied by the desire to have them reciprocated and with the almost obsessive intent of doing something for the city. All of his cultural initiatives are for Parma. Pietro: «Barilla owes Parma much: its growth is intimately linked to the growth of this city.» At the same time, nothing that he has done in any field has a provincial or local character, not the great work and enormous expansion of the company, nor the various acts of cultural support for many different initiatives. All of them have a European character, outlook and relationship. Parma and Europe: it is a very precise and natural fact solidly rooted in the tradition of the city itself. This concept is immediately reflected in the choice of works making up the collection, and also, therefore, in its overall character.

The point has now been reached in which the relationship between the company and the collection is sealed in a way I believe unique in all of Italian enterprise. Barilla relates that the idea came to him one time when he entered the Ciba offices in Basel. The vice-president, a man of culture, had hung a painted panel with a gold background and alongside it a painting by Picasso. This made a great impression on him and stimulated an idea already pre-existent but not well defined, that works of art would have to enter the business, or better, as he says, he would have to «transfer the spirit of art into the business.» These concepts matured and developed to the point of becoming almost an ideology and since, in the end, the experience was successful, the offices, corridors, meeting rooms and other parts of the firm have now become small museums extending outside into the various open spaces between one building and another where the large sculptures are placed. This fact has meant that many works have been bought over the years, not only masterpieces — even if these are not lacking — but also more normal works, yet all of them always rich with excellent qualities so that daily contact with them could be educational, even if in an unconsciously habitual way.

Very often the research of the works and artists is carried out by Pietro Barilla, also to satisfy his natural passion; he has not carried them out systematically, but across the free and meandering course of opportunities, trips and discoveries. The suggestions of specialists and writer friends are quite rightly taken into consideration, but in the end, what steers the way, almost always in a determining fashion and always with great discretion, is Pietro's taste. He has also made mistakes, but not many and later often corrected, and they became increasingly rare as his experience grew and his taste stronger and more refined. His taste, accompanied by an innate intuitive sense, had already manifested itself in a number of cultural initiatives undertaken parallely with his uninterrupted acquisition of works of art, initiatives taken both inside the firm as well as completely independent of it for the benefit of the city. Two episodes in the field of advertising should be mentioned. One is the choice, starting in 1952, of Erberto Carboni as graphic artist, a person who in Pietro's eyes had the two great advantages of being from Parma and being brilliant, and who in fact gave a creative imprint, extremely innovative, perfect and enduring, to the Barilla logo as well as to everything else. The other episode, to me even more subtly imaginative and cultural and even more courageous, was the series of television advertisements starring Mina. Desired by Pietro against the opinion of his advisors, and entrusted to director Valerio Zurlini, to this day they are very lovely and exert great charm, and for the years between 1965 and 1970 they were courageous and challenging. Mina exhibited unbridled bravura and creativity, García Lorca would have said she sang with *duende*, and delivered the advertising message with a voice that was sometimes persuasive, sometimes imperative and sometimes sensuous. Zurlini's skill came through in some almost-Surreal sequences in which only Mina's hands were seen; nervous, loving, delicate and feverish hands that brushed, caressed and encircled packages of pasta as if they were a man's body.

It is also useful to mention the thirty-three issues of *Palatina* with the cover design by Carlo Mattioli who employed the same refined elegance as in the one he had recently created for *Paragone*, as well as the volume of photographs of the city in which emerged the creative imagination of Carlo Bavagnoli, still manifest today on the occasion of its reprinting, and whose title, *Cara Parma*, came to Pietro Barilla spontaneously, prevailing, with its simple truth, over all other suggestions.

The choice of the works that make up the exhibition was made from a very extensive reservoir distributed throughout the firm's various buildings and both Pietro Barilla's home as well as those of his family. They were chosen from among the various works of art of varied techniques with different qualities and values that make up the overall fabric of the collection of which these exhibition works are the skeleton, its very flesh and blood. A sense of imbalance and preponderance in some cases was respected, and in others lightened or eliminated with the intention not only of imparting a certain style to the exhibition, but also of reproducing the taste, passions, predilections, relationships and instincts of the man who created the collection so that the exhibition would be the projection of a very personal story, of a life, and take on the illuminating truth of something experienced.

Because Pietro Barilla did not follow a pre-established plan throughout the entire thirty-five years of the search for and acquisition of the works of art, but only quite variable considerations such as his own inspiration, his own imagination, his own passions, the vicissitudes of fortune and chance meetings to bring together the various elements of the collection, one might think that the result could prove to be quite casual, if not chaotic. But faced with the expanse of the works chosen, one understands immediately that this feared chaos has taken on a sense of order and that within its expanse can be perceived various lines, tendencies or nuclei, that render it harmonious, precise and strong with tension and cultural rationality. Very likely arbitrariness does not exist, and the dark forces, impulses or intentions freely circulating within a person and in his unconscious, work in an ordered and resolute manner. Certain events mentioned in the beginning of this introduction are useful in the attempt to throw some light on these obscure aspects.

We now turn to some of the features of the collection, above all the decidedly unusual number of sculptures present. This is perhaps its most important and striking characteristic and it lends the collection a very particular tone and style. Sculpture is an extraordinarily beautiful art. It gives us a sense of presence, of body, of material and it emerges from the space with a power that draws us in. It is absolute and cumbersome at the same time, essence and weight, purity and plasticity and elusive overall, endlessly many-sided and yet fixed in its immobile pose. The collection ranges from the human aspect of Manzù to the music of Melotti, the dialectical essentiality of Pomodoro to the truth of Vangi, the archetypical sense of Marino to the ambiguity of Perez, and the epic proportion of Ceroli to the «stoniness» of Pietro Cascella. The taste for sculpture could indicate a tendency towards concreteness, but it also contains a desire for the ideal.

Another overall characteristic of the collection that touches on its style and its innermost sense is the absence of formalism. It is its most evident aspect and most avoided defect. Not to accept formalism means to negate mannerism, fashion, abstraction, and to possess the sense of the truth, the figure and the emotion embodied in the material, to pay attention not to what is exterior but to what is deep inside, to not fear fable and imagination, and to feel how much art can be a part of nature. It could seem contradictory to see many examples of Informal art gathered together in this collection. This was the only avantgarde tendency accepted, but it is also the avantgarde tendency which is less subject to formalistic results than any other. On the contrary, it is the only one, mid-way through the century in the 1950s, that founded an artistic renewal, especially in painting, without negating it, and modifying it from deep inside. Because of this foundation, it is also the most enduring as well as the true heir, or at least the continuation, of the avantgarde movement.

A third, consequent, characteristic of the collection is the exclusion of the neo-avantgarde tendencies, all those which, alongside or in contrast to the Informal, or attempting to supersede it, abounded in that decade and the ones that followed. The important thing to the person who assembled the collection was that the work remain painting and sculpture. It is not a restriction but rather, in addition to being a question of taste, a conception of art which is not even that moderate and more attentive and understanding of the existential than the intellectual sense.

But these characteristics, as well as some lesser ones, would not be sufficient to give an overall sense, tendency or unified shape to the works collected. And on the other hand, choices entrusted, as these were, to pleasure or momentary whim and sometimes at the very moment offered, in short, to free vagabondage within art's dominions, do not create rigid, rigorous or thematic collections prearranged around a single idea or purpose. So much the better, I believe. For my taste, freedom and variability are precious elements; in collections freely assembled one never finishes making discoveries, creating relationships, weaving plots, marveling, and making with great pleasure those leaps that history itself never would. As I have already said, arbitrariness does not dominate in this collection. One can identify various connecting threads and nuclei that give a sense to the entirety and show it to be not mechanical, but alive.

Before pointing out the most important thread, two very beautiful and rare works should be mentioned, works that indicate, in quite different ways, a keen sensitivity for having been chosen: the *Study for Garland Weavers* by Edward Burne-Jones and the *Mouvement de danse A* by Auguste Rodin. The former contains a refinement so delicate it immediately becomes poetry rhymed in a long-limbed meter broken only by the flowering of the roses and the golden splendor of the woman's head. The latter is like a knot made up of tensions, moving volumes, curved lines, parts in equilibrium and empty and circumscribed spaces, like a concentration of forces and dynamism compressed into the material and on the point of exploding. Together with the other six «dance movements» that accompanied it, but of which it is perhaps the most harmonically original, this sculpture shows how much plastic and dynamic energy its seventy-year-old sculptor still possessed. Placed as it is at the beginning of the collection, it is one of the first signs of a great, instinctive love for sculpture. The work by Ensor, *Coquillages et draperie bleue*, also remains a bit outside the various groupings and is one of the most bewitching examples of his still lifes. In fact, Claude Vignon calls it the most important and most representative of the year 1903. With its unusual and discordant composition, it accumulates secrets between the various objects — the pitcher, the basin and the numerous shells scattered on the table that are so alive with color sprayed with reds and pink as if still damp from the sea — and has descend, in order to conceal who knows what other mystery, a sumptuous drape of intense blue that unbalances, but at the same time encloses, the composition. Like all of Ensor's works, it is both natural and magic, rich with color and irony, crowded and free, so much so that, as we shall soon see, it also enters into the realm of fantastical painting.

But what seems to me to be the most important tendency — almost a central, sustaining area — is difficult to define since it appears to be made up of hidden and poetic relationships of distant references, but it acts as the very heart of the collection nonetheless. It comprises a style of painting that finds a basic expressive element in the *matière*, whether thickly congealed or applied lightly, and includes passion, feeling and sometimes even drama. A light that comes from deep inside, at times violent and almost always natural, impregnates the material and does not give rise to chiaroscuro since it also spreads into the shadows. It is a painterly style that does not know abstraction. It keeps its distance from it, just as the semblances of the world and the soul are removed from it. On the other hand, it knows the sinking of life and can reach the Informal since it finds in it a poetic that in some ways contrasts with the abstract. It often draws inspiration from nature to the point of touching on an extreme, modern naturalism that is, if you will, avantgarde. It works with form, breaking it up or corrupting it, making the edges vibrate, sometimes fusing it with a nearby form for a transfer of tones, light and colors, and sometimes dissolving it into the surrounding space. This tendency in painting had a number of artists and illustrious champions in Emilia and Lombardy, but also had its heirs in other parts of Europe.

It begins with the mythological, but also dramatically natural, landscape, *Prometheus*, by Böcklin, the exhibition's great opening work, from which many things proceed, but also recognizes Courbet, its even earlier and true pioneer, who is not represented in the collection for purely external reasons. It evolves through the works of Soutine, Morandi, Permeke, de Staël, Morlotti and Burri. It is not insignificant that paintings by artists such as Böcklin, Soutine, Permeke and de Staël, rarely, or extremely rarely, found in either public or private collections in Italy, are found here.

Here, the work by Böcklin is mysterious and supreme with Nordic spirit and Mediterranean imagery, a Dyonisiac work that could form the origins for fantastical and naturalistic art. Soutine has a landscape in which, during the last, terrible year of his life, he was able to make flow a deep and tender lyricism that restrains but does not cancel out the basic, desperate agitation of its form and spirit. Morandi appears with six works, three of which landscapes imbued with his purest poetic sense. The two Permekes, *Marine* and *Winderlandschaft*, reveal an intense naturalistic expressionism with lights, layers, clouds and sadness of a Nordic stamp, quite correct in this context and a clear example of it. On the other hand, *Ciel à Honfleur* by de Staël is one of the artist's most moving and lyrical paintings and seems to stand at the very core of his work, summing it up in an infinite, celestial light, culminating in a point in which the concepts of abstraction and naturalness of form, space and figure, almost no longer have any place. Morlotti is represented by a group of paintings belonging primarily to that period between 1955 and 1959 when he reached the high point of a Panic and absolutely new naturalistic style in which the material and color seem distorted by passion. Burri's *Rosso plastica 3* is a magical and powerful drama, an innovation so new and unexpected as to create deeply emotional poetry removed from any guidelines. It fits well into this context, even if at its extreme, since, like all of the other works named, it touches on the areas of existence, sometimes dark, sometimes light, but always with a passion and deep involvement. This is also true for Morandi's landscapes which, with all their purity and apparent distance, nonetheless almost physically adhere to our most deeply-stirred emotions. Here we should also mention, since it is part of this group, the acquisition of a beautiful painting by Mafai, *Fiori* done in 1954, that unfortunately cannot be exhibited since it is no longer part of the collection.

Other artists are found at the margins, on the sidelines, or near-by this contextual group, and even if in different ways, they are nonetheless a part of it. They are primarily Informal painters and works: a refined example of the more subtle Dubuffet as «materialogist;» an airy Sam Francis at his best; two dense paintings by Alfredo Chighine, sometimes delicate and sometimes vivid, but always poetic; Tancredi's *Strarococò no. 2*, one of the most important paintings by this extroverted and creative artist, a tangled, whirring, interminable work, reminiscent of Pollock with Venetian color and light; plus Riopelle and Afro. On the other hand, Mattioli, with his original style, sits apart, between the figurative and informal, nature and *matière*, refinement and sentiment, just like Goliardo Padova with his spontaneous inspiration of the Po Valley.

Even more removed, but not completely extraneous or opposed to this context, are two great painters with their livelier attention to reality, the pair that dominated English art in this century: Sutherland and Bacon. Sutherland is present with a *Standing Form*, like an idol coming from the «origins of the earth,» a metaphor located between the barbaric and refined of an erect human and vegetable body that the curtain in the background encloses in an aura of sacredness, as well as with one of his «articulated forms» of mechanical and tree-like limbs immersed in woodland foliage like a mysterious vessel voyaging within a natural setting that is both brand-new and ancient. Bacon is represented with *Two Americans*, one of his first works, in which the simple structure of the space, the lack of lament, the dark everydayness of the color and the erasure of the faces lend a sense of a repressed and infinitely sad drama. And finally, isolated because of his delicate and tragic poetry, Zoran Music.

Another tendency, completely different from the first but developing alongside it throughout the entire exhibition, is that of the fantastical. It starts from the other aspect of Böcklin's *Prometheus*, pauses briefly over the pulsating work *Coquillages et draperie bleue* by Ensor, and then finds a great open stretch of powerful imagination and invention of poetic and ironic height in the four works by de Chirico and the four by Alberto Savinio that together form a nucleus, almost an island, of a lofty visionary sense within the exhibition. From this follow the Surrealistic episodes of Max Ernst and Magritte or, going a bit ahead and changing the situation somewhat, of Fabrizio Clerici with one of his legendary levitations, Domenico Gnoli with his hyper-realistic Metaphysical art, and Carlo Guarienti with his unparalleled excavations.

One can also identify in the collection a space in which 20th-century masters magnificently appear, and standing out among these is that masterpiece of light, moving chromaticism, intimacy and supreme spatial composition, the *Il romanzo di una cucitrice* by Boccioni. Here we also find three different paintings by de Pisis, all beautiful in different ways — the airy, celestial and erotic lightness of the *Figura con flauto*, the intense *Ritratto di giovane* with its dark and withering gaze, and the nervous stenography and throbbing of the Parisian scene. Also included here are Picasso, Léger, Chagall and Sironi, with naturally the addition of Morandi. Moving on to the next generation we find very well-chosen works by Rosai, Guttuso, Gentilini and Maccari. Set apart from these tendencies in order to partake in solitude his elegance and diversity, almost a bit ill-at-ease within a crowd so different from him but yet bolstered from a distance by the poetic friendship of Burri, Melotti and also somewhat that of Atanasio Soldati, is Lucio Fontana with the defenseless purity of *Concetto Spaziale. Attese.*

And now we come, finally, to the youngest generation in which we find Cremonini, Ferroni, Gianquinto, Vallorz, Ruggero Savinio and Guccione, each one with an early example of his presence in the most-recent history of Italian art, ending with a French painter who lived in Rome, Jean-Pierre Velly, rich in poetry and hope, and who died at an early age.

Having reached the end of this incomplete and a bit simplistic inventory, the only thing left for me to mention is that this exhibition is not, and absolutely does not intend to be, the manifestation of a display or affirmation of power. But according to the sentiment of the person who played a leading role in it, and also to a much lesser extent mine, its intention is to be an act of optimism and trust in the midst of a dark, uncertain, confused and adverse period in Italian history. Not, however, an opposition to the sadness and pain of this period, but rather the desire and attempt to believe in something, to have some sense of certainty that in contemplating a cultural act, small but necessary if united with others, one can once again begin to build, to rise up and be renewed simply by reviving and putting back in circulation values from a previous age.

The Barilla Collection of Modern Art

1
Arnold Böcklin
Prometheus
1882

3
James Ensor
Coquillages et draperie bleue
1903

4
Umberto Boccioni
Il romanzo di una cucitrice
1908

5b
Umberto Boccioni
Testa di donna
1908

6
Giorgio de Chirico
Le consolateur
1929

7
Giorgio de Chirico
Chevaux sauvages
1929-1930

8
Giorgio de Chirico
Bagni misteriosi
1934

9
Giorgio de Chirico
Ippolito con i compagni
su i monti dell'isola di Creta
1955-1956

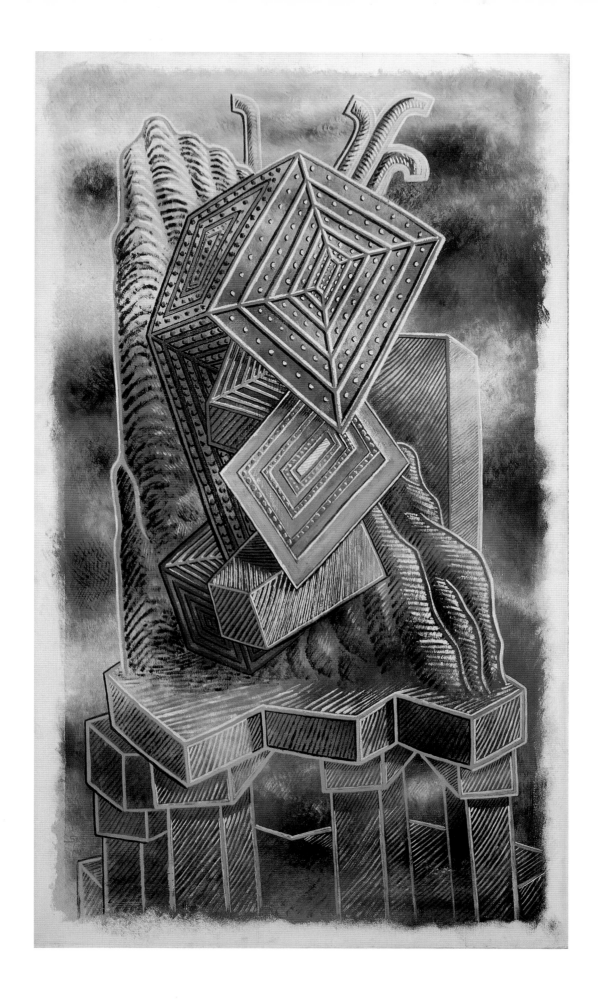

11
Alberto Savinio
L'ira di Achille
1930

50

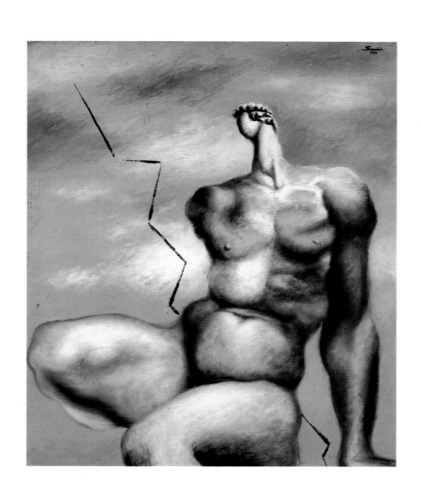

14
Max Ernst
Divinité
(1940)

17
Marc Chagall
Violoniste
1938

18
Pablo Picasso
Femme sur un fauteuil. Buste
1962

19
Fernand Léger
Des oiseaux dans les arbres
1953

21
Giorgio Morandi
Natura morta
1935

24
Giorgio Morandi
Fiori
1953

25
Giorgio Morandi
Natura morta
1957

26
Giorgio Morandi
Paesaggio
1961

29
Chaïm Soutine
Le printemps à Champigny
(1942)

33
Ennio Morlotti
Paesaggio sul fiume (Adda)
1955

34
Ennio Morlotti
Paesaggio (Brianza)
1958

36
Ennio Morlotti
Autunno
1958

37
Ennio Morlotti
Studio per bagnanti n. 2
1959

39
Ennio Morlotti
Tre bagnanti
1992

40
Alberto Burri
Combustione F
1960

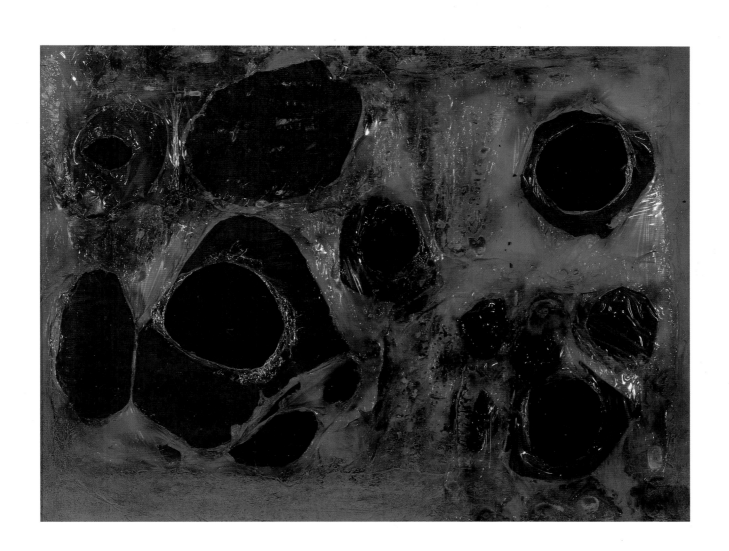

42
Lucio Fontana
Concetto Spaziale. Attese
1961

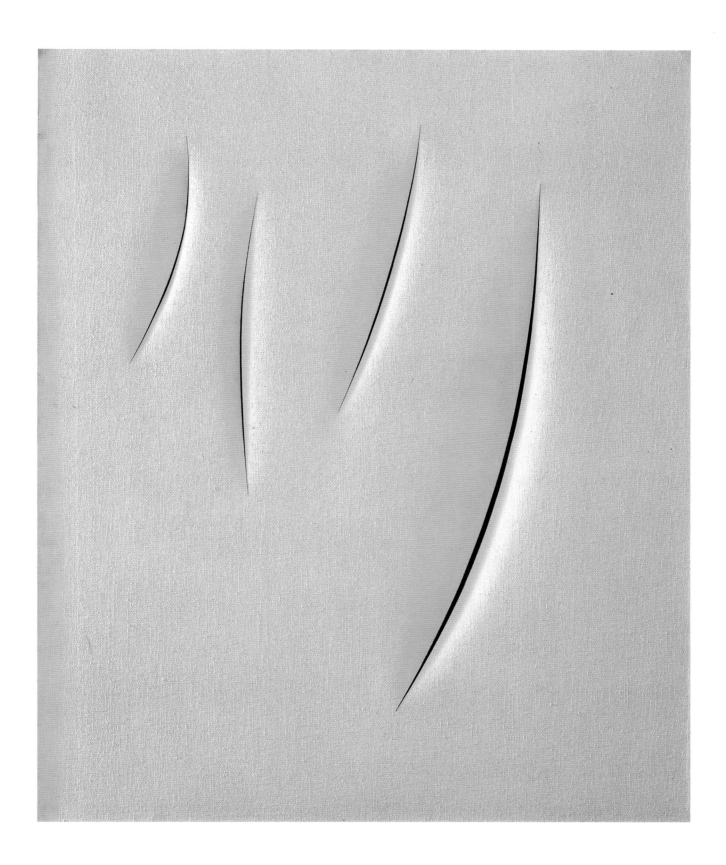

43
Afro (Basaldella)
Sagra delle ciliegie
1960

45
Jean-Paul Riopelle
Composition
1955

46
Sam Francis
Painting
1957

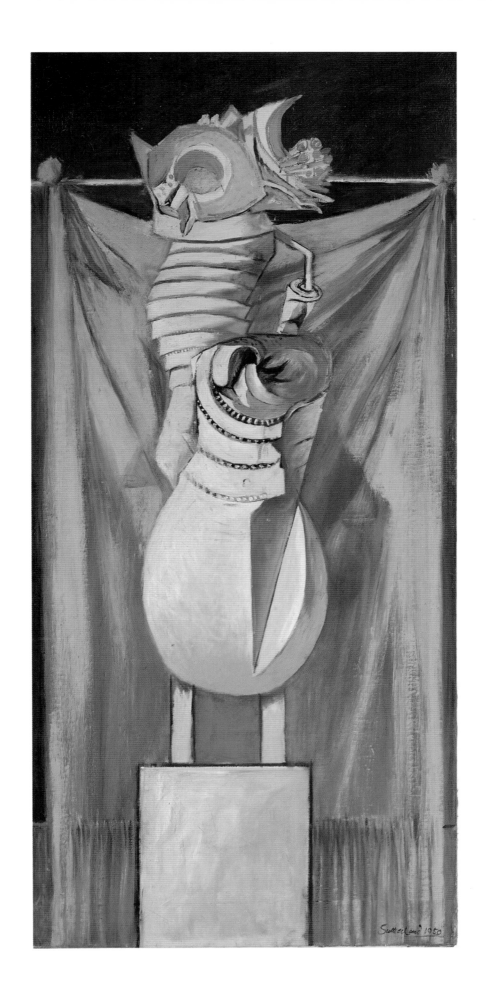

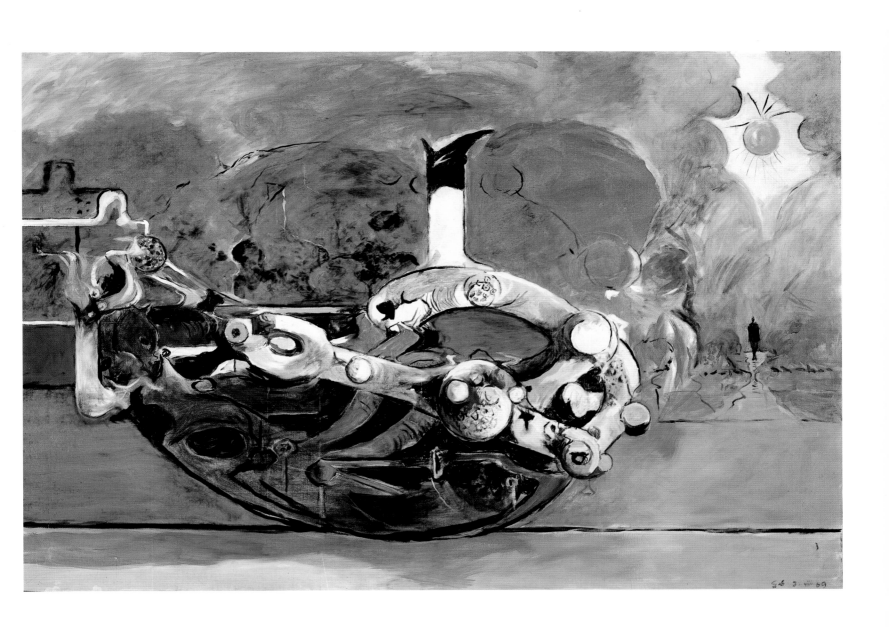

49
Francis Bacon
Two Americans
1954

51
Zoran Music
Point de repère sombre
1963

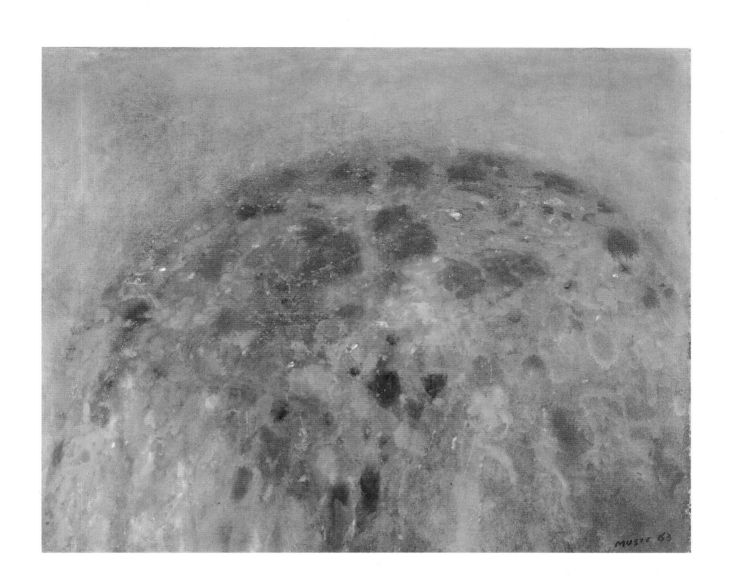

52
Zoran Music
Collina dalmata
1966

53
Zoran Music
Autoritratto
1989

54
Zoran Music
Doppio ritratto
1990

55
Carlo Mattioli
Nudo coricato
1961

56
Carlo Mattioli
Piccola natura morta
1965

58
Carlo Mattioli
Aigues Mortes
1979

59
Goliardo Padova
Paesaggio
(1967)

60
Goliardo Padova
In un piccolo giardino (Siepe)
(1974-1976)

61
Ottone Rosai
San Gimignano
1954

62
Mino Maccari
Gruppo di personaggi
1974

63
Franco Gentilini
Washington Bridge
1959

65
Renato Guttuso
Interno dello studio a Velate
(Grande natura morta)
1961

66
Fabrizio Clerici
La poltrona di Nonza
1979

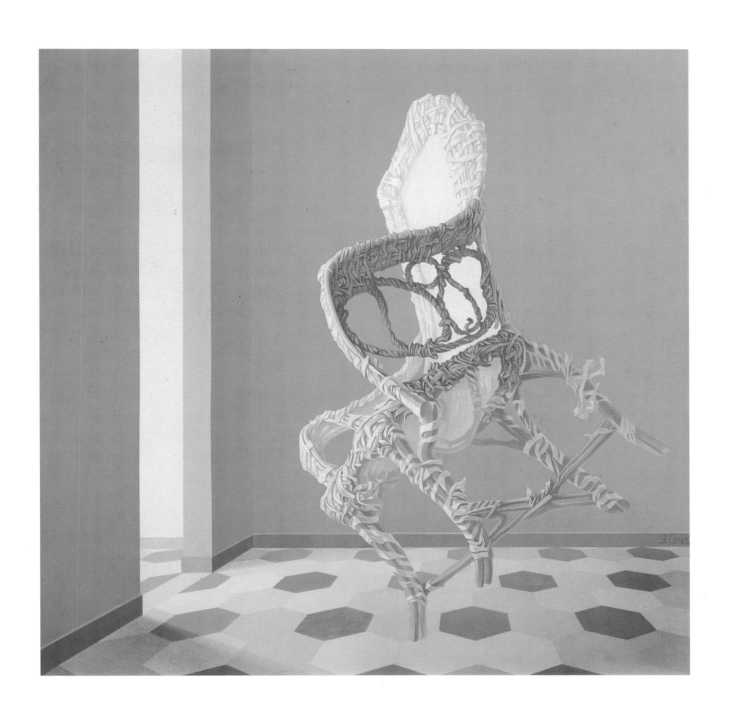

67
Atanasio Soldati
Composizione
(1935)

69
Domenico Gnoli
Desk
1968

70
Alfredo Chighine
Composizione blu e rosa
1956

73
Carlo Guarienti
La sera di Anversa:
metamorfosi dell'angelo
e del capitano generale
1975

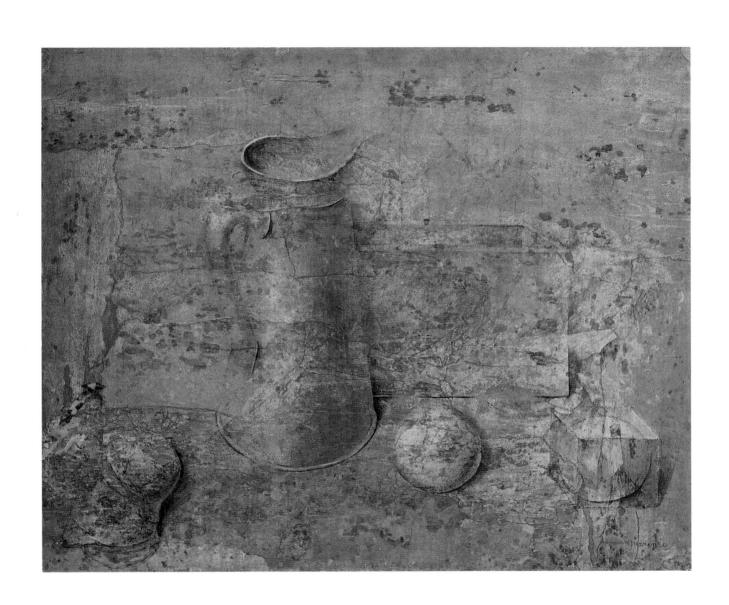

76
Carlo Guarienti
Natura morta
1992

77
Carlo Guarienti
Natura morta (Omaggio a Villa)
1992

79
Gianfranco Ferroni
Interno - quasi sera
1981-1982

80
Alberto Gianquinto
Luce a Venezia: finestra n. 3
1962

83
Piero Guccione
Spiaggia 91
1991

86
Jean-Pierre Velly
La quercia
1989

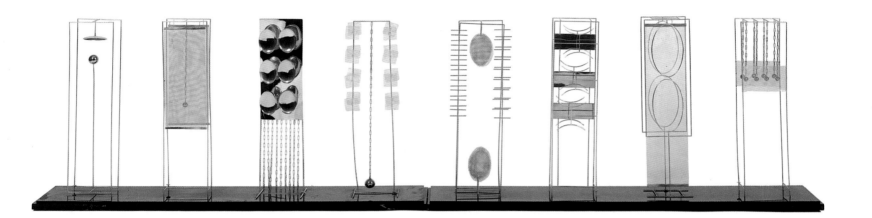

92
Marino Marini
Cavaliere
1951

93
Marino Marini
Cavaliere
1951

214

94
Marino Marini
Composizione
(Cavallo e cavaliere)
1955

96
Giacomo Manzù
Passo di danza
1954

97
Giacomo Manzù
Cardinale seduto
1958

98
Giacomo Manzù
Testa di Papa Giovanni XXIII
1963

100
Giacomo Manzù
Amanti
1965

101
Giacomo Manzù
Sedia d'argento
1966

102
Giacomo Manzù
Pittore con modella
1966

103
Giacomo Manzù
Grande chiave
1967

104
Giacomo Manzù
Idea per un monumento
1968

106
Giacomo Manzù
La Famiglia nel Risparmio
(bozzetto)
1970

107
Giacomo Manzù
Muro di Odissea
1985

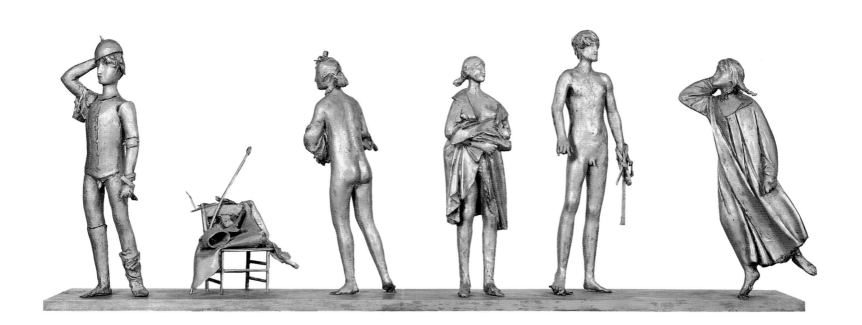

108
Reg Butler
Girl (Chrysanthemum)
1959

109
Andrea Cascella
Aurora
1989

111
Arnaldo Pomodoro
Cubo IV
1965-1975

113
Augusto Perez
Narciso (Grande Narciso)
1966

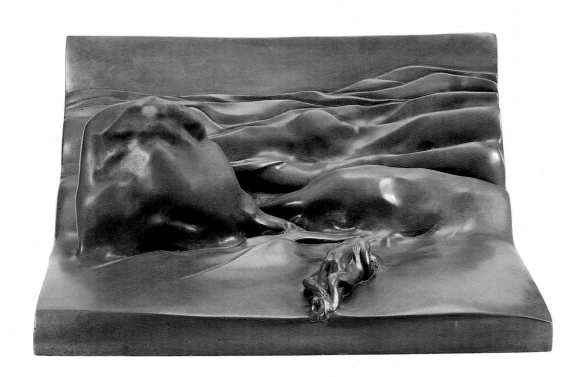

116
Giuliano Vangi
Donna vestita di azzurro
1991

117
Giuliano Vangi
Il nodo (bozzetto)
1992

118
Giuliano Vangi
Il nodo
1993

Catalogue of the Works

1
Arnold Böcklin. 1827-1901
Prometheus
1882

Oil on canvas, 115.5 x 150.5 cm.
Signed on bottom left: «A. Böcklin».
Provenance: Fritz Gurlitt Gallery, Berlin; Eduard Arnhold Collection, Berlin; heirs of Eduard Arnhold, Florence.
Exhibitions: Berlin, Gurlitt Gallery, 1883; Dresden, Böcklin Exhibition, November-December 1883; Berlin, Academy Exhibition, 1884; Berlin, Böcklin Exhibition, 1897, pag. 37; Hamburg, Böcklin Exhibition, 1898, pag. 60; Basel, Kunsthalle, Böcklin Exhibition, Centenary of his birth, 1927, no. 120; London, Böcklin Exhibition, 1971, no. 40; Düsseldorf, Böcklin Exhibition, 1974, no. 49, ill.; Basel, Kunstmuseum, Böcklin Exhibition, June 11-September 11, 1977, no. 162, col. ill. no. 46; Fiesole, Palazzina Mangani, *Arnold Böcklin e la cultura artistica in Toscana*, July 24-Sept. 30, 1980, no. 19, b/w ill.; Milan, Finarte, auction 701, 1989.
Bibliography: H. A. Schmid, *Arnold Böcklin*, I, Munich, 1892, pl. 23; C. Gurlitt, «Arnold Böcklin» in *Die Kunst für Alle*, Munich, 1894, pp. 17, 18, ill. pp. 32-33; A. Rosenberg in *Kunstchronik*, no. 18, 1883, col. 433; A. Lichtwark, «L'anima e l'opera d'arte,» *Böcklin Studies*, Berlin, 1899, p. 43; F.H. Meissner, *Arnold Böcklin*, Berlin, 1901, pp. 97-100; H. Mendelsohn, *Böcklin*, Berlin, 1901, p. 157; H. A. Schmid, *Catalogue of the works of Arnold Böcklin*, new edition, Munich, 1903, no. 317; E. Berger, *Böcklin Technik*, Munich, 1906, pp. 4, 13, 14, 113; A. Grabowsky, *La battaglia di Böcklin*, Berlin, 1906, pp. 70-72, 98; C. Gurlitt, *L'arte tedesca del XIX sec.: suoi scopi e opera*, Berlin, 1907, pp. 571, 572; *Böcklin Memoiren*, selections from the diary of Angela Böcklin, his wife, with the complete collection of his posthumous letters, F. Runkel ed., Berlin, 1910, pp. 228, 293; G. de Chirico, «Arnold Böcklin» in *Il Convegno*, 4, 1920, found in *Il meccanismo del pensiero*, M. Fagiolo ed., Turin, 1985, p. 171; H. A. Schmid, *Arnold Böcklin*, Munich, 1922, pp. 22, 36, 45, 47, pl. 69; F. van Ostini, *Böcklin*, Bielefeld, 1925, pp. 79 (pl.), 101, 103; A. von Schneider, «Böcklin» in *Der Kunstwanderer*, Berlin, 1926-27, p. 374; H. Floerke, *Arnold Böcklin*, Munich, 1927, pp. 21, 22, 84, 85; W. Barth, *Böcklin*, vol. 11 of *La Svizzera nella vita spi-*

rituale tedesca, Frauenfeld, 1928, pp. 27-28; G. J. Wolf, «La supremezia di Böcklin nel nostro tempo: In occasione del centenario della nascita del maestro, 16 ott. 1927» in *Die Kunst für Alle*, 1928, p. 3 (pl.); O. Fischer, *Arnold Böcklin*, Burg bei Magdeburg, 1940, pp. 7, 37 (pl.); U. Christoffel, «Natura e uomo in Arnold Böcklin» in *Die Ernte*, 1947, p. 57 (pl.); R. Andree, *Arnold Böcklin. Contributi all'analisi della sua struttura figurativa*, dissertation, Freie Universität of Berlin, 1960, Düsseldorf, 1962, p. 74 (fn. 106); G. Kleineberg, *Lo sviluppo della personificazione della natura nell'opera di Arnold Böcklin (1827-1901). Studi sull'iconografia e i temi dell'arte del XIX sec.*, dissertation, Gottingen, 1971, pp. vi, 92, 174, 175, 177, 178; R. Andree, «Arnold Böcklin, A proposito dell'esposizione al Kunstmuseum di Düsseldorf» in Bollettino dei Musei di Düsseldorf, 1/74, p. 186; M. Bringmann, «Annotazioni su Arnold Böcklin, H. Thoma e W. Leibl in occasione delle esposizioni a Düsseldorf, Karlsruhe, Monaco del 1974» in *Kunstchronik*, January 1975, vol. 1, pp. 5, 16 (pl.); R. Andree, *Arnold Böcklin. Die Gemälde*, (paintings), Basel, Friedrich Reinhardt Verlag and Munich, Prestel Verlag, 1977, no. 370, p. 442, col. pl. 38; *Arnold Böcklin*, exh. cat., Basel, 1977, pp. 125, 129, 151, no. 162 p. 204, col. pl. 46; C. Nuzzi in Catalogue of the Fiesole Exhibition, Rome, De Luca, 1980, p. 105; M. Fagiolo dell'Arco, «Böcklin e de Chirico. La pittura letteraria» in Catalogue of the Fiesole Exhibition, Rome, De Luca, 1980, pp. 180-183; R. Monti, *Un'opera fiorentina di Böcklin*, Milan, Finarte, 1989; R. Tassi, «*Prometheus*: un drammatico inno alla natura, di Arnold Böcklin» in *Arte all'incanto*, Milan, 1990, p. 134.

Arnold Böcklin is one of the great men of northern lands attracted by the light and waters of the Mediterranean who dream of the shores on which Greek Classicism was born and the plains inhabited by the gods. The luminosity of the south, where during the midday hours nature arouses and gathers together mythical apparitions among the transparent shadows, is a lost paradise. A powerful, blue-eyed man of the north, Böcklin tried to recapture this paradise, and for this reason went to Rome

where he lived and married. The culture he assimilated in Basel, his birth-place and where he returned following his Rome period, was probably not extraneous to this unceasing search. Basel was also the homeland of Jacob Burckhardt, and in the period around 1870 Nietzsche lived there, anticipating in some of his lectures the basic tenets of *The Birth of Tragedy* published in 1872. The book began: «We will have acquired much in the science of aesthetics when we have arrived not only at the logical understanding, but also the direct certainty of the insight that the development of art is linked to the duality of the *Apollonian* and the *Dionysian*.» Once again, the northern spirit enchanted by Greece.

Within that duality, even if he seems to remain balanced between the two, Böcklin is part of the latter: he is Dionysian, inebriated, and only in rare moments is he perhaps able to unite the two aspects. In the Greek mythology of Nietzsche there is too much joy, too much radiant splendor, too much light.

Böcklin's muse is Melancholy: the mythological journey, that of springtime, leads him to drama, to dealing with death, to autumn. Böcklin is not a Classicist. The nostalgia from Greek Classicism, and thus the desire to revive it, are manifestations of the Romantic spirit. Exactly because of his faithfulness to his northern nature, to the deep melancholy and the modernization of the myth, in the second half of the nineteenth century Böcklin awakened a return to Romanticism, establishing a great Neo-Romantic style.

One of the purest and most richly fascinating examples of this is *Prometheus*. It is the crowning point of a series he had begun in 1859 with *Castle on the Sea* (or, *Murder on the Castle Grounds*). It includes the subject of *Villa on the Sea* for which a sketch dated 1858 as well as five later examples done between 1864 and 1878 are known, *Undertow* from 1879, *Ruins on the sea* from 1880, and ends with the five versions of *Island of the Dead* made between 1880 and 1886. This series of works evolved over the span of more than twenty years and ran parallel with others of a more serene spirit,

Arnold Böcklin, *Prometheus*, 1885

crystalline light, calm ambiguity and mythology based in nature. The works that make it up have in common aspects — exhibiting a completely new creativity perhaps not yet well appreciated for its poetic grandeur — that make Böcklin one of the greatest painters of the nineteenth century.

In them is a dramatic hymn to nature and a profound relationship between nature and events, human or mythical, that take place within it. Thus, they manifest their derivation from the original German Romantic movement, i.e., from Caspar David Friedrich, clearly Böcklin's inspiration in his first landscapes. The fantastical and natural heart, or center, of these works lies in the image of the rocks on the sea: rocks covered with thick vegetation and plunging sharply into the water which calmly laps or breaks against them. The solid earth, powerful, unmoving, and eternal, and the translucent water, boundless, turbulent and also eternal — the two basic elements of nature contrasted and united — express the supreme beauty of their contrast and unity. On the rocks amidst the vegetation — that of a park, woodland or wild growth — appears a villa, or sometimes a castle, ruins, or tombs. Between the sea and rocks a human presences peruse and prolong the mystery.

These works, saturated with a melancholy, afflicted and loving sense of *Stimmung*, are among the most mysterious and enchanting ones Western culture has left us. In *Villa on the Sea*, the presence is human and in the *Island of the Dead* from both the human and spirit worlds. In both paintings the myth is hidden, yet hovers about like an occult spirit or an unseen presence. But in *Prometheus* the myth is evident and is located in nature, lives in it and is assimilated by it. The giant Prometheus is outstretched on the highest peak of the rocks at the point the vegetation ends and over which the clouds hover. In the distance, almost unreal, almost a dream, his great body seems to be either an appendage of the rocks or a thickening of the clouds so similar are the colors and the play between light and shadow. He seems to enter into the great natural harmony of the cosmos.

Because of the distance and visionary sense, he

contrasts with the lower part of the mountains and rocky coastline where the dense shadows hide in the hollows and intense gashes of light reveal in places the pink and yellow of the rock and the green of the trees. Little waterfalls cascade among the crevices to become united with the sea and are of a dark blue which becomes lighter when they break up in the waves. This landscape, pushed so much into the foreground, without a horizon and almost in contact with the observer, is of great beauty, drama and involvement. It is not a scene, but a land which attracts and, at the same time, frightens us and draws attention to itself with a power of attraction produced by something greater than its beauty. The martyrdom of Prometheus seems almost hidden, secondary, and yet creates the mystery in the landscape, it sharpens the drama, as if amidst the luxuriant natural surroundings and the salty sea air which gusts through the trees, we expect some human presence or the unforeseen manifestation of an event, an escape, a struggle, or a metamorphosis, to rise up unexpectedly.

De Chirico, a great admirer of Böcklin, drew inspiration from this work in his own *Prometheus* of 1908-1909 published by Fagiolo dell'Arco who wrote: «The painting, *Prometheus*, shows a tall rock crowned by the tragic mythical figure (as in Böcklin's famous painting) which can be seen in a careful analysis of the picture.»[2] De Chirico himself mentions this work in his 1920 essay on Böcklin: «In his *Prometheus*, he marvelously portrayed that aspect of the divine giant come to live on earth, an aspect for which perhaps the first idea arises seeing Poussin's painting entitled *Sicilian landscape*, now in the St. Petersburg art museum, in which in the background atop a high rock and behind a valley inhabited by nymphs, one sees the gigantic back of Polyphemus playing reed-pipes.»[3] If we look at Poussin's work, now known as *Landscape with Polyphemus*, we find in the difference between the two depictions the meaning and novelty in Böcklin. In fact, the Polyphemus playing a hundred-reed flute while perched on the mountain almost as if he were an extension of it, is an image similar to

that of the Prometheus, grey and violet like the stones and clouds amongst which he is exposed. In Poussin, the countryside is completely inhabited but everything appears fixed, immobile, crystalline, old, timeless. In Böcklin the landscape is dense, wild, divided between veils of shadow and flashes of light, and is the protagonist of the work, the triumph of nature. It is as deeply Romantic as Poussin's landscape is Classical.

Prometheus was painted in Florence in 1882. Böcklin's financial situation was precarious, his paintings were sold only with great difficulty, but things changed after he met Berlin businessman Fritz Gurlitt who, starting in 1880, began to exhibit his works regularly in Berlin and later in Dresden. *Prometheus* was shown in an exhibition at the Gurlitt Gallery in 1883. On this occasion, referring to the painting, critic Adolf Rosenberg wrote in the *Kunstchronik*: «A creation so completely balanced and full of sublime poetry, gives us once again the welcome proof that the original vigor of the Florentine hermit has not been exhausted.»[4] But the public received the painting with great incomprehension, charging that it was unintelligible. What they probably found disturbing is the very thing that to us today seems so fascinating and poetically inspired: the dramatic pre-eminence of the landscape and the mythological scene lost like a cloud among the other clouds. Eduard Arnhold's acquisition of the painting provoked a scandal. In the exhibition at the Berlin Academy the following year (1884), Böcklin was to have won the gold medal for *Prometheus*, but as he insisted on also showing *Denianira and Nessus* which the judges did not like, the award with its medal vanished into thin air.

Böcklin had previously painted the Prometheus subject in 1858 over a door in the dining room of consul Paul Wedekind in Hanover. In 1885 Böcklin made a copy of *Prometheus* in oil on a panel of reduced size (98.5 x 125 cm.). The idea and spirit of the painting are the same. This is also a painting of Romantic-style nature, dramatic in the contrast between the illuminated areas and the darker ones, while the martyrdom of the giant chained to the

2
Edward Burne-Jones. 1833-1898
Study for Garland Weavers
1866

The Garland, 1866   *Garland Weavers*, 1867

most distant mountains becomes an event of secondary importance. It is currently housed in the Hessisches Landesmuseum in Darmstadt (see the color reproduction). Speaking of this copy, Rolf Andree wrote in the museum catalogue: «in comparison with the 1882 painting, it is clear that the visual power of the Darmstadt painting is weaker. But, even though it does not equal the penetrating force of the earlier version, this copy also expresses the revolt of the elements which for the viewer represent the torment of the chained Prometheus.»[5]
Roberto Tassi

1. M. Fagiolo dell'Arco quoted in bibl., 1980, p. 183.
2. M. Fagiolo dell'Arco, op. cit., p. 180.
3. G. de Chirico, quoted in bibl., 1985, p. 171.
4. Quoted by Von Lutz Tittel in the catalogue of the Basel Exhibition, 1977, p. 125.
5. R. Andree, quoted in bibl., 1977, p. 461.

Tempera, 76 x 48 cm.
On the back: «Galleria Galatea, 1866».
Provenance: Galleria Galatea, Turin.
Bibliography: M. Bell, *Edward Burne-Jones, a Record and Review*, London, 1892 (updated & rev. 1898), p. 39; Burne-Jones, cat. of the Mappin Art Gallery, Sheffield, 1971, W. S. Taylor ed., pp. 19-20; A. C. Sewter, *The Stained Glass of William Morris and his Circle*, 2 vols., New Haven and London, 1974-75, vol. I, ill. no. 269, vol. II, pp. 103-104; *The Paintings, Graphic and Decorative Work of Sir Edward Burne-Jones 1833-98*, cat. of the Arts Council, London 1975-76, J. Christian ed., p. 68; *Burne-Jones dal preraffaellismo al simbolismo*, cat. of the Galleria Nazionale d'Arte Moderna, Rome, 1986, M.T. Benedetti and G. Piantoni eds., p. 157.

This work is part of a group of five, all of which center upon a solitary female figure drawn either from the front or behind. The most famous is in the Cecil French Bequest, Borough of Hammersmith Public Libraries, London (now in the Leighton House) and bears on the reverse side the inscription: «Edward Burne-Jones/Watercolour/The Garland/A series of five pictures/was (?) in hand ... left(?)/for this and the others are/unfinished — See the windows/..... Refreshment.» The reference is to the six windows that offer identical likenesses carried out, based on Burne-Jones's drawings for the *Green Dining Room* of the Victoria and Albert Museum, by Morris & Co. in the years 1866-68 (Sewter, vol. II, 1975, nos. 267-70). Two other versions of the painted series are in the collections of John Nicoll and Terence Rowe, the fourth was put up for auction at Sotheby's on June 16, 1970 (Lot 152), and the last has been on the international market and could be the work under examination. A group of drawings (Birmingham City Art Gallery; Witt Collection Courtauld Institute of Art, London) treats, in its details, the same subjects; relevant to our *Study* is a drawing at the Fogg Art Museum, Cambridge, Mass. (1902, 15). Confirmed once again is Burne-Jones's characteristic osmosis between pictorial and decorative works. Starting with the drawings, he develops a series of variants which

often take on their own independent directions, thus feeding the vast Corpus of his work. Stylistically we are at the moment in which the rudimentary and Rossettian matrices are left behind, when the artist adopts an animated line, has the drapery take on a decorative cadence, makes the colors sparkling and delicate, and organizes the space in a less schematic manner. All of these are elements that signal his adherence to the ideals of the Aesthetic Movement which were put forth in the poetry of «Art for Art's Sake» circulated by Whistler, theorized about by Swinburne in his essay on Blake (1866) and cultivated by Albert Moore, to whose work figures like those of the *Study for Garland Weavers* can be put alongside. Although never completely identifying with the dictates of the Aesthetic Movement, Burne-Jones is attentive to the formal elements of its painting style and to its language of color and line. In addition, in the young girl's clothing there is an echo of the interest in «China blue» which was made popular during that period by Rossetti, Whistler and Howell. According to B. Waters (*Burne-Jones*, in collaboration with M. Harrison, London, 1973, p. 82), the work's iconographic prototype can be seen in the drawings for *The Tale of Cupid and Psyche* (1864-66) and in *The Earthly Paradise* of William Morris which in turn was taken from the Renaissance illustrations of the *Hipnerotomachia Poliphili*. In any case, it is certain that, at the time, the artist had already come in direct contact with great Italian art of the fifteenth and sixteenth centuries during the voyages he made with Ruskin in 1859 and 1862, also documented by extensive notes and copies. In the little figure seen from behind, of light step and elegant gestures wrapped in a vaguely classical peplum, who passes through the narrow, flowered courtyard rich with Italianate spatial suggestions united with references to a Flemish ambience, a multiplicity of inspirations is combined into a single composite typical of this artist who, free of academic conditioning, delves without inhibition into the art of the past in the belabored search for a style and constantly sustained by a unique aesthetic calling.
Maria Teresa Benedetti

<table>
<tr>
<td>

3
James Ensor. 1860-1949
Coquillages et draperie bleue
1903

</td>
<td>

4
Umberto Boccioni. 1882-1916
Il romanzo di una cucitrice
1908

</td>
</tr>
</table>

Oil on canvas, 79 x 96 cm.
Provenance: Galleria Galatea, Turin.
Bibliography: «Il paese delle meraviglie,» chronology, in *James Ensor*, exh. cat., C. Vignon-Janus ed., Ferrara, 1986, p. 28.

At the time this still life was signed and dated, James Ensor was forty-three years old. The new century had just begun and would hold out for him a very long life, active up to the very end. Ensor, however, had already made his choices early on, and the catalogue of his works would continue to be enriched for another forty years, but always with variations on the same themes without lending an ear to the upheavals which art in his time underwent. Just as, at the age of twenty or so, he had had no confidence in the serene and happy objectivity of the Impressionists who did perhaps help him in lightening up the palette — dark, bituminous and allegorically bereft of light — of the artists more anxious to lend figurative dignity to the other side of the coin, i.e., to the terrible social conditions of the workers, artists like Charles De Groux and later Constantin Meunier (and Van Gogh in his dark paintings from the Eighties). Even before he turned thirty, therefore, Ensor had abandoned those dark hues. The *Fall of the Rebel Angels* with its opening up onto an apocalyptic sky, is from 1889 and it is a very light-hued painting even if its subject is demonic. From the year before is the famous *Christ's Entry into Brussels* which is an anarchic insult to bourgeois society, painted, however, with unprecedented Carnival-style festivity with light, sparkling colors. In short, the bitter *vis polemica* and the use of grotesque themes in Ensor goes hand-in-hand with his never-ending inquiry into the plastic and visual qualities of the painting as well as the materials of which it is made. Additionally, in the numerous still lifes, this bitterness is often softened and tempered by his way of studying the objects and their breaking up of the light. It is exactly this natural and omnipresent diffusing of the light which shatters the compactness of the objects and which, in the end, enlivens them with a slimy, ambiguous vitality. Ambiguous be-

cause it gives them, as also happens here, a sort of excited, unexpected, mobility which compels one's gaze to never halt on the surfaces or known volumes which are still or at rest, but rather forces one to bounce from one point to another on the canvas, from one sparkling object to another without a central point. In his first still lifes, Ensor adopted a style which was fixed on the object. Such is the case with the first version of *Skate*, 1882 (Antwerp, Royal Museum), or in the *Red Apples* of the following year (Lens Fine Art, Antwerp). In these paintings, it is easy to trace the antecedents and models from among the famous canvasses of Chardin and the seventeenth century Dutch masters, and from among the canvasses (and apples) of Courbet. But already starting in 1889 (in the *Flowers and Butterflies* of the Hotel Charlier in Brussels, for example, where I recall that the same green ceramic sugar bowl that is seen here appears there in the same position on the right), the ductus of the brush-stroke breaks up and the eye begins to search for resting points which are not to be found. Here, that scattering tendency is complete. And Ensor is winking at us because yes, he establishes a lovely, geometrically exact center in the composition (the fake-Japanese- or Louis Philippe-style pitcher which is placed within the circle of the copper basin — once again, reminiscences of and references to Willem Kalf and Chardin), but then disperses the attention in a mass of chromatic sparks, lights and reflections of illuminated, shadow-less whiteness which are scattered throughout the entire canvas without let-up. And from that apparently fixed point, the eye inevitably drifts away to count the oysters and shells littered on the table (the artist's grandfather, collected and sold them), to the veining in the marble table itself, whether real or fake, and to the thousand disruptions in the material and light which make the entire surface seem to crackle. And, as always in Ensor, they transform a completely normal still life into a scene enlivened by annoying and disturbing sprites who undermine our tranquility in contemplating the beauty of the objects.
Eugenio Riccòmini

Oil on canvas, 150 x 170 cm.
Signed and dated on upper left: «Umberto Boccioni 1908».
Provenance: Procida Collection, Rome; Palazzoli Collection, Milan.
Exhibitions: Milan, Palazzo della Permanente, *Concorso Mylius*, 1908; Milan, Palazzo Cova, *Grande Esposizione Boccioni*, 1916-1917, no. 15; Venice, Sala Napoleonica, *Mostra Primi Espositori Cà Pesaro*, September-October 1958, no. 7; Frankfurt, Frankfurter Kunstverein Steinernes Haus, *Italien 1905-1925*, 1963-1964, no. 18; Reggio Calabria, Museo Nazionale, *Omaggio a Boccioni*, June-October 1966, no. 22; Milan, Società per le Belle Arti ed Esposizione Permanente, *Mostra del Divisionismo Italiano*, March-April 1970, no. 123; Milan, Finarte, November 1988, auction lot 600; Trento, Museo d'Arte Moderna e Contemporanea di Trento, Palazzo delle Albere, *Divisionismo italiano*, April-August 1990, no. 146; Verona, Galleria dello Scudo, *Boccioni 1912 Materia*, December 1991-January 1992, no. 16.

Bibliography: G. Borelli, «Concorso Lylius alla Permanente,» *La Perseveranza*, July 27, 1908; «La Mostra Boccioni a Milano,» *Emporium*, XLV, January 1917, p. 77; G. C. Argan and M. Calvesi, *Boccioni*, Rome, 1953, p. 29; M. Drudi Gambillo and T. Fiori, *Archivi del Futurismo*, Rome, 1958-1962 (2nd ed. Rome-Milan, 1982), no. 48 p. 415; G. Ballo, *Preistoria del Futurismo*, Milan, 1960, no. 140, p. 76; R. De Grada, *Boccioni*, Milan, 1962, no. 157; G. Ballo, *Boccioni*, Milan, 1964 (2nd ed., 1982), no. 75, p. 85; E. Crispolti, «Vicende dell'immagine tra naturalismo, divisionismo e fauvismo» in *L'Arte Moderna*, vol. VIII, Milan, 1967, p. 30; F. Bellonzi and T. Fiori, *Archivi del Divisionismo*, Rome, 1968, no. 2253, p. 186; G. Bruno, *L'opera completa di Boccioni*, Milan, 1969, no. 40; M. Calvesi and E. Coen, *Boccioni: L'opera completa*, Milan, 1983, no. 309, p. 240; E. Coen, *Boccioni: A Retrospective*, New York, 1988, pp. 44-45.

5a
Umberto Boccioni. 1882-1916
Testa di donna
1908

5b
Umberto Boccioni. 1882-1916
Testa di donna
1908

Pencil on paper, 12.4 x 12.2 cm.
Signed on bottom right: «Boccioni.»
Study for the painting *Il romanzo della cucitrice*
Exhibitions: Lugano, Finarte, October 10, 1992, no. 96.
Bibliography: J. C. Taylor, *The Graphic Work of Umberto Boccioni*, New York, 1961, no. 127 (1909-1910); M. Drudi Gambillo and T. Fiori, *Archivi del Futurismo*, Rome, 1958-1962 (2nd ed., Rome-Milan, 1982), no. 82; G. Ballo, *Boccioni*, Milan, 1964 (2nd ed., 1982), no. 83; M. Calvesi and E. Coen, *Boccioni: L'opera completa*, Milan, 1983, no. 318 (on the back of no. A4).

Pencil on paper, 16.8 x 11.8 cm.
Signed on bottom right: «Boccioni.»
Study for the painting *Il romanzo della cucitrice*
Exhibitions: Lugano, Finarte, October 10, 1992, no. 95.
Bibliography: J. C. Taylor, *The Graphic Work of Umberto Boccioni*, New York, 1961, no. 127 (1909-1910); M. Drudi Gambillo and T. Fiori, *Archivi del Futurismo*, Rome, 1958-1962 (2nd ed., Rome-Milan, 1982), no. 83; G. Ballo, *Boccioni*, Milan, 1964 (2nd ed., 1982), no. 81; M. Calvesi and E. Coen, *Boccioni: L'opera completa*, Milan, 1983, no. 320 (on the back of no. 479).

In Boccioni's output, the *Il romanzo di una cucitrice* represents one of the most important stages in his artistic development. In fact, it was painted in 1908 during one of his most exuberant and intellectually intense phases but which was also one of deep internal torment. The pages of Boccioni's diary are an extraordinary testament to these years and, above all, to the stylistic and mental evolution of some of his paintings, among which this *Il romanzo di una cucitrice*. May 13, 1908. «I have started the painting with Ines for the competition. Unfortunately it is nothing new, and what's more, it is a motif I have been rebuked for repeating too much and in fact I want this painting to sum up and bring to a close the past period.» May 28. «The only hope that guides me is that from now on, what I do become strong and original and that others can see what I, unfortunately cannot. [...] it is in the painting with Mrs. Ines which I take up again at 11 o'clock after an hour's rest that I cannot explain my recklessness. I saw it clearly; I dreamed of it as silvery and I painted it red!! Now I go back to it but I don't understand a thing. Prepared the sketch carelessly and painted the details extremely unwillingly. Seeing the figure, it realistically seems to me (although I always recall a certain ideal figure) to be drawn in such a way as to remind me of Previati. Perhaps this is due to the abolition of the varnishes and using only vermilion. I started with the window empty, dwelling a bit on the details (perhaps secondary) of a window on the house in front with red

shutters and flower pots on the windowsill inside and out, now everything is changed with the flowers in the windowbox thus covering the window in front. I forgot to say that I am changing the figure again in the direction of what seems to me to be reality. Why this? Perhaps for the nearness of a young woman for whom I harbor affection? I don't think so. [...] It also seems to me that working now I am not doing anything but watering down what little I have learned and lost in vigor what I have acquired in speed. The painting (170 x 150 cm.) has already been sketched out in one sitting. Today after three or four hours it is already at the point that I must begin on the details. [...] In short, I don't understand anything anymore. I am afraid to always repeat the same colors and so I hurry even more.» June 15. «On the other hand, I have strong doubts about the Ines painting. I'm afraid the structure is weak.» June 27. «Despite everything, my work seems to be going fairly well. Ines' head and other things are satisfactory, thirteen more days and everything will be finished.» In the painting *Il romanzo di una cucitrice*, Boccioni did not move away from the initial idea, already well-shaped and quickly sketched with a pen at the bottom of the page in his diary dated May 13. While working, moments of strong skepticism alternated with others of extreme confidence about the final outcome of the work which was to be presented at the Milan Permanente for the Mylius competition.

Exhibited in July 1908, it received a cold reception. Borelli, journalist for *La Perseveranza*, criticized its extreme painterly skill to the detriment of a conception of modernity: «With *Il romanzo di una cucitrice* [Boccioni] appears to be a catechumen of technique. The young working girl, in a dressing gown and seated near a sewing machine which is near — I must mention — a flower-covered window through which a stream of light breaks in, is intently reading a novel. Brightly-colored fabric is scattered on the floor to intensify the pictorial motifs. But we have the same cold strain of the light with some even heavier angular and emaciated aspects in the dressing gown and in the «embalming» of the objects. There is a bit of feeling in the

character of the protagonist's stylized intent. However, it is not adequate either for doing a painting or for emerging from a mold which has already been abused.» The writer for *Il Secolo* noted that, in general, the young artists who exhibited displayed a certain lack «of imagination in the choice of subject,» and added, «Umberto Boccioni painted a woman who is reading in front of a sewing machine and calls it *The Seamstress's Novel*! It is not worth much: the floor has the same pictorial value as her attire.» Disappointed with the reaction of the critics for the two paintings he presented at the Permanente — he also exhibited a *Paesaggio lombardo* — Boccioni entrusted his sense of deep discouragement to his diary. July 28: «Paintings sent to the competition. General indifference! Very rare praise here and there, cold and perhaps dictated by good manners. The papers are indifferent or speak about them as if they were completely nothing! Do I deserve this? I'm not questioning the works, but no one realized the intent. Almost everyone judged with an old or conventional painterly sense. No one noticed if looking at my paintings one saw something different from the others which is personal in its tone and vision. They saw nothing. They said I am cold, monotonous and labored, and just think, in almost all the ones spoken about I can see the trick, all the conventionality and the complete lack of experimentation. Am I mistaken? Am I really labored and weak?»

Recent criticism has also underscored his close dependence on already well-known literary ideas or iconographic models. Argan discovered a wellspring of inspiration in the post-Impressionist painting of Toulouse-Lautrec, while Ballo identified it in the composition of a 1905 painting by Balla, *Il Proprietario*. Settled in Milan for just a few months having moved there following a long stay in France and Russia, Boccioni, with his profoundly analytic spirit, was tormented, as it appears from his writing, in wanting to overcome that viewpoint which in Balla seemed to him to be still too realistic and in creating forms that would correspond to his desire for modern ideals. Involved in a solitary quest and full of doubt and anxiety, the artist strove to translate onto canvas the thoughts which were going through his head. «The constant striving for truth, the awareness of my shortcomings in reproducing it in comparison with how I see it, the never having worked with imagination, mean that the few ideas I have had have remained dead letters for fear of carrying them out badly,» the artist wrote just a few days before beginning to paint *Il romanzo di una cucitrice*. But the subject, with its strong references to the late 19th century and still tied to a traditional compositional structure playing with intense chromatic shifts, is lit up by such an extraordinary luminousness that it transforms the scene and also fuses the internal and the external into a single reality. This was an idea that Boccioni had already pursued from his very first portraits until he developed it a few years later in his strong visions of futuristic interpenetration. «The same immobile poses,» wrote the artist during these months, «continually women near windows. To tell the truth, I, lover of the open air, find it to be the only place which approaches my way of seeing. I hate darks. Light, light, light!»

Using studied timbral harmonies, the atmosphere which surrounds the young girl in the *Il romanzo di una cucitrice* illuminates and delves into the traits of her character, almost letting shine through «the poetry of the blood, of the flesh and their reflections with the poetry of the lights and darks of the glazings.» These same traits, marked in the preparatory sketches of the face by an extremely sensitive and incisive pencil which, within the range of the blacks and greys, anticipate the subtle passage of pictorial tones.

Inspired by a deep admiration for Previati's work, through its intimate affinity between line and color, *Il romanzo di una cucitrice* expresses a sense of profound naturalness and a tension with the absolute that Boccioni's work tends towards that here seems to find a form of spiritual elevation in the careful description of a forlorn reality which seemingly lacks mystery. A long-suffering meditation, born of the restless pursuit of the correct balance between ideas and technical perfection.
Ester Coen

Oil on canvas, 190 x 130 cm.
Signed on upper right: «G. de Chirico».
Provenance: Galerie de l'Effort Moderne, Paris (Archives Rosenberg, no. 1241); Rino Valdameri, Milan (1942); Galleria del Milione, Milan, no. 3753; Carlo de Angeli Frua, Milan; Galleria Gissi, Turin (1964); Private Collection; Galleria Sprovieri, Rome (1986).
Exhibitions: Rome, Galleria di Roma, *LI Mostra della Galleria di Roma — opere di Rino Valdameri*, January 27-February 10, 1942, no. 64 (dated 1927); Turin, Galleria Gissi, *De Chirico degli anni Venti*, L. Carluccio, curator, April 1964, (*Grandi figure*, pl. 12 dated 1926); Switzerland, *Arte italiana in Svizzera*; Verona, Galleria dello Scudo, Museo di Palazzo Forti, *De Chirico: gli anni Venti*, M. Fagiolo dell'Arco, curator, December 1986-January 1987, exh. cat., col. ill., pp. 122-123.
Bibliography: Lo Duca, *Giorgio de Chirico*, Hoepli, Milan, 1936, pl. XXVI; *Valori Primordiali*, F. Ciliberti ed., vol. I, pl. XIV; Lo Duca, *Giorgio de Chirico*, Hoepli, Milan, 1945, pl. XXXVI; C. Bruni Sakraischick, *Giorgio de Chirico, Catalogo Generale*, vol. II, book 1, no. 137 (*Grandi figure*, dated 1926); P. Baldacci, M. Fagiolo dell'Arco, *Giorgio de Chirico, Parigi 1924-1930*, Daverio-Mondadori, 1982 (2nd ed. 1983), cover, pp. 302, 303, 509, no. 106.

History of the painting
I quote the evaluation from my catalogue *De Chirico — gli anni Venti* (1986) because there have been no new discoveries about exhibitions or collections since that time. This painting, the greatest of its age, must have been done before May 1929 (when *Le bal* went on stage in Monte Carlo). Perhaps a unique case in the history of de Chirico, it had the good fortune to be photographed on a roll of film (I have reconstructed it over the years between Paris, New York and de Chirico's home) by Lipnitzky, photographer of the Ballets Russes.

The painting entered the Rosenberg Gallery but was not shown, partly because these were disastrous times for art (I am referring to the major crisis caused by the collapse of Wall Street which also spurred de Chirico to return to Italy). Lo Duca pub-

Iconography of the mannequin

1. *Les tragédiens d'Eschyles*, 1925, Private Collection.

Diffusion.
2. Etching from the *Grafica nova* series, 1927.
3. Lithograph from the *Metamorphosis* suite, 1929.

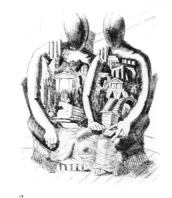

1

2

3

Composition.
4. De Chirico before a painting with mannequins (lost) in which one has a hand on the other's shoulder.
5. *Les navigateurs*, 1928, Paris, Centre Georges Pompidou.
6. *Gli araldici*, 1929-30, Private Collection.

4

5

6

A Roll of Film

The painting, *Le consolateur*, was executed during the period of the rehearsals and sketches for the last season of the Ballets Russes. Diaghilev's official photographer, Serge Lipnitzky, took a series of photos of de Chirico in front of the painting (one would be used for the New York catalogue, October 1930). De Chirico is with Raissa; it is at the end of their relationship. The series is (also) extraordinary because it allows us to enter de Chirico's studio (not bohemian but *ancien régime*), to see the paintings being worked on and to understand his melancholy demeanor.

277

lished the painting in Scheiwiller's small monograph (1936); Rino Valdameri included it in his collection which has fifty or so of de Chirico's works. In 1938 it was published in *Valori Primordiali*, the journal in which Franco Ciliberti tried to find an accord between Rationalism, Abstraction and Metaphysics. The painting also appeared in the second edition of the monograph edited by Scheiwiller (1945). It passed from the Valdameri collection to that of De Angeli Frua (inappropriately broken up in recent years).

Iconography (and lapsus)

A painting of great painterly command, it is the most extensive of its age, and is, in fact, the largest canvas available on the market (120 «points figure»). Does it perhaps stem from the colossal nature of the canvasses for the Rosenberg home? It is a solemn painting which presents itself as a point of arrival for the thematic style explored over twelve years (in Ferrara and later in Paris). A hand on a wrist, a melancholy pose, an arm on a shoulder, faces without features, the two mannequins fuse the various themes which had come to light during those years: Orestes and Electra, the poet and his muse, the prodigal son (also overlapping with the states of mind, from the «soliloque enchanté» to the «tendresses cruelles,» which the titles of some of the mannequins speak of).

It is one of the most aggressive paintings of the period for the definition of its image and solidity of painting style. Two mannequins in an interior against a cloudy background, seated on a red armchair, hand in hand, one foot curiously turned out towards the foreground, the ancient pose of melancholy. Inside the stomach is a concretion of discordant elements: a fragment of blue sky with stars and cirrus clouds, rainbow-hued breakers, a medieval edifice and heraldic designs. The unconscious appears openly, assuring a physical form for metaphysical thought.

The mannequin appears in approximately forty of the canvasses done between 1925 and 1929. The titles, often generic and referring either to the mannequin or to archaeology, conceal the first profound meaning: the mannequin is a Philosopher. As in ancient iconography, it appears melancholy or meditative, solemn or skeptical (SUM SED QUID SUM can be read on a little slate that issues from the stomach of the philosopher of Manchester). He strikes a warlike stance or is calm in repose, sometimes placed on a wharf stretching out to sea (Nietzsche was the one who spoke of philosophers among «the waves of insanity and perversion»), placed in front of chunks of houses or sections of Greek temples.

As always, de Chirico himself is the best analyst of his own visions, often years later. I quote three excerpts from the years between 1938 and 1942: «In the buildings and houses of New York, I found what I myself had felt and expressed in a part of my work as artist: homogeneity and harmonic monumentality made up of disparate and heterogeneous elements. Just as in my *Manichini seduti*, ascending and clinging to the trunks of the figures sunk in the armchairs or resting on pedestals and stools there are motionless breakers, deep blue and capped with solidified foam, aqueducts in ruins, temples closed to any sort of liturgy, fragments of very ancient columns coupled together like bosom friends in the midst of lands swept away by historic event after historic event that the charioteer Destiny has driven with a firm hand and tight rein.» (from «Metafisica dell'America» in *Omnibus*, Rome, 1938).

«The lyric sense and plastic development of my mannequins, from the first ones standing like actors in front of the footlights to the others sitting with their massive trunks and short legs like apostles in Gothic cathedrals [...].» (from «Barnes collezionista mistico» in *L'Ambrosiano*, Milan, 1938).

«As for the mannequin, the more it resembles man, the colder and more unpleasant it is. The pathetic and lyric side of my mannequins, especially the seated ones as in *Archeologi*, resides in their *estrangement from man*. The mannequin seems so unpleasant to us because it is a kind of parody of man. [...] The mannequin is not a fiction, *it is a reality*, or better, a sad and monstrous reality. We will disappear, but the mannequin remains.

The mannequin is not a fragile and ephemeral plaything that can break in the hands of a child; its purpose is not to entertain man but, in making it, man assigns it a specific function: for painters, tailors, in clothing store windows, training police dogs, etc. It is not the pretense of death, of nonexistence we search for on stage. If this were the pretense man asked of the theater, the mannequin would perhaps be a consolation. But, instead, life is the pretense we ask of the theater, we ask for life which is unreal, without beginning or end, as in fairy tales» (from «Discorso sullo spettacolo teatrale» in *L'Illustrazione Italiana*, Milan, October 25, 1942).

Maurizio Fagiolo dell'Arco

7
Giorgio de Chirico. 1888-1978
Chevaux Sauvages
1929-1930

Oil on canvas, 100 x 82 cm.
Signed on bottom right (diagonally): «G. de Chirico»; inscriptions on the back: the number 6597 pencilled on the frame; label: «G. de Chirico - Chevaux sauvages - 40" x 52" canvas size»; label: «James St. L. O'Toole, Inc. - 33 East 51 St., New York»; label: «Wild Horses 1035»; label: «Courvoisier Penthouse, 133 Great V St., San Francisco.»
Provenance: Léonce Rosenberg, the painting is registered in the Archives (unnumbered); James St. L. O'Toole, New York; Courvoisier Gallery, San Francisco; Bill Acquavella Gallery, New York (1972).
Exhibitions: New York, Demotte Gallery, 1930 (six paintings were shown with the generic title of *Horses*; this could be the occasion for which the painting was transferred to the U.S.). The exhibition then moved to Chicago, The Arts Club, December 1930.
Bibliography: C. A. Bruni, *Giorgio de Chirico — Catalogo Generale*, vol. II, book 1, works from 1908-1930, 1972, no. 161 (referred to as belonging to Acquavella); M. Fagiolo dell'Arco, *De Chirico — gli anni Veni*, exh. cat., Galleria dello Scudo, Museo di Arte Contemporanea, Verona, 1986 (cat. Mazzotta, Milan), p. 184 (entitled *Cavalli-trofeo*).

Dating
From various clues, above all stylistic ones, the work seems to have been painted in the winter of 1929. This was the date of the cancellation of the contract with Léonce Rosenberg which (judging from the photograph preserved in the Archives of the Caisse des Monuments Historiques, Paris) this painting was part of. Another element which associates it with this period is the diagonal signing of his name which de Chirico started in 1929 following the triumphal season of the production *Le Bal*, part of the last season of Diaghilev's Ballets Russes (de Chirico's was the great choreographer's penultimate production). But above all, it is the painterly style belonging to this period, fluid but secure and solid at the same time.

The subject of the «horse trophy» remains fairly isolated in de Chirico's work. I can point out a gouache executed during the same period (27 x 35 cm., private collection) in which the group of horses is smaller (five of them), but the spirit of an absurd aggregate, a trophy, is analogous.

The interesting fact is that this subject appears again on his return from the U.S. I know of two paintings in which the tangle of horses poses as a trophy. One was printed by Carrieri in 1942 in his classic monograph published by Giò Ponti, and the other is a «variation on a theme» (cfr. M. Fagiolo dell'Arco, *I bagni misteriosi — de Chirico anni trenta: Parigi, Italia, New York*, Milan, Berenice, 1991, p. 314).

Iconography
A horse was the first subject Giorgio de Chirico painted as a child (as his brother Savinio related), and a horse would be his final painting at the end of his life. In the middle there were the enigmatic horses of the Parisian period, the non-denominational and mysterious horses of his period in Paris (1925-1930), the large, tragic horses of the '30s, the baroque horses and the neo-Metaphysical horses.

But this painting has a special charm since it is not a group of horses, but rather, it would seem, a *Horse Monument*, a subject he delved into that same year with gladiators. We begin with the colors. Unnatural. Horses of childhood have been spoken of as well as the four-legged beasts of the Metaphysical school and merry-go-round horses. Paolo Uccello and Umbrian marquetry have been cited. In reality, this «monument» is but another tribute to the fantasy of the «variation on a theme.» One horse is purple, another bright pink, and the others are grey or whitish with their solid tails anchored to the ground (a kind of desert worthy of a «piazza d'Italia.») It was during this period that he devised enigmatic paintings like the *Les constructeurs de trophées* (on the back of the most beautiful one of the series there is an inscription in his own hand: «pas changer le titre») and in *Hebdomeros* one reads (and it is necessary to excerpt the whole passage in order to understand the visionary sense of the Metaphysical school): «Trophies ... constructions that took the form of mountains because, like mountains, they were born of the act of inner fire and, once the upheaval of their creation was past, with their restless equilibrium they attested to the fiery thrust which had provoked their appearance. Thus they were *pyrophiles*, that is, like the salamander, they *loved fire*. They were immortal since they knew neither sunrise nor sunset, only eternal midday. One always found in them the same correctly proportioned men, perfectly sound of body and spirit and engaged in their favorite occupation: «the building of monuments.» And so there sprung up in the middle of the rooms that strange scaffolding that is severe and entertaining at the same time ... the rooms housing it were like those islands that found themselves off the beaten track of the major navigational routes where the inhabitants sometimes wait for entire seasons to pass before an oil tanker or good-willed sailing ship tosses them some crates of spoiled preserves.» (from *Hebdomeros*, Paris, 1929).

Two or three years earlier he had painted a memorable series of Trophies, in which the old suits of armor or mythical figures protect themselves like an organic mass, exactly like the «playthings» which emerge from the stomachs of his mannequins. (Exactly like the agglomerations of «playthings» that his brother Alberto Savinio introduced in Paris between 1928 and 1929, even making an entire room of them for Léonce Rosenberg in that house which, in another room, contained the enigmatic *Gladiateurs* of his brother who had taken on a Late-Empire style for the occasion). But this subject has distant roots. To tell the truth, its panoply of forms recalls his *Grande Metafisico*, the painting he did in Ferrara in 1917 and repeated in Paris in 1926. A gigantic figure in the middle of a square (de Pisis, a witness from the period, mentioned the Piazza Ariostea in Ferrara) constructed with squares and painter's rags, pieces of mannequins and easel fragments. In short, it is a figure constructed with the instruments at-hand in a studio. Experience has taught me that nothing is accidental in Giorgio de Chirico's *imagérie*. Does the group of nine stallions (or Thessaly mares) allude to the magic number nine of the Muses?
Maurizio Fagiolo dell'Arco

1. Alberto Savinio, *L'île des jouets*, Paris, 1928 (a trophy of toys, childhood and the island of the dead).

1

Continuity of the «trophy»

2. *Il Grande Metafisico*, 1917, Private Collection.
3. *Trofeo*, 1926, previously belonging to Anna Laetitia Pecci-Blunt (has been stolen).
4. *La cohorte invincible*, 1928, Private Collection (gladiators assembled as in a trophy).
5. *Les constructeurs de trophées*, 1927-28, Private Collection. Inscription on the back reads «pas changer le titre.»

2

3

4

5

The «Trofeo di cavalli» from 1930 to 1938

6. A miniature version.
Les chevaux sauvages, 1930, gouache on cardboard, 27 x 35 cm., Private Collection.
7. *Cavalli selvaggi*, ca. 1938, location unknown (from R. Carrieri, *De Chirico*, «Stile» monograph, Milan, 1942.

6

7

Giorgio de Chirico. 1888-1978
Bagni misteriosi
1934

Oil on canvas, 50 x 43 cm.
Signed on upper right: «G. de Chirico»; inscriptions on the back: label: «V. Barbaroux 149»; written in pencil «Bagni» and then the number «8»; written in pencil on the frame: «Sig. Pallini.»
Provenance: Galleria Barbaroux, Milan (1938); Adriano Pallini, Milan.
Exhibitions: Rome, Palazzo delle Esposizioni, *Seconda Quadriennale d'Arte Nazionale*, February-July 1935 (not identified with complete reliability); Milan, Galleria Barbaroux, 1938 (no catalogue exists).
Bibliography: unpublished.

An unpublished masterpiece
The *Bagni misteriosi* series is one of Giorgio de Chirico's most admired (almost equivalent to the Italian Piazzas of twenty years earlier), but also one of the rarest. There are just a dozen paintings (often small in format) which I documented in my book dedicated to de Chirico in the 1930s (*I bagni misteriosi - De Chirico anni Trenta: Parigi, Italia, New York*, Milan, Berenice, 1991, chapter 12).

This painting is almost certainly part of the first series of paintings on this theme (he did others in New York when he was there in 1936-37) exhibited at the Quadriennale in Rome. Correspondence with the painter Nino Bertoletti regarding this exhibition is known (see E. Coen, in *I pittori di Villa Strohl-Fer*, Rome, De Luca, 1983, pp. 141-145). De Chirico had entrusted him to open the crates of paintings, restore any flaws and arrange them by groupings. He also said that behind each painting he would find a reference number in pencil. In our painting, the number («8», to be exact) is still legible on the frame.

The reasons behind the iconography and «visions» of de Chirico will be seen. Dominant in our painting are the two Post-Modern colored cabins (orange and aquamarine) with the two portholes that make them seem like wide-eyed individuals. In the foreground is a kind of lake and on the left a kind of river, like parquet because de Chirico does not paint the water but almost brings an interior setting outside. Two nudes in the lake and

one in the tributary contrast sharply with a standing figure: a man dressed, almost like a tailor's mannequin or a statue clothed as in a store window. A photogram of absence.

History of the painting
The work's previous change-of-hands can be found on the back of the painting. De Chirico exhibited it in the gallery of Vittorio E. Barbaroux who first opened with a personal showing by Giorgio de Chirico in the spring of 1938.

The press reports said that de Chirico, returned from his success in America, was passing through Milan on his way back to Paris. The critiques appeared in *Corriere della Sera*, *L'Ambrosiano* (written by Carrà) and *Meridiano di Roma* (by Raffaele de Grada). Carrà spoke of an uneven exhibition, but his conclusion was not nasty: «The sincerity of action and principle in de Chirico is unquestionable. What is more, he is one of the very few who has never tried to do slick paintings.» The work passed into the collection of tailor Adriano Pallini who possessed many masterpieces of the Metaphysical school. In a pamphlet prepared at the time of his death (1956), there is an (unknown) reminiscence by de Chirico: «Twenty-five years ago or so, I went from Paris to Milan for a show of mine at the Barbaroux gallery which at that time was located in Via Croce Rossa. It was then that I came to know Adriano Pallini. I needed a spring coat; it was April. As soon as I spoke of the overcoat I wanted and that I desired information about tailors located in Milan, Vittorio Barbaroux and others who frequented his gallery immediately told me to go to Adriano Pallini.

«I went to find him. At the time his workshop was in Via dell'Orso in one of those old Milanese houses in which the stairways and rooms are dark even at noon and so, at first glance, seem depressing, but are really full of their own special poetry. They are full of dignity and a charm that unfortunately insatiable time and so-called «progress» systematically destroy. In the dark rooms of that workshop, located in the old Milanese street called dell'Orso, Adriano Pallini appeared before me. A little because of the lack of light in the surroundings, but

more so because of the color of his reddish-blond hair, he seemed to me to be *luminous*, almost phosphorescent. This is how I perceived this polite and gentile young man with a friendly smile, and I immediately took a liking to him.

«While he spoke to me and showed me the paintings hung on the walls, every once in a while I watched him and imagined him in the *salons* of our embassy in Paris or London as a secretary or cultural attaché, maneuvering between and conversing with the ladies and gentlemen of the Faubourg Saint Germain or the baronets of the Crown in Belgrave Place.

«Adriano Pallini also imbued the cut and manufacture of his garments with his gentlemanly style and manner. Not to mention the quality of his fabrics. I still own a dark blue winter overcoat which Pallini made for me many years ago, and every time I wear it, everyone thinks it is new. [...]»
The painting arrived in the Barilla collection where it remained unknown until now.

Chronological history of the Bagni misteriosi
On his return to Paris in 1934 following the disappointments in Italy (the Maggio Musicale and Milan Triennale), de Chirico was struck by a new revelation. Throughout that spring he worked on drawings and paintings (one was shown in April). The Galerie des Quatre Chemins which had previously commissioned the *suites* of lithographs for *Metamorphosis* and the lithographs and etchings for *Le mystère laïc* of Jean Cocteau, offered to publish a portfolio of ten lithographs accompanied once again by the poems of Cocteau. Once again de Chirico was in the printworks of Edmond Desjobert who four years earlier had printed the sixty-six lithographs for the *Calligrammes* of Apollinaire published by Gallimard.

Ten lithographs: they begin to fill up with pools and cabins, nude swimmers and fully-dressed visitors, centaurs and wayfarers, water solidified like parquet, a swan and a boat, colored balloons, a parquet cascade...
In the winter of 1934, the paintings begin to multiply in his studio, ten or twelve of them. One painting is shown in the spring in the exhibit at the Gale-

The «Baths» on exhibit

1. The accrochage of the Giorgio de Chirico room at the Rome Quadriennale, January 1935. On the extreme left are seven paintings dedicated to the subject of the «Mysterious Baths» (the painting analyzed here is probably the last on the bottom left).
2-3. The «Baths» in New York: the catalogue from the Julien Levy exhibition in 1936; the painting from the Chrysler Collection (from the 1941 catalogue).

1

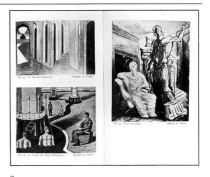

2

3

rie Billiet-Worms and as Jacques de Laprade recalled in the periodical *Beaux Arts*: «une toile qui n'amorce toute une série; une singulière piscine ou l'eau est représenté par un parquet.» At the end of the year, a painting entitled *The Mysterious Baths* appeared in the catalogue of an exhibit put together by Dario Sabatello that toured museums in California. In February 1935 the second Rome Quadriennale opened; there were seven *Bagni misteriosi* shown. We know from his letters to Nino Bertoletti how much these «still wet» paintings meant to de Chirico.

«In addition, there were some paintings which were still wet when they were packed, and they are: painting no. 13 (*I bagni misteriosi*), no. 23 (*La bàrca nei bagni misteriosi*) and no. 45 (*Le due cabine*). The number of each painting is written behind on the wood of the frame. Take a look to see if they are still wet and if they are, have them put aside until they are to be hung.» Luckily, we know of a photograph of the accrochage (in an article published in *La Tribuna*). One can see some of the paintings collected into a compact group as de Chirico had suggested in the same letter to Bertoletti. Among the echoes of the exhibit (very few make note of de Chirico's achievement), should be pointed out the article by Italo Cremona, the Turin intellectual and friend of Savinio, who perfectly recorded the presence of the *Bagni misteriosi*. «Metaphysical and surreal elements reach an understanding: the reasons are extremely comprehensible and the genesis and clearness of the pictorial explanation is astonishing, the artificiality of the color is almost always sustained and the reconstruction and correlation of the events and surprises is one of the most complete we know.»

But, above all, it was in the U.S. that paintings of this sort were successful. De Chirico brought some there from Paris, others he painted on site. They often appeared in catalogues and became part of the most prestigious collections (Walter P. Chrysler, Albert C. Barnes). When de Chirico returned to Italy, he took with him a group of canvasses of *Bagni misteriosi*. In his personal exhibition that opened in May 1938 at the Galleria Rota in Genoa,

he showed three works on this theme and (given the provenance of the painting analyzed here) he evidently also exhibited them in his personal show organized by Barbaroux the same year.

And here the story comes to a halt, to start up again in some late exhibitions, like the commemorative exposition at the Palazzo Reale in Milan in 1970 that presented two paintings from the series. We owe the equating of Metaphysical painting with the bagni misteriosi to certain critics such as Luigi Carluccio. On the cover of the catalogue *Le muse inquietanti* (1967), marking a new period in de Chiricoian history, he published one of these very baths, *Il nuotatore misterioso*, to be precise.

Not by chance, this iconography would erupt during the Neo-Metaphysical period, above all around 1970, when formats were enlarged and the copies multiplied, sometimes inlaid with the theme of the illustrations for Apollinaire. Themes blossomed in the life of Giorgio de Chirico: they were born, developed and then died to be reborn in a shifting metempsychosis. And when, by chance, the themes came to die, they behaved like the «extinguished suns» created for Apollinaire: they always mysteriously light something else.

A newly-unearthed subject

The mechanism of Giorgio de Chirico's thought process functioned by association of images (this was the way he defined his method in a memorable text from 1943). In essence, the mysterious baths were born by accumulating memories from his life (summers with his father and brother at the Pireo), books from his childhood (the antediluvian world of the Figuier) and culture (the etchings of Klinger).

We start with this last-mentioned motivation. In 1920, De Chirico wrote an essay on Max Klinger for the publication *Il Convegno*, and it is useful to quote this piece to see the unwinding of de Chirico's thought process at length: «Observe the etching entitled *Accordo*, once again from the *Brahmsphantasie* series: above a structure erected on the swirling and foaming sea, a black-garbed pianist is sitting by a piano on which he is playing as if he found himself in the warmth and tranquility of a

concert hall. Seated next to him is a woman. The folds of a curtain hung behind the two individuals hide a mysterious horizon. Underneath, in the water, a triton has difficulty handling an enormous harp which the wind batters against his forehead; mermaids play the harp. [...] To render this paradoxically lyrical scene more real, Klinger has placed near the pianist a small wooden ladder similar to those of the cabins at ocean resorts, of which one sees the first steps that enter the water. *The idea* of this ladder is extremely ingenious. Recalling the memories of my childhood, I remember that the ladders of the oceanside cabins always upset me and were very disturbing. Those few wooden steps covered with seaweed and mold and immersed at least a meter under water, seemed to me to descend for leagues and leagues, right into the heart of the oceanic pale. I relived this same emotion when I saw Klinger's etching. But in it the ladder also has another meaning: it unites the real with the unreal, and the latter, having been expressed with the same means as the former and not clouded over and confused as some painters do in compositions that contain unreal components (for example, Detaille's *Reve*), it seems that on leaving his instrument, the pianist could go into the water or that the marine creatures, by climbing the ladder, could come sit on top of the structure. It is a dream, and at the same time a reality; to those looking at it, it seems to be something they have already seen, but without remembering when or where.»

Giorgio de Chirico is speaking of Max Klinger, but he seems to be analyzing his own work. When he mentions a «paradoxically lyrical» scene, he seems to be defining a «Piazza d'Italia» in which every particular is faithful, but the combinations (paradoxical) transform the vision and reach the true objective: the poetic-lyric ambience. (It is no accident that he is one of the most-loved painters of poets, including Apollinaire, Cocteau, Breton, Ungaretti, Carrieri and Sinisgalli.) And finally, another point of his research: the dream which ends up coinciding with reality. The thing which appears impossible or non-existent has perhaps

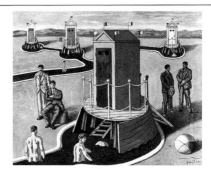

4. One of the masterpieces of the series, oil on canvas, 54 x 64 cm., Private Collection. (Returned are the motifs of the little lake, the stream, the large and small cabins, the dressed figures in contrast with the naked ones; the desert-like terrain is that of the old «Piazze d'Italia»).

4

already been seen in another world or at another time.

Unconscious and collective unconscious
An enrichment of this explanation is found in a passage from Martha Davidson's article in *Art News* as marginal notes to the 1936 personal exhibition in New York at Julien Levy's, that clearly record the painter's statements: «Apart from a feeling of suspended existence these paintings must depend on a literary transcription for an exposition of their esoteric meaning. When Chirico was a child in his native Greece, his father, a Sicilian engineer working in Volo, occasionally took him to the baths. The boy was deeply impressed by the difference he perceived between the clothed and unclothed figures. They seemed like different species of animals in different spheres of existence. The clothed men, like overwhelming and majestic statues, towered over the swimmers, who appeared exposed and defenseless. The little cabins, with their pierced windows were like masked heads looking on the scene.» In a certain sense, the painter's statement on the occasion of the reworking of a life-size mysterious bath for the 1973 Triennale in Milan is a repetition of this (from *Contatto, Arte/Città*, G. Macchi ed.): «The idea of the *Bagni misteriosi* came to me when I found myself once in a house in which the floor tiles were waxed to a high shine. I watched a man who was walking in front of me and whose legs were reflected in the floor. I had the impression that he could sink into that floor, as in a pool, and that he could move about and even swim. And so I imagined strange kinds of pools with people immersed in a kind of water-parquet, who stayed still and who moved, and sometimes they stopped to talk with other people who were outside the pool pavement.»
Maurizio Fagiolo dell'Arco

Iconographic motifs

5-6. *L'uomo che traversa il ruscello.* Two lithographs from the *Mythologie* collection, published by Quatre Chemins, with text by Jean Cocteau, in the Summer of 1934.

5

6

7. *L'uomo manichino stante.* Etching from the album *25 gravures de Arp, Calder, de Chirico, Ernst, Fernandez, Giacometti, Ghyka, Gonzales, Hélion, Kandinsky, Léger, Lipchitz, Magnelli,* by A. Jakovki, Orobitz Editeur, Paris, July 5, 1935.
8. *La vasca di bagni misteriosi* (with two figures), ca. 1936. Oil on canvas, Private Collection.

7

8

9
Giorgio de Chirico. 1888-1978
Ippolito con i compagni su i monti
dell'Isola di Creta
1955-1956

Oil on canvas, 148 x 144 cm.
Signed on the back.
Inscription on the back: «G. de Chirico»; label from
the 1956 Venice Biennale, no. 120; stamp of the art
supply company, A. Paciosi in Piazza San Carlo,
Rome.
Provenance: Galleria d'arte Medea, Milan (1971-
1972).
Exhibitions: XXVIII Venice Biennale, 1956, personal room, no. XVI, ill. no. 33; Milan, Galleria
d'Arte Medea, November 18-December 20, 1971,
col. ill. no. 31; Cortina d'Ampezzo, Galleria Medea,
July 1972; Montecatini Terme, Galleria Internazionale, September 1972, col. ill. no. 30.
Bibliography: F. Bellonzi, *Giorgio de Chirico*,
Rome, La Barcaccia, 1961, double page color
spread.

Dating
According to the «vox populi» (which had also said
the same about de Chirico of the Twenties and
Thirties), «baroque» style de Chirico is ugly, amoral
and out of date (today we would say «anachron-
istic»). The consequence: not only is this period not
studied philologically, but the problem is not even
touched on. To this very day, the date this masterpiece, *Ippoliti e i compagni su i monti dell'Isola di
Creta*, was painted is not even is known. I do know
a post-quem: the painting *Ippolito* with horse was
printed in a monograph with text by Isabella Far
published by Bestetti (Rome, January 1953). A simplified version compared with our painting here, it
centers around three figures. I know an ante-quem:
its exposition at the Venice Biennale in the summer
of 1956. The inscriptions on the back of the canvas
are no help to us (strangely, the signature is even
placed on the back), and there are no publications
or statements by the artist to assist us (at the end of
the exhibited works published in the catalogue of
the Biennale, the artist appended this polemical
annotation: «By the express declaration of the
artist, the works have no indication of date: just one
bears the year of execution on the canvas.») Not
even the autograph shipping form to the Venice
Biennale (four entry forms filled out in pen by

Giorgio de Chirico preserved in the ASAC archives)
give us supplementary help.
A number of reasons convince me not to distance
the work too much from its exhibition date. Above
all the effort in painting it, plus the impressiveness
of the format, the price attributed to the work — far
and away the most expensive (3000 lire according
to the accompanying sheet mentioned above) of
the ones sent to Venice, and finally, the reworking
of a previous painting enriched with details and an
enlarged setting. In addition, on the entry form,
this work is the last on the list of the paintings
sent (which later, in the exhibit, is numbered 36).
Therefore, I believe this large canvas was executed
especially for this exhibit.
Parenthetically, the Biennale removed it from its
rooms following the (warranted) protest by the
artist who, in the room dedicated to him, found a
Manichino he had not painted (one of the group of
32 works I have linked to Oscar Dominguez and
which I will publish with a complete dossier). At the
time, de Chirico responded with an «Anti-Bien-
nale» (also involving young painters like Carlo
Guarienti and old colleagues like Romano Gaz-
zera). In short, *Ippolito con i compagni su i monti
dell'Isola di Creta* is a demanding painting because
it also marks an eagerly awaited comeback.
Iconography
The story of Hippolytus derives primarily from the
Euripedean tragedy, but there are many sources
listed by the major «mythographers» (among the
most important ones: Carlo Kerenyi, *Gli dei e gli
eroi della Grecia*, Ital. ed., Milan, Il Saggiatore,
1963; Robert Graves, *I miti greci*, Ital. ed., Milan,
Longanesi, 1955). We know about the moment in
which following her marriage to Theseus, Phaedra
sends her bastard son Hippolytus away and we
know about Hippolytus's stay in Thessaly, the
young man's return and his (incestuous) love for
Phaedra, as well as the story's epilogue, Phaedra's
accusation of violence against Hippolytus and his
self-sacrifice by hanging. But I do not believe that
anything about the stay of Hippolytus and his companions on Crete emerges from any source (the
«embryonic» painting of the series, the one pub-

lished in the January 1953 monograph, in a certain
sense, is much-simplified and generic). Is it another
de Chirico enigma or, more simply, a way of throw-
ing the viewer off-track? The viewer, rather than
being attracted to a precise theme, is drawn to the
hero's statuesque position, the picturesque movement of the dogs, by the dynamism of the trainer of
the rearing horse, the rhetorical gesture of the
nude in the foreground, the richness of the red
drape and the oddity of the countryside in the
background in which a storm is breaking. The purpose of the very long title (so *unusually* long) is perhaps to sidetrack us away from the theme: de Chirico has painted an ancient «academy,» anti-
Modernist par excellence.
On the other hand, themes of this sort frequently
return in his works during these years: for example,
Lo sbarco di Alessandro with similar characters,
published in the monograph by I. Far (Milan,
Fabbri, 1968, no. 94.) or *Ippolito e i suoi compagni*
in which Hermes even appears in flight (I. Far,
ibid., no. 160). Am I venturing too much to suppose
that it is an image of antiquity in itself (that is, anti-
modern)? An antiquity that is not textual but
simply evocative, coming from the memory, or better, from the overlapping of memories since, from
an iconographic standpoint, Alessandro could be
superimposed on Ippolito.
Anti-Modernism
In the 1956 Venice Biennale in which the painting
was exhibited, the most recent abstract tendencies
(the rooms of Consagra, Afro and Corpora) and
informal tendencies (Mannucci, Vedova) could be
seen, but also realism (Ziveri, Pirandello). France
was represented by a classicist, Juan Gris, Germany
by Emil Nolde, the United States, with the odd
exhibit «American Painters and the City,» brought
face-to-face old and modern tendencies, nonetheless still «avantgarde» (Willem de Kooning and his
rival Edvard Hopper, Franz Kline, Max Ernst, Jack-
son Pollock, Reginald Marsh, Marc Tobey and Ben
Shann).
De Chirico who, alongside Picasso, Chagall,
Apollinaire and Max Jacob, «invented» the avantgarde in Paris, some time before had in fact taken a

1. *Autoritratto col manto giallo* (1947): exhibited work.
2. Page from the catalogue with an *Ettore ed Andromaca* (reworked) along with the painting analyzed here.
3. Autograph loan form for the painting at the Venice Biennale. It appears as no. 53 and is valued at 3000 lire (the highest price of the 33 paintings sent). Archivio ASAC (Courtesy of Sergio Pozzati).

1

2

3

step backwards. The press nurtured its venomous writings against «Modernism,» while the polemics intensified against «forgeries» (*Oggi*, March 16, 1956; *Il Tempo*, February 5, 1956; *La Domenica del Corriere*, February 26, 1956). We had arrived at the furthest point: the craving for avantgarde had led some unscrupulous forgerers to copy those works, the fruit of the «Modernist dictatorship.» But in the meantime there had appeared the monograph of James Thrall Soby for the Museum of Modern Art in New York: de Chirico hinted at some protests, but by this time, no one could deprive him of his pivotal role in the 20th century avantgarde movement. (At base, it was a double-track analogous to that of the 1955 Quadriennale. In the exhibit *Antologia della pittura italiana dal 1910 al 1930*, Giorgio Castelfranco presented his avantgarde paintings. In the rooms of the Quadriennale, five canvasses with the presentation of Isabella Far showed his current, touchy, Rubensian style).

But what was the meaning of this rebellion by de Chirico against «the modern»? It was in 1938, on the eve of the war, that he started to immerse himself in other worlds (the Renaissance, the Baroque, Romanticism) which were different from the Hellenic dream, but for him, simply complementary. It was the celebration of disguise and freedom which

every artist should be constrained to allow himself (and this also explains the self-portraits in which he masquerades as a Turk, a toreador, a warrior or Venetian gentleman).

«Only by following me will they save themselves,» wrote the prophet of anti-Modernism, but this crusade had begun many years before. I remember that it was Jean Cocteau himself who began the struggle: «L'antimoderne par excellence» he signed a dedication to Jacques Maritain which I found in a book entitled *Moderno* in my library. This really is a modern statement, it was only noted around 1880 when Arthur Rimbaud uttered his famous anathema «Il faut être absolument moderne.»

A relentless crusade (and a somewhat ridiculous one, as all crusades are). An apparently losing battle. In reality, the example of Giorgio de Chirico, who became a sacrificial lamb, returns to the limelight every time an artist wants to abandon for a moment the Salon or Lobby of the Biennale, or the Gallery and air-conditioned and fast-paced surroundings (jet or Ferrari). However, there is no longer any need for that young artist to replicate the crusade, to play the fool as Nietzsche said. Metaphysical painting did it once and for all.

Did no one speak of technique any more? He

returned to the old recipes and painterly «kitchen» secrets, just as he had done in Paris in 1928 with the *Piccolo trattato di tecnica pittorica*, when the Surrealists had adopted him as their father (and he, Nietzschian par excellence, wanted no part of any family). And so he refused what was on the market and he «perfected» it (as he said) or «improved» on it (oh, deceit!). He felt the need of expanding the material in the painting without knowing exactly what to aim for (but, as Christopher Columbus taught, it is difficult for an explorer to know the outcome of his search). During these years, it seemed important to him to enlarge the territory of the artificial, expand the materialness of thought and, as always, build the phantom of an idea. One only need go through his writings from those years to understand that his search was the same as always: «We love the *not true*,» «Everything but reality.» The last period. Many painters today are still heavily underestimated in their activity in old age, for example, Francis Picabia, Giacomo Balla, Salvador Dalì, or (even) Pablo Picasso. It almost seems as if towards the end of their lives, they suddenly discover that one can also cast off true painting since the real problem (metaphysical) is the end of life, and therefore also the end of painting.

Maurizio Fagiolo dell'Arco

Prototype and variations on the same theme

4. *Ippolito con cavallo* from the monograph by I. Far, 1953.
5-6. *Ippolito e i suoi compagni* and *Lo sbarco di Alessandro* (published in the monograph by I. Far, 1968).

4

5

6

10
Alberto Savinio. 1891-1952
Le cadran de l'espérance
1928

Oil on canvas, 126 x 72 cm.
Signed and dated on lower left: «Savinio 1928»; title appears on the frame.
Provenance: Léonce Rosenberg Collection, Paris; Galerie Rive Gauche, Paris; Galleria Marescalchi, Bologna; Cavazza Pier Leda Collection, Bologna.
Exhibition: Bologna, Galleria d'Arte Moderna, *La Metafisica, gli anni Venti*, May-August, 1980, vol. I, 81, 95, b/w ill.
Bibliography: *Les ventes publiques en France. Répertoire general des prix 1945-1946 et 1946-1947*, Paris, 1947, p. 95, b/w ill.; E. Benezit, *Dictionnaire des peintres, sculpteurs, dessinateurs et graveurs*, Paris, 1947, p. 543, pl. 7; *Alberto Savinio*, Milan, 1949, b/w ill. (title: *La torre*); M. Fagiolo dell'Arco, *Alberto Savinio*, Milan, 1989, pp. 105, 241, no. 25, col. ill. (along with another work painted in 1928, *La tour du bonheur* and bibl. relating to it); P. Vivarelli, in *Savinio, gli anni di Parigi, dipinti 1927-1932*, exh. cat., Verona, Galleria Civica d'Arte Moderna, Palazzo Forti and Galleria dello Scudo, December 9, 1990-February 10, 1991, p. 186, b/w ill.

Sold in an auction at the Hotel Druot in Paris on January 28, 1946 for 2,800 francs,[1] the painting had been part of the decoration in an area of the apartment of Léonce Rosenberg, the dealer of both de Chirico brothers at the end of the 1920s. Rosenberg had invited eleven important artists connected with his gallery, the Effort Moderne, to collaborate in the major project of decorating his Paris home, located in 35 Rue Longchamp which was inaugurated on the evening between June 15 and 16, 1929. Among them Ernst, Léger, Giorgio de Chirico, Severini, Picabia and Metzinger.[2] The decorative series Savinio realized for Rosenberg during 1928-29 included — as the artist himself stated in 1950[3] — six canvasses with «transparent cities» as their subject: *L'île des charmes* and *La cité des promesses*, both horizontal in format, and three vertical works with the specific theme of «towers,» *La tour du bonheur*, this 1928 painting from the Barilla collection and *Monument* from 1929.[4] We have no documentary evidence with which to defi-

nitively identify the sixth painting of the cycle. However, two other small versions are known that have on the back the title *Les Grâces insulaires*[5] and which, because of their small size, were probably sketches for the large work destined for the Rosenberg home.

The geometrical objects of de Chirico's Metaphysical canvasses or his «trophies» from the '20s, certainly offered Savinio an iconographic starting point for this accumulation of heterogeneous elements. But, in comparison with de Chirico's absurd style deriving from the presence of incongruous objects, Savinio favors instead the theme of a deep ambiguity concerning all that is real, a basic and constant concept in his poetic style. The conceptual oddity of the miniaturized rock placed on pedestals and platforms reminiscent of the theater, is reabsorbed in the overall reduction of all the composition's elements into playthings, united by a uniform linear schematization of the masses which are defined by almost phosphorescently colored borders. A process of metamorphosis runs through the whole scene, therefore, a scene in which the naturalness of the rock and the artificiality of the decorated polyhedrons do not emerge as distinct categories and together contribute to defining a sense of reality on a «marvelous» level, not perceptible in abstractly rational terms, but as the hope or expectation (as the painting's title itself suggests) of miracles of a prelogical nature. In their ambiguous way of appearing simultaneously as both natural and transparent images, the seductive «cities of incantations» present themselves, in essence, not as pure and unrealistic visions, but as plausible apparitions, even if imagined.

In his literary and theoretical writings, Savinio himself continually tends to reaffirm that his ideational processes are not completely imaginary — and as such, incapable of catching the truth of the objective world — but rather derive, as for all German Romantic artists as well as for Breton in *Le Surréalisme et la peinture*, from a visual potential that makes them more acute and sensitive. For an artist, imagining is to see with «a perspective capable of reaching farther [...] deeper [...] more into

the past. [...] His eyes see [...] the stuff of the air, the light blue landscapes [and] the images of the most ancient skies still intact and with their original shine and colors.»[6] Savinio also traced back the elaboration of the transparent cities and towers to this theme of «extraordinary visual perception» as well as to hermetic-religious allusions. In fact, the artist affirms in a late reference that the memory which prompted the paintings in the Rosenberg decorative cycle, «I found in a phrase I read in a book by Anatole France, *La Rôtisserie de la Reine de la Pédauque: Les paysages de l'air*. Monsieur d'Asterac, the alchemist who pronounced these lines, said that acquiring sharper perception through the intervention of Paraclesian art, one could see landscapes in the air. Added to this memory was that of the New Jerusalem announced in the Apocalypse. The city floating in air, as white as one made out of sugar which at certain times of the day, at sunrise and sunset, could also be seen by the human eye. *La città meravigliosa* and the other paintings similar to it were painted, or better *painted* and *written*, under the dictates of these memories. *Painted* against a profane background, i.e., in the earthly atmosphere as the profane eye sees it. *Written* in the more subtle part and which only an extremely trained eye is able to see, that is, in the configurations which *against the light*, are delineated in the midst of the earth's atmosphere. In other words, these configurations are like the vision of the New Jerusalem which, at sunrise and sunset, even the human eye can see.»[7]
Pia Vivarelli

1. This is the first documented report relating to the painting, contained in *Ventes publiques, op. cit.*, in the bibliography of the work analyzed here. Evidently, Savinio was not aware of this 1946 auction since, in personally compiling the small monograph released by EPI in 1949, he published the work as still belonging to the collection of Léonce Rosenberg.
2. We owe the most replete analysis of the decorative project for the Rosenberg apartments to C. Derouet, «Un problème du baroque tardif à Paris» in *Giorgio de Chirico*, exh. cat., W. Rubin, W. Schmied, J. Clair eds., Munich, Haus der Kunst, November 1982-January

11
Alberto Savinio (Andrea de Chirico).
1891-1952
L'ira di Achille
1930

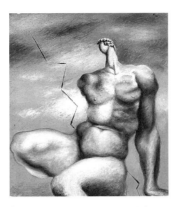

1983; Paris, Centre Georges Pompidou, Musée National d'Art Moderne, February-April 1983, pp. 111-135 of the French edition of the catalogue.
3. A. Savinio, quoted in R. Carrieri, *Pittura e scultura d'avanguardia 1890-1950*, Milan, 1950, p. 249.
4. All of the cycle's canvasses are reproduced in the catalogue of the 1990-91 Verona Exhibition (*op. cit.* in the Bibliography of the work), pp. 181-187.
5. The two canvasses are also reproduced in the Verona exhibition catalogue indicated above, pp. 184-185.
6. A. Savinio, *Casa «la Vita»*, 1943, pp. 269-270, from the 1971 Milan edition.
7. Idem, quoted in R. Carrieri, *op. cit.*, p. 249.

Alberto Savinio. *L'île des charmes*, 1928

Oil on canvas, 54.5 x 45.5 cm.
Signed and dated on upper right: «Savinio 1930.»
Provenance: Galleria Galatea, Turin; Galleria il Fauno, Turin; Galleria L'Approdo, Turin; Galleria Medea, Milan; Mario Cambi Collection, Rome; Galleria Dello Scudo, Verona.
Exhibitions: Milan, Galleria Levi, 1963, no. 8, b/w ill.; Rome, Palazzo delle Esposizioni, *Alberto Savinio*, May 18-June 18, 1978, no. 38, b/w ill.
Bibliography: E. Crispolti, «Savinio un surrealista autonomo» in *Arte Illustrata*, October-December 1970, p. 62, b/w ill. no. 9 (with the title *La stanchezza di Achille*); P. Vivarelli in *Savinio, gli anni di Parigi, dipinti 1927-1932*, exh. cat., Verona, Galleria Civica d'Arte Moderna, Palazzo Forti and Galleria dello Scudo, December 9, 1990-February 10, 1991, p. 246, b/w ill.

The motif of the distortion of the classical nude is present in Savinio's paintings throughout 1929 in a series of numerous variations both on the individual characters as well as the compositional settings. This theme also continued over into 1930, enriched with new metamorphic «taints.» In a compact group of paintings the nudes appear as angelic figures with ring-like heads, in other canvasses we encounter animal heads or, in still others, the colossal figures are reduced to just linear outlines as in *Le départ de la colombe* in the Barilla Collection.

The common characteristic of all these heroic figures is an explicit alteration of the form that distorts the original models of the past, even if Savinio's immediate models are those taken from late-nineteenth century plates found in the artist's studio along with photographs of youths in academic poses.[1] Even in the first two years of his activity as a painter, between 1927 and 1928, Savinio made wide use of classic models, taking them, during this period, from the reproductions of Salomon Reinach's repertory of ancient painting and sculpture which at the time was quite diffuse among archaeology and art students and also known to de Chirico who used them as a source of inspiration for many of his pictures. But, if in 1927-28 the

examples of classic statuary appearing in Savinio's canvasses retain all the characteristics of truly «plaster» figures lacking real human substance, vice versa the nudes from the works of the two years following have — because of their color and design — an insistent plasticity, one would say a mannerism of Michelangelesque origin, also because of the preference given compositional schemes in chiasmal and spiral form. These figures, which are so vigorous, collide with processes that deform them and paroxysmally elongate or decisively broaden their limbs. From this is derived a substantially ambivalent humanity in which co-exist an extant sense of heroism of the bodies and a general sense of uselessness in the apparently titanic gestures performed by legendary giants but with heads reduced to the small egg-shaped ones of mannequins. Of the entire series, *L'ira di Achille* — directly comparable to *Oreste et Pylade*, also from 1930, for the iconographic and stylistic solutions it employs — presents the novelty of the epically tragic emphasis the nude assumes, isolated without visible support in a spatial situation lacking Savinio's customary and rich scenographic apparatus. The absolute vacuum surrounding the hero is only furrowed by the menacing omens of a thunderbolt.

The near-contemporary criticism of these canvases already caught their contradictory nature. «Savinio,» wrote Cheronnet in 1934, «is that of the demi-gods from a legendary age. He loves the epic mass of planetary systems which guard heroes with brutish and deformed muscles and a head that is atrophied...useless.»[2] A comprehensive analysis of the entire cycle of titanic nudes in the context of Savinio's output during these years clarifies the overall significance of these ambiguous figures: for Savinio, painting is the exercise of the memory, retrieval of one's own individual past or of the history of the world. The phases of greatest truth in history are for Savinio — bringing together Vico's philosophy with Nietzsche's thought — the initial moments in the development of the world, those in which nature is free to expand and display its vitality outside the rational schemata of logic. Therefore, the titanic figures, whether Adam or Prome-

287

12
Alberto Savinio. 1891-1952
Le départ de la colombe
1930

theus, Daedalus or Achilles, the builders of paradise or sirens — according to the titles of some of his works between 1929 and 1930 — are representatives of an original and primordial nature, of a human stock both mythical and primitive, magnified from an heroic standpoint and, at the same time, still chaotic and undefined, so as to present, only apparently incongruously, gargantuan bodies and minuscule, feature-less, heads.
Pia Vivarelli

1. The three plates with academic nudes found in Savinio's studio are reproduced in L. Cavallo, P. Vivarelli, *Savinio, disegni immaginati (1925-1932)*, Milan, 1984, 140.
2. L. Cheronnet, «Les peintres oniriques» in *L'Amour de l'art*, March 1934, p. 327.

Alberto Savinio, *Oreste et Pylade*, 1930

Oil on canvas, 55 x 65 cm.
Signed and dated on left-center: «Savinio 1930»; title appears on the frame.
Provenance: Ch. Pomaret Collection, Galerie de la Renaissance, Paris, no. 576; Galerie A.-F. Petit, Paris; Galleria Galatea, Turin, no. 1690; Galleria Gissi, Turin, no. 2679; Galleria Medea, Milan.
Exhibitions: Turin, Galleria Gissi, *Savinio*, February 28, 1967, no. 21, b/w ill.; Milan, Galleria Medea, *44 opera di Alberto Savinio*, March 14-April 1970, no. 34, b/w ill.; Milan, Palazzo Reale, *Alberto Savinio*, June-July 1976 (later, Brussels, Société des Expositions du Palais des Beaux-Arts, August-September 1976), no. 33, b/w ill.; Verona, Galleria Civica d'Arte Moderna, Palazzo Forti and Galleria dello Scudo, *Savinio, gli anni di Parigi, dipinti 1927-1932*, December 9, 1990-February 10, 1991, no. 68, col. ill.
Bibliography: L. Carluccio, «Alberto Savinio» in *Le Arti*, XVII, 1967, p. 55, no. 3, b/w ill.; *Alternative attuali 3 — Rassegna internazionale d'arte contemporanea*, exh. cat., L'Aquila, Castello Spagnolo, July-September 1968, 161, b/w ill.; P. Vivarelli in *Alberto Savinio*, exh. cat., Rome, Palazzo delle Esposizioni, May 18-June 18, 1978, 93, b/w ill.; Idem. in L. Cavallo, P. Vivarelli, *Savinio, disegni immaginati (1925-1932)*, Milan, 1984, pp. 84, 142, b/w pl. no. 31; L. Cammarella Falsitta in *Alberto Savinio dipinti e disegni 1929-1951*, exh. cat., Milan, Galleria Spazio Immagine, April 22-June 15, 1988, p. 44, b/w ill.; M. Fagiolo dell'Arco, *Alberto Savinio*, Milan, 1989, pp. 154, 243, no. 67, b/w ill.

The motif of the images «against the light» — born of the example of various Cubist works by Juan Gris — over the course of the 1920s became the common legacy of a wide range of figurative currents and, at the end of the decade, circulated above all in the ambience of painters connected to Surrealism or who revolved around Léonce Rosenberg's gallery, including Ernst, Picabia, Léger and Giorgio de Chirico. But these points of tangency between artists who worked in the same cultural climate at the same time have a more interesting significance on a general historical level than from

any real analogy between their poetic styles.

With an ambiguity peculiar to Savinio, the human forms in *Le départ de la colombe* seem to be temporary concrete expressions of a single luminescent linear stamp which, with the same feverish and irregular tendency, defines both the dense embellishment of the setting as well as the anatomical details of the central group. Thus, in a certain way, the transparent figures are expressions of a vital force that permeates the entire reality and also manifests itself in the expansion of the spatial context of the painting with the proliferation of other undefined spaces above and beyond the curtain at the side.

The reasons for this agitated dynamism are indicated by the title of the work itself. In fact, in Savinio's painting and writing, frequently the theme of the point of departure or the voyage is, in itself, a recapitulation of that continuous and volatile course of the world which, for the artist, constitutes the truest essence of reality. In addition, here, as well as in other paintings of the same period, Savinio always links the presence of the dove to its traditional function as the harbinger of momentous tidings.

According to a precise and constant narrative volition in Savinio's painting, despite being so strongly estranged from the bodies appearing as pure, multi-colored arabesques, the effects should not be taken to harken back to an obscure, dreamlike Surrealist dimension. On the contrary, they are, even if indefinable, the result of a declared and objective extraordinary event, capable of overturning physical laws and have emerge arcane revivifying natural forces. With subtle playful irony, only the animals — taken from the illustrations in children's books and found in the artist's studio — seem to be excluded from this global subversion of reality and retain a residual realistic substance in the heads with their blank and unwitting expressions.
Pia Vivarelli

13
Alberto Savinio. 1891-1952
Fruits et orage
1930-1931

Alberto Savinio, *Le goûter*, 1930

Page from a children's book found among the material in the artist's studio (Archivio Savinio, Rome)

Oil on canvas, 44 x 54 cm.
Signed on upper left: «Savinio»; title appears on the frame.
Provenance: Ch. Pomaret Collection, Galerie de la Renaissance, Paris, no. 807; Galerie A.-F. Petit, Paris; Galerie de France, Paris; Galleria Medea, Milan.
Exhibitions: Milan, Galleria Medea, *44 opere di Alberto Savinio*, March 14-April 1970, no. 25, b/w ill.; Verona, Galleria Civica d'Arte Moderna, Palazzo Forti and Galleria dello Scudo, *Savinio, gli anni di Parigi, dipinti 1927-1932*, December 9, 1990-February 10, 1991, no. 77, col. ill.

A small group of paintings precisely dated 1930 — from *Le réveil du Carpophage* to *L'annonce faîte à la Vierge* — presents the disturbing metamorphic personalities of the «sea dinosaurs» or the human figures with animal heads next to luxuriant still lifes. And taken almost completely faithfully from a painting of this 1930 series, *Le goûter*, is the group of fruit seen in this current painting on display which thus constitutes — together with the *Nature morte bleu* — the first example of the still life subject in Savinio. The subject continues, even if in isolated instances, in his output throughout the 1930s up to the *Natura morta con fiori ricamati* exhibited in Milan in his 1940 personal exhibition at the Galleria del Milione. Five works by Savinio with the specific title of *Nature morte* are documented in the paintings exhibited in Paris in 1930 at the *VIII Salon des Tuileries*. But there is no documentary evidence that would allow us to link these titles with works which have come down to us except for the case of the *Nature morte bleu* cited above with the precise date of 1930 on the painting. The other (few) famous works having a still life subject or bearing a more specific title on their frames — as in the case of *Fruits et orage* — either because of the tempera technique or choice of colors used, must date back to a period subsequent to 1931, as in the case of the painting previously belonging to Paris gallery owner, Léonce Rosenberg.[1]

Giorgio de Chirico, starting with the Rome Bien-

nale in 1923 and throughout the 1920s, had already devised complex still lifes placed on windowsills framed by puffy curtains and opening out onto external landscapes. In Savinio's *Fruits et orage* this iconography takes on more explicitly theatrical connotations, both for the accentuated precariousness of the narrow boxed space in which the walls open up like stage wings as well as, and above all, for the intense contrasts of light that cut across the essentially monochromatic structures of the setting — thus presenting itself as a stage backdrop — and the composition of the sumptuously colored fruit as a seventeenth century still life. The strong contrast between the monochromatic parts making up the background to the area rich with color is part of Savinio's painting style already starting from the earlier *Objets dans la forêt* of 1927-28 and it contributes to lending this still life, although realistically shaped, the sense of a true «apparition.» The still life does not change in its concreteness, nor does it become an explicit metaphor for symbolic meanings. In its unblemished objectivity it becomes the moment summarizing that natural vision of reality belonging to Savinio's poetic sense. For the artist, in fact, every facet of the real, even that which is inanimate, is permeated by a universal and cyclical dynamism which is not just boundless vitality or the quiet flow of events, but also the potential for violence and the menacing force of nature. The dramatic tension circulating in the landscape ribboned with lightning is thus reflected in the isolation of the still life which, as the title suggests, is charged with the premonitions of a «storm» passing through the external space.
Pia Vivarelli

1. The *Natura morta* that reappeared in Italy in the *Savinio* exhibit at the Galleria Gissi, Turin, February 28, 1967 (reprod. in the catalogue, no. 26, with the erroneous date of 1910).

14
Max Ernst. 1891-1952
Divinité
(1940)

15
Max Ernst. 1891-1952
Le Romantisme
(1960)

Oil on canvas glued to cardboard, 36 x 27 cm.
Signed on bottom right: «Max Ernst».
Provenance: Galleria Galatea, Turin.

On the back, this small painting bears an inscription in the artist's own hand: «A' Leonor Fini/Divinité/Max Ernst.» This Argentinean woman painter who moved from Milan to Paris in 1933, was strongly influenced by paintings such as this one from which she derived many of her extremely sophisticated female figures. Although not dated, the painting can be easily ascribed to the year 1940. In fact, it seems to be a preparatory sketch to the famous *Vestizione della sposa* (Venice, Peggy Guggenheim Collection) painted during that period. And if it is not exactly a sketch (a very unusual practice for Ernst), it is certainly a study for the central figure of the Venice painting. The final version is larger, seems more complex and is charged with a more restless sense of mystery. There are two female figures in mute dialogue; both are naked and surrounded by nightmarish monstrous creatures and they pace within a flight in perspective partially enclosed by a wall on which is hung a picture that repeats part of the scene using the technique of frottage. In this painting, of all this there appears only the figure of the «bride» completely enveloped in a domino of red feathers. From under the hood can be made out her profile (while in the Guggenheim painting her face vanishes under the plumage of an owl and just one eye can be glimpsed). The hands emerge from under the cape: the outstretched left hand would remain almost the same in the larger version while the right, here just hinted at, would maintain the same pose but be precisely drawn following museum examples (from Botticelli or Parmigianino). Further, the winged outstretching of the cape, on the right of this painting, is transformed, with the same profile and spatial placement, into the hair of the second female figure in the Guggenheim painting, while the harpy crouched on the right becomes, in the same position, a finned, four-teated monster which is, nonetheless, masculine. In any case, the link between the two works is clear,

and the more refined complexity of the Venice painting suggests a slight pre-dating for this study.

The feminine form appearing here is that of the young English artist Leonora Carrington whom Ernst had met in 1937. We recognize them from the photographs taken in Cornwall and at their house in Ardèche which Ernst fled from in 1940 after having been captured twice by the Germans, going first to Madrid, then Lisbon and finally the United States together with Peggy Guggenheim. That face, beloved and then lost, Ernst had painted with obsessive photographic detail in `Leonora in the Morning Light` (Julien Levy Collection, Bridgewater, Connecticut) in 1940, and a little later in *Napoleone nel deserto* (New York, Museum of Modern Art, 1941) and in *Antipapa* (this also formerly belonging to Peggy Guggenheim in Venice and dated 1941 or 1942). In all these paintings, Ernst frequently made use of the technique of «frottage,» rehabilitating for new expressive ends a technique he had already tried fifteen years earlier. But here, in this little painting, a singular inversion of the procedure takes place shedding some light on the artist's insatiable curiosity about painting methods and his readiness to interchange them and have them coexist often in the same context. In fact, at first glance the overall effect brings to mind the random and partly unforeseeable texture of frottage. But only in that wing-like form on the right is one able to recognize the imprint of a foreign material (fabric, it seems) on the still-wet painted surface. All the rest is carefully painted with short strokes which imitate the thread of a carpet, a web of thick fringe. Here, in short, the most traditional and imitative technique faithfully follows the appearance of an automatic and surreal device, confirming the idea (typical of Ernst and other Surrealists, all now advanced beyond the first steps of the avantgarde) of the absolute preeminence of invention in the face of linguistic instruments that render it manifest.
Eugenio Riccòmini

Oil on panel, 41 x 31 cm.
Provenance: Galleria Alexandre Iolas; Galleria Galatea, Turin.
Exhibition: *Max Ernst, oltre la pittura*, Palazzo Grassi, Venice, June 17-October 2, 1966, no. 57, b/w ill.
Bibliography: *Max Ernst, oltre la pittura*, Venice, 1966.

This painting, signed but undated, is probably from the year 1960. It is very similar, in fact, to the *Quasi feu le romantisme* (P. Marinotti Collection, Milan) which all the literature ascribes to that year even if the date is not visible on the back. Also here, as in the other picture cited, Ernst applies the well-proven technique of frottage, making use of the same twigs of two different plant species evoking a fairy tale-like undergrowth through which a cold lunar light is filtered. Here the star dominates the center of the composition in a perfect circle, probably obtained by exactly tracing the outline of a coin, while in the Marinotti painting, Ernst makes use of a variant, compressing the circle into a flattened ellipse. This use of the frottage technique is typical of Ernst's work following his return to Europe at the end of the war and was already quite evident in *Pour les amis d'Alice* in '57 (Anne Doll Collection, Paris) in which the jumble of figurative and geometric elements combined in kaleidoscopic fashion recalls similar experiments by Klee. I would also mention that in 1960 Ernst made a long trip to Germany and it is not unlikely that the abundance of plant forms in his paintings of that period (here the sole theme of the composition) is an echo of his revisiting the forests of his native environment.
Eugenio Riccòmini

16
René Magritte. 1898-1967
La belle captive, II
1935

Oil on canvas, 45 x 65 cm.
Signed on upper left: «Magritte».
Provenance: Robert Strauss Collection, London.
Exposition: New York, MOMA, *René Magritte*, 1965, no. 28.
Bibliography: J. T. Soby, *René Magritte*, New York, MOMA, 1965, p. 79, b/w ill. p. 35.

There is a previous version of this «exceptionally lyric»[1] painting, *La belle captive*, from 1931. Depicted in this painting is a rustic landscape with an artist's easel on which is placed a canvas showing a country village with a farmer leading a horse-drawn cart. This 1931 work is the first of a group in which Magritte reflects upon the relationship between reality and artistic representation. This process of reflection had already been foreshadowed in images from the second half of the 1920s, as in *Nocturne* (1925), *Les signes du soir* (1926) and *Le message à la terre*, and gave life to «two great series: that of the *Belle captive* in which a painting on an easel seems to have substituted part of the landscape behind it, and the paintings from the *Condition Humaine* series, in which the same idea is made more complex by placing the painting on the easel in an interior setting which opens up onto the landscape.»[2]

As usually happens in Magritte, an idea is elaborated in multiple variations or modified in combination with others. For the *Belle captive*, there also exist numerous subsequent versions up until the 1940s. Magritte stated: «Following my first exhibition [...] I painted a thousand pictures, but I only devised about a hundred of these images [...]. These thousand pictures simply derived from the fact that I often painted variations of my images: this is how I better delimit the mystery, possess it better.»[3] The crux of the problem Magritte took on in this group of paintings is clarified by Jean Clair in discussing the *Condition Humaine*: «The painting which 'represents' is well-overlayed in the painting which is 'represented', as in inlay work. But it does not repeat it in depth; it prolongs it without interruption. It hides it quite a bit more than it lets it appear: the painting hides what is real,

and instead of revealing it, masks it. The wall of pure glass, as Leonardo defined painting, the perfect *intersection* of Alberti, here becomes the pitiful miracle of a conjurer who shakes screens to have the images appear and disappear. [...] This has a number of consequences. In 'classical' painting, a body, an object or a figure does not really hide another body. On the basis of the visible parts of this body, the crystallographic structure of the mathematical space allows one to deduce the hidden parts. Contrarily, in Magritte's painting, one can never be sure of the nature of what is hidden; the veiled part could differ from the part that is visible and, should it become uncovered, reveal some unexpected aspects.»[4] In other words, Magritte is working with one of the themes which most excited him, what is inherent in the relationship between signs and things with the intent of highlighting a «divergence between the object and its symbol,»[5] a divergence, this, which confers upon his depictions a great sense of ambiguity and mystery. As for style and technique, Magritte considered them secondary aspects, only useful for rendering, with the maximum sense of illusionism, a fantastical and disturbing image: «I always force myself,» he told Pierre Descargues, «to not have the painting call attention to itself, that it be as invisible as possible. I work somewhat like a writer searching for the simplest tone, avoiding any stylistic aspect, so that the reader cannot discern in the work anything but the idea the author wanted to express.»[6]
Claudio Zambianchi

1. Soby, p. 14.
2. D. Sylvester, *Magritte*, Turin and Houston, Umberto Allemandi & Co. and the Menil Foundation, 1992, p. 88.
3. P. Descargues, «René Magritte, le plus célèbre des surréalistes belges, parle du mystère,» *Feuille d'avis de Lausanne — Magazine*, November 1, 1961; published as «Intervista rilasciata a Pierre Descargues» in A. Blavier, ed., *René Magritte. Tutti gli scritti*, Italian trans. by L. Sosio, Milan, Feltrinelli, 1979, 162, p. 471.
4. J. Clair, «Le visible et l'imprévisible. Sept prolégomènes à un petit traité des tropes magrittéens» in Brussels, Palais des Beaux-Arts (later publ., Paris, Musée National d'Art Moderne Georges Pompidou), *Rétrospective Magritte*, exh. cat., October 27-December 31, 1978, p. 37.
5. S. Gablik, *Magritte*, London, Thames, 1970 (6th printing), p. 75.
6. P. Descargues, «René Magritte: Faire la peinture qui se remarque le moins possible,» *Tribune de Lausanne*, January 15, 1967; publ. as «Intervista rilasciata a Pierre Descargues, II» in Blavier, 204, p. 574.

17
Marc Chagall. 1887-1985
Violoniste
1938

Tempera and pastel on paper, 34.5 x 25.5 cm.
Signed on bottom right: «Marc Chagall».
Provenance: Private Collection, Frankfurt.
Exhibitions: Verona, Galleria Comunale d'Arte
Moderna, Palazzo Forti (later Rome, Galleria
Nazionale d'Arte Moderna), *Da Cézanne all'arte
astratta. Omaggio a Lionello Venturi*, G. Cortenova
and R. Lambarelli eds., March 1-May 10, 1992, exh.
cat., Mazzotta, Milan, col. ill., p. 42.

The theme of the violinist continuously reappears
in Chagall's work. In some paintings, in particular
in the *Violinista verde* of 1918, the musician represents the «Devil when he wants to appear in disguise.»[1] In other works, on the other hand, the
violin appears in paintings dedicated to lovers
(*Sonate de violon*, the first version as well as the
definitive one of 1929), is an attribute of angels
(*L'ange aux ailes rouges*, 1933-36), of clowns
(*Femme clown au violon*, 1937-38 ca.) or superna-
tural animals (*Le bouc au violon*, 1937-38 ca.).[2] In
particular, *Le Violoniste* exhibited here is linked to
an oil painting from 1929 — *Le violoniste au monde
renversé* (1929) — and presents an identical composition, including the small flying woman, but with
the world «right side up.»[3] In both instances, the
violinist seems to be playing a lover's serenade. For
Chagall, the violin was associated with memories
from his childhood in Russia in the Jewish ghetto
of Vitebsk. Russia is, in fact, alluded to in the shape
of the house on whose roof the player is sitting. In
addition, his Uncle Neuck and a neighbor who left
an indelible impression on the painter, both played
the violin.[4] Here, as in many of his paintings, Chagall gives free rein to his imagination, mixing familiar images and dreamlike fantasies into a totality of great symbolic power. «I have [...] psychic
reality — the fourth dimension — enter into the
plastic one, and the two realities merge,» Chagall
said.[5] The result is that of «constructing a world in
which a tree can be something else, in which I,
myself, can immediately verify that I have seven
fingers on my right hand, but only five on my left; a
universe, in short, in which anything is possible.»[6]
Claudio Zambianchi

1. E. Debenedetti, *I miti di Chagall*, Milan, Longanesi,
   1962, p. 158.
2. Reproduced respectively in F. Meyer, *Marc Chagall.
   La vita e l'opera*, Milan, Il Saggiatore, 1962, figs. 537
   and 538, plate p. 408, fig. 640 and fig. 642.
3. Meyer 1962, fig. 543.
4. See Paris, Musée des Arts Décoratifs, *Marc Chagall*,
   exh. cat., June-October 1959, pp. 88 and 188.
5. *Chagall, Peintures 1942-45*, Paris, Les Editions du
   Chêne, 1947, p. 6; quoted in U. Apollonio, *Chagall*,
   Venice, Alfieri, 1949, p. 6.
6. *Chagall, Ernst, Miro, Propos sur l'art recueille par
   Edouard Roditi*, Paris, Sedimo, 1967, p. 29.

18
Pablo Picasso. 1881-1973
Femme sur un fauteuil. Buste
1962

Oil on canvas, 116 x 89 cm.
Signed on upper left: «Picasso»; dated on the back:
«18/11/1962 II».
Provenance: Kahnweiler Gallery, Paris.
Bibliography: C. Zervos, «Pablo Picasso», Paris,
Cahiers d'Art, vol. 23, no. 83 (b/w ill. no. 43.)

«She looks like her portraits: the model of the
lovely arlésienne, the Roman woman with an
aquiline nose on the medallion. Her face has the
same sweet sadness of her voice.»[1] This is the way
André Malraux described Jacqueline, Picasso's
companion in the last twenty years of his life and
the subject of this and very many other portraits.
Picasso met Jacqueline Hutin in the summer of
1952, but it was only two years later, in June 1954,
that he began to draw her. Three months later they
began to live together: it was the beginning of the
époque Jacqueline.[2] In this late period of Picasso's
life, up until the artist's death in 1973, the portraits
of Jacqueline (who became his wife in 1961) pro-
liferated, not just on canvas, but in engravings,
drawings, sculptures and ceramic pieces.[3] Especially in his late period, however, Picasso painted series
which always remained open-ended.[4] «Picasso expresses his mental wanderlust, this refusal to stay
put or to regard anything as definitive, in a maxim:
'To finish an object means to finish it, to destroy it,
rob it of its soul, to give it the *puntilla* as to a bull in
the ring'.»[5] Octavio Paz states: «[Picasso] is not the
painter of movement within painting: he is movement that has become painting. He paints out of
urgent necessity, and what he paints is urgency
itself. He is the Painter of Time.»[6] A large part of
Picasso's late paintings, like this one, bear a precise
date with the day, month and year, and thus have
almost the quality of a diary of images. The artist
once said to Françoise Gillot: «I paint the way some
people write their autobiography.»[7] As for the style
of this painting, it seems to connect up with an
expressive style that would have its full development a few years later. «Picasso's late style, which
first emerged in the course of 1964, is characterized
by the juxtaposition of two ways of painting: one
elliptical and stenographic, made up of ideograms,

codified signs which can be inventoried; and the other thick and flowing, a hastily applied *matière* of runny, impastoed, roughly brushed paint. [...] This schematic approach [...] correspond[s] to the desire to paint and draw at the same time: 'What has to happen, when you finally look at it, is that drawing and colour are the same thing'.»[8]

From a compositional standpoint, this painting has an affinity with the work of artists Picasso felt particularly close to in this phase of his life: Velazquez in the dark, resonant, undifferentiated background from which the figure emerges; Van Gogh — the true tutelary deity of late Picasso — in the cut of the figure and the direct way of seeing it. The illumination of the face is completely artificial. Malraux observes: «In thinking about his collection, there is not even one Impressionist painting or any painting in which light plays a role [...] His work only recognizes the candles, beacons and the sun; the sun of bullfights and of Cannes, unified as a gold background or the black skies of Goya.»[9] It is an anti-naturalism which defines the otherness of the artist with respect to the world: «I also believe that everything is unknown, is the enemy,» Picasso said.[10] And this non-involvement with the world is found in the wide-open eyes of his figures, as in this Jacqueline. Eyes which are, as Alberto Boatto says, «dazed and huge, like fish drawn to the light from the darkness of the depths. [...] There are artists who make the world familiar and bring it closer to us. [...] On the other hand there are others, like Picasso, who glorify non-involvement, our irreducibly unnatural condition.» [11]

Claudio Zambianchi

1. A. Malraux, *La tête d'obsidienne* (1974); also in idem, «Le Miroir des Limbes II. La corde et les souris,» *Folio*, Paris, Gallimard, 1976, p. 292.
2. J. Richardson, «L'epoque Jacqueline» in London, Tate Gallery, *Late Picasso, Paintings, Sculpture, Drawings, Prints 1953-1972*, exh. cat., June 23-September 18, 1988, pp. 17-18.
3. See, Carsten-Peter Warncke, *Pablo Picasso. 1881-1973*, Ingo F. Walther, ed., vol. 2, *Opere 1937-1973*, Cologne, Benedikt Taschen, 1992, p. 722.
4. M.-L. Bernadac, «Picasso 1953-1972: Painting as Model» in London, Tate Gallery, *Late Picasso*, p. 88.
5. R. Penrose, *Picasso*, Harmondsworth, Penguin, 1971, p. 486; quoted in Bernadac, *Picasso 1953-1972*, p. 88.
6. O. Paz, *Marcel Duchamp, or the Castle of Purity*, London, Cape Goliard Press, 1970; quoted in Bernadac, p. 88.
7. Quoted in Richardson, p. 28.
8. H. Parmelin, *Le peintre et son modèle*, Paris, Cercle d'Art, 1965, p. 40; quoted in Bernadac, p. 85; the rest of the excerpt is from Bernadac, p. 85.
9. Malraux, p. 343.
10. *Ibid.*, p. 299.
11. A. Boatto, «L'ultimo Picasso e la 'reinvenzione' della pittura» in Rome, Accademia di Francia — Villa Medici, *Pablo Picasso. Gli ultimi anni*, B. Bauer, ed., exh. cat., Rome, Carte Segrete, 1987, p. 435.

Oil on canvas, 92 x 60 cm.
Signed and dated on bottom right: «53/F. Léger».
Provenance: M.me Léger; Beyeler Gallery, Basel.
Exhibitions: San Paolo, Museo d'Arte Moderna, *III Biennale*, 1955, no. 24 (Léger section); Paris, Musée des Arts Décoratifs, Palais du Louvre — Pavillon de Marsan, *Fernand Léger 1881-1955*, June-October 1956, no. 150 (cat. b/w ill., p. 363); Zurich, Kunsthaus, *Fernand Léger*, July 6-August 17, 1957, no. 131; Dortmund, Museum am Ostwall, *Fernand Léger 1881-1955*, September 29-October 27, 1957, no. 47.

«The idea of the contrast between natural and artificial [...] runs through all my work. Think of the so-called animated landscapes from the 1920s with human figures and trees contrasting with the bare walls of the apartment houses flanked — or crisscrossed — by electrical pylons or posters.»[1] Thus Léger declared to Duilio Morosini in 1946. And in fact, the theme of the relationship of art and man with the modern landscape renovated by technology and the advent of the machine age, is one of the recurrent motifs in his work: «Machines interested him, but above all the relationship between man and machines and thus machines and the city and machines and the landscape.»[2]

In the last years of his life, a certain amount of doubt crept into this attitude of complete trust in progress which characterized Léger's work, a «warning light»[3] regarding the progressive disappearance of nature. Thus, the relationship between the latter and technique is increasingly more tense, «every year the painting becomes a site of conflict not only between objects of different origins and functions, but also between geometric and organic forms.»[4]

Léger is not a pessimist, however. Pictorial space is never for him the site in which to emphasize conflicts, but rather where they are resolved in balanced compositions of vast breadth and classical in nature. Here, for example, birds perch on electrical lines or tranquilly fly around them, not at all intimidated by the impending urban landscape, and bring to mind somewhat those of *San Fran-*

20
Mario Sironi. 1885-1961
Studio in bianco e marrone
1958

cesco che predica agli uccelli in the upper church in Assisi. Léger's deftness in reducing the scene to a few elements positioned according to decorative intent, make this artist one of the great mural painters of this century (it was exactly during these years that Léger worked on his last great decorative works, painted, in ceramic or mosaics). And yet, Léger was convinced that «the easel painting dominates and will continue to dominate for a long time to come contemporary artistic evolution [...] It incarnates plastic life organized within a frame with precise limits and controlled emotion. It is a precious and rare object, and is more than a jewel, a diamond, gold, or silver, it is something fundamental that throbs, captured in a frame.»[5]
Claudio Zambianchi

1. D. Morosini, *Il fabbro della pittura. Conversazioni e ricordi su Léger*, Rome, Editori Riuniti, 1983, p. 16.
2. M. de Micheli, «Le immagini e i problemi della modernità» in Milan, Palazzo Reale, *Fernand Léger*, exh. cat., November 2, 1989-February 18, 1990, p. 33.
3. Morosini, 1983, p. 50.
4. *Ibid.*, p. 43.
5. F. Léger, «Couleur dans le monde,» *Europe*, 1938; reprinted in idem, *Fonctions de la peinture*, R. Garaudy ed., Paris, Editions Gonthier, 1965, p. 92.

Oil on canvas, 60 x 80 cm.
Signed on bottom right: «Sironi;» signed and dated on the back: «Mario Sironi/Cortina Agosto 1958.
Provenance: Private Collection, Venice; Galleria Hausammann, Cortina d'Ampezzo.
Exhibition: Cortina d'Ampezzo, Circolo Artistico, *Mario Sironi*, August 6-September 15, 1961, no. 52.
Bibliography: G. Cavazzini, I. Consigli, R. Tassi eds., *Pittura e scultura del XX secolo 1910-1980*, Parma, 1982, p. 69, col. ill. p. 69.

On a formal plane, the last period of Sironi's work is characterized by the atomization of the composition into a number of isolated scenes which stand out against large, undifferentiated backgrounds. These «fragments meet on the surface of the canvas and combine, mysteriously, into a pictorial unity. Every section of these strangely elaborate paintings can have a different subject, a different colour scheme, or even a different painterly style, and yet each is a comment on its neighbour and each enlarges on the meaning of the whole.»[1]

Such a way of organizing the painting leads back to the world of mural painting (an environment in which Sironi worked intensively during the fascist years), that is, it brings to mind «the plastic spatial organization of large murals in which the image responds to the search for architectural relationships internal to the narrative and to its link with the environment it is a part of. The ideal reference point for Sironi's work has always been the wall.»[2] According to A. Pica, Sironi reaches «full ripeness» in his «vocation of mural painter»[3] exactly in this late period. But the reference to the frescoed wall gives rise to nostalgia since the painter, given the human and political events which affected him, wrapped himself up in a haughty and desperate public silence. The fragments appearing in this cycle of paintings are of a simultaneously autobiographical and philosophical nature. Autobiographical because each fragment has its origin in motifs present in Sironi's previous paintings. Philosophical because it is meditations on time. In works such as this «Sironi seems dazzled by time, time as a source of inspiration, time as material for construc-

tion, the whole of time from the beginning of memory, including that following oblivion.»[4] This is where that atmosphere of archaeology which pervades the painting comes from, that reference to very ancient eras appearing especially in the upper part of the painting. It is, as G. Mascherpa observed, «archaeology of the soul and the memory. The historical world either appears in lifeless monumental contemplations of grandiose structures in barren silences or caverns in the center of the earth, or else in tumultuous visions of death and universal drama, past, present and future fused into a single portrayal of things and realities which are short and as stabbing as visions, but as necessary to the stratified geology of history as time and its age-old mutations.»[5] It is the desolate sense of history expressed in the depiction of a petrified and obtuse reality, an expression of that «modern malaise» which, according to Jean Clair, distinguishes Sironi: «The melancholy conscience is that which turns its back on life, on the world of the living, to let itself sink into the inert, into the world of things.»[6]
Claudio Zambianchi

1. E. Newton, *The Guardian*, February 6, 1964; published as «Documentazione della fortuna critica» in Milan, Palazzo Reale, *Mario Sironi*, exh. cat., February-March 1973, Electa Editrice, p. 158.
2. G. Bruno in Acqui Terme, Palazzo «Liceo Sarracco,» *Mario Sironi*, exh. cat., July 24-September 12, 1982.
3. A. Pica, *Mario Sironi, Painter*, Milan, Edizioni del Milione, 1955, p. 40.
4. C. Cagli in Florence, Palazzo Corsini-Il Prato, 56, *Mostra di Mario Sironi*, exh. cat., September 1969, Moneta.
5. G. Mascherpa, «Sironi e il suo dramma» in Milan, Galleria San Fedele, *Mario Sironi e il religioso*, G. Mascherpa ed., exh. cat., May 15-June 15, 1984, p. 7.
6. J. Clair, «Nato sotto Saturno. Su due allegorie di Sironi» in Milan, Palazzo Reale, *Sironi 1885-1961*, C. Gian Ferrari ed., exh. cat., October 4-December 8, 1985, Milan, Mazzotta, p. 36.

21
Giorgio Morandi. 1890-1964
Natura morta
1935

22
Giorgio Morandi. 1890-1964
Paesaggio
1941

Oil on canvas, 60 x 58 cm.
Signed top center: «Morandi 1935».
Provenance: Pecci Blunt Collection, Rome.
Exhibition: Florence, Palazzo Strozzi, *Arte Moderna in Italia 1915-1935*, February 26-May 28, 1967, no. 1223, b/w ill.
Bibliography: A. Beccaria, *Giorgio Morandi*, Milan, 1939, b/w pl. no. 29; C. Brandi, *Morandi*, first ed., Florence, Le Monnier, 1942, b/w pl. no. 41; second ed., 1952, p. 23, b/w pl. no. 42; published in C. Brandi, *Morandi*, Rome, 1990, p. 31; L. Vitali, *Morandi, catalogo generale*, 1977-1983, no. 190, b/w ill.

Appearing in this famous still life are some objects already familiar to those accustomed to viewing Morandi's paintings. The blue-striped flower vase is present in his work from 1921 (Vitali no. 64, location unknown) and appears etched for the first time in 1924, after which it is a constant presence, especially in works from the 1930s. The bottle on the extreme right first appears in a painting from 1929/30 (Vitali no. 152) and then in others from the years immediately following (Vitali nos. 169, 171) and are, as is known, among the things most densely charged with *matière* Morandi ever risked, so much so that this object appears vivid with its own light with an almost electric yellow, even jarring, sharp, and lacking a plastic roundedness. This bottle also has the same lack of volume in the etchings of that period, the one from 1931 in which its profile, white and intact, is carved out against the dark background (Vitali no. 82) as well as the other engraving of the same year called «a grandi segni» (Vitali no. 84). Instead, the dark octagonal bottle with its long neck appears, along with the striped bottle, in a painting from this same year (Vitali no. 191). From 1929 up until 1936, Morandi seems to carry out a true series of experiments on the painting material itself in order to enliven and set free, one could say, the somewhat dull plasticity of many contemporary results of twentieth century taste. It is exactly this inquiry of his (intense and varied, despite an apparent solidity of the images) which gave nourishment, even from this period, to

the painting of Mafai and a few years later to that of Morlotti, just beginning. In those years (and here inside this painting) Morandi alternated a style of applying the paint, rich and full of impasto, with one that was thin and almost without body and left, as here, clear traces of a laborious trailing of an almost completely dry brush, and in places, the white of the canvas shows through, opening up perforations of light in the background. Here the composition emerges like a walled curtain as in the contemporary, extraordinary landscapes without sky with their dry painting style, in which the hill rises up without perspective to occupy the entire space of the canvas. Similar ideas can also be seen in the engravings, for example in the 1933 still life (Vitali no. 100) in which, as here, the plane of support has the hint of a curve, almost as if from bearing the weight of the bastion crowded with objects that overhangs it.
Eugenio Riccòmini

Oil on canvas, 52.5 x 47.5 cm.
Exhibition: Bologna, Galleria Comunale d'Arte Moderna, *Giorgio Morandi, 1890-1990: Mostra del Centenario*, May 12-September 2, 1990.
Bibliography: M. Pasquali, *Morandi*, Milan, Electa, 1990, no. 83, p. 409; p. 149, col. ill.

Morandi, as is well-known, is a painter of variations, and he demonstrated in a thousand ways how, with a few bottles, boxes and other odds and ends placed on a table, one can paint almost into infinity. All that is required is to change, even just slightly, the disposition, angle of vision, inclination or intensity of light. This is also is true in his landscapes. The same familiar outline of a hillside or the same group of houses along a lane occupy different spaces on the canvas and are tinged with different colors according to the time of day or simply by moving the easel a few yards. All of this is generally known. This painting, however, occupies a very special place (in my view, even unique) in the artist's entire output. For example, it escaped the extremely attentive cataloging of Lamberto Vitali, and it must be said that its absence does have a plausible explanation in the sense that the catalogue's editor could have been fooled, confusing it with another painting. In fact, the Vitali catalogue reproduces (as number 285 in its inventory with the date of 1941, that which also appears here) a landscape that is not at all a variation of the same place drawn from the same point of view, but the very same scene compositionally cut in the same, identical manner. So much so, that to distinguish one painting from the other, unusual and acute attention is required. The variations that allow us to confidently affirm that we are faced with two different paintings are fairly elusive. The only one which appears plainly is the placement of the signature (here on the left and written in light ochre, while in the painting catalogued by Vitali it is on the right and traced in a dark color). But the angle as well as the manner of applying the paint almost merge and overlap, except that here, on the wall of the house on the upper left one can perceive an open window which does not appear in the other

23
Giorgio Morandi. 1890-1964
Paesaggio
1941

Giorgio Morandi, *Paesaggio*, 1942

painting, plus the hint on the bottom right of the exit to a tunnel missing in the other, and here the group of trees in the foreground is more compact and not animated, as in the other, by some flashes of white. Thus, we have run across the only copy which Morandi ever painted. And to me it seems certain, given the identical scene and the complete similarity of the pictorial ductus, that it is, indeed, a copy, in the sense that the artist (here, or in the painting catalogued by Vitali since it is completely impossible to determine which came first) made uncustomary use of a practice common in ancient times, copying one painting from another instead of returning a second time to the site of the subject (which, unquestionably, would have induced him to change, even just slightly, the angle and way of painting, something which did not happen).

The view depicted here does not seem to be from around Grizzana. More likely it is one of the hills near Bologna which Morandi went to when he could not get to his beloved Apennine village. This habit of his is clear in various landscapes from the previous year, 1940 (Vitali nos. 270, 272, 274, 276), in which, from the tops of the hills, one can glimpse the distant line of the plain. Here the point of view is reversed, from the base towards the ridge and the site is certainly familiar to the artist. The same group of houses appears other times in various paintings from 1940 in different variations, in closer views (Vitali nos. 291, 280) and with solutions of a Cézannesque flavor with large patches of color (Vitali no. 279), sometimes with more expansive touches (Vitali no. 319) or slightly modifying the angle (Vitali no. 321, dated the same year, 1941, and dedicated on the back «a Pietro Feroldi»).
Eugenio Riccòmini

Oil on canvas, 38 x 47 cm.
Signed and dated on bottom center: «Morandi 1941».
Provenance: Lionello Santi Collection, Milan.
Bibliography: C. Brandi, *Morandi*, Florence, 1942, col. ill. p. 16; L. Vitali, *Giorgio Morandi*, Milan, 1964, col. ill. no. 125; M. Valsecchi, *Morandi*, Milan, 1964, col. pl. no. 10: F. Arcangeli, *Giorgio Morandi*, first ed., Milan, 1964, p. 229; second ed., Turin, 1981, p. 216; L. Vitali, *Morandi, catalogo generale*, Milan, 1977, b/w ill. no. 325; S. Calabrese and S. Canerini, *L'immagine dell'Appennino bolognese: dai disegnatori dell'Ottocento a Giorgio Morandi*, Bologna, 1984, col. ill. no. 42, p. 72.

Morandi always drew landscapes and right from the very beginning since landscapes were the first of his paintings to become known. But there are fewer of them in relationship to his still lifes which, in the context of his total output, are five times as numerous. There are many reasons why it can prove useful to separate the landscapes from the still lifes in this way, including from a critical standpoint, even more so because the distinction between genres, even of the same artist, is credible and born out by the most recent studies in linguistics and rhetoric. Morandi is not an abstract painter and although the unity of his language is prodigious, seamless and formally undifferentiable, the difference in subject matter implies a structural and psychological diversity in its outlook and meaning.

The number of landscapes increased suddenly in 1927 when, for the first time, Morandi went to Grizzana, a small town in the Apennines not far from Bologna, and continued to vary according to the time he spent there. They are most numerous during the period of the war when he stayed there uninterruptedly for four years instead of just during the summer months. From 1940 to 1943 Morandi painted eighty-seven landscapes and this painting is one of them. Thus we see that he became a complete, and very great, landscape painter when he discovered the Apennines, a natural subject which fully and profoundly corres-

ponded to his sensitivity, his spiritual make-up and his way of painting. And we also discover that in order to paint, he needed a direct relationship with the reality from which he drew the image. Only in Grizzana, or after having been in Grizzana, could he draw that natural setting, that landscape; the interdependence is unquestionable. These two factors are the basis of a poetic style that must always be kept in mind when interpreting his landscape painting.

But a comprehensive critique of this group of paintings from 1940-43 is very difficult, and perhaps impossible. It is not much use pointing out references to the Italian Corot of the years 1825-28, even less so evoking the shadow of Cézanne or attempt other associations and comparisons. Morandi is removed from any historical reference, removed from the painting which preceded him and that which surrounded him. He had little or no rapport with his age, if anything he anticipated what was to come. In those years he carried out what is perhaps the most solemn and moving meditation on nature that European art has known in our century.

This landscape has very special characteristics which distinguish it from the others done in 1941 and from almost all those of the entire group. Just one work from 1942, in a Rome collection (Vitali no. 396) has very similar features, angle and figures, so much so that it seems a copy of this one, but with less detail in the shapes and less spaciousness. The first characteristic is the sequence of plastic blocks, three houses and the hill, like a successive disengagement which traverses the entire painting and creates an indication of spatial opening towards the bottom. It is a way of creating space that is unusual in Morandi and which finds an analogy only in two still lifes, that of Falk from 1940 (Vitali no. 112) and that of the Fondazione Magnani Rocca of 1942 (Vitali no. 384) in which the theory or procession of the objects in a sequence towards the bottom is similar, as is the dramatic sense and mystery created by an intense contrast between light and shadow.

In fact, the other characteristic of this landscape

24
Giorgio Morandi. 1890-1964
Fiori
1953

25
Giorgio Morandi. 1890-1964
Natura morta
1957

is the sharp alternation between violent light and deep shade which, in addition to creating that sense of plasticity and space, lend more drama than usually appears in Morandi and also lend mystery, but not more than is lavished in almost all of his other works. Arcangeli noted in 1962: «this is the almost Expressionist drama, but serious, of the *Paesaggio* from the Santi Collection in Milan.» The miraculous thing in this work is that almost-geo-metrical surfaces — but with that trembling at the edges in which all the poetry lies concealed, in almost-abstract shapes and interlacings, less natur-alistic than ever and not directed by any logical tenets or ascribable to any reality — together make up three houses, the brow of a hill which rises gently, a noonday sun, trees and fields, in a corner of the Apennines. From reality to the painting is a very long, slow, revolutionary transition. What takes place in it, from the meditation on nature to the absolute of the form, is incomprehensible and mysterious. The result is very removed from the real image, and yet it cannot be put aside nor express the internal truth, the spirit and the aura.

As always in Morandi, but here with a way of painting, mastery and imagination that is even more intense, the entire painting is based on the tone and its minute variations. What dominates is that dull green, a bit faded, almost as if it had been delicately covered with dust, which is one of the great chromatic inventions of Morandi, the land-scape painter. But it is continuously transformed into a green that is sometimes paler, sometimes more intense and sometimes almost withered; and then with the flickering ochres, in the light earth colors and the browns just barely illuminated. Everything in this painting is suspended, still, not subject to the passing of time. But everything also vibrates silently, in the flickering coming together of the hues, in the imprecise suturing of the forms and in the irregular spreading of the shadow. It is like an imperceptible and hidden throbbing, an internal shiver. It is the long and difficult breath of poetry.
Roberto Tassi

Oil on canvas, 40 x 30 cm.
Provenance: Galleria Marescalchi, Bologna.
Exhibition: Cortina d'Ampezzo, 1991, no. 22.
Bibliography: L. Vitali, *Morandi, catalogo generale*, Milan, Electa, 1977-1983, no. 843, b/w ill.; M. Pasquali, *Morandi, riflessioni sull'opera*, Piacenza, 1991, no. 35, col. ill., p. 52.

This theme, with its bare concentration and dusty, arid painting style, was already one of Morandi's early habitual ones. Traces of it can be found in the very famous tempera (on cardboard, the material most suitable for avoiding the temptations of fine painting) done in 1916 and owned by the city of Jesi, as well as in a later painting from 1918. A sim-ilar simplicity of invention is also seen in a painting from 1920 (Vitali no. 56), containing the same form and the same vase (making its first appearance). In his unshakeable certainty that the diapason of painting could be infinitely varied even maintain-ing just the same few things in view, on more than one occasion Morandi tried to constrict his field of vision to the bare minimum (just as he had done the opposite, crowding all the very same objects onto the table). And so, just one vase, as here, was sufficient along with four or five dried flowers (or perhaps even the artificial porcelain ones that can be seen in his studio). This task of reduction to the minimum, to the essential, was something he did more frequently in the later years, almost as if to save his remaining strength, and perhaps because saying more would be superfluous when every-thing could be conveyed with very, very little, almost keeping silent. During his last decade, the light, often probed, seems to be the sole protagonist of his painting, as happens here, in a very slow brushing of different shades of white, barely re-vivified by the rosy pallor of the petals or the blue and grey deposit of the shadow.
Eugenio Riccòmini

Oil on canvas, 35.5 x 30.5 cm.
Provenance: Galleria del Milione, Milan.
Bibliography: *Palatina*, no. 4, Parma, 1957, col. ill., p. 60; L. Vitali, *Morandi, catalogo generale*, Milan, Electa, 1977-1983, no. 1066, b/w ill.

The squat bottle appearing almost in the center of this painting is the same one Morandi often chose, beginning approximately in 1930, when he had to arrange the composition around the insertion of a simple mass heavily invested with light. Thus it is also seen in a painting from this same collection dating back to 1935. As was said, the bottle is almost in the center, but, in his later works, Morandi keenly avoided any possible symmetry between the volumes, crowding his objects, as here, into compact blocks, but gathered in positions off-center with respect to the plane of support and also to the surface of the canvas. At times the nucleus of the whole was completely displaced to the edge, leaving a vast empty space to balance the visual weight. Sometimes, as here, the play was much more subtle and the object which most attracts attention is slightly off the axis and thus the eye is compelled to linger over the other things present, to extort the spaces involved in order to re-estab-lish a sense of equilibrium. As is usually the case with the paintings from the last decade, again here the careful compositional mix is wrapped in a very clear and diffuse light. The scanty areas of shade seem to be applied *après coup* with the tip of the brush almost dry, as happens in the drawings when, at the end, a little bit of relief must be indi-cated in an area which appears flat. The color also almost seems to vanish in the light, if it were not for that sudden and unexpected clash of green and vermilion which mitigate the relief in an incongru-ous, flag-like effect. In the same year (see Vitali's monograph, Milione, 1964, ill. 217) Morandi had used a composition quite similar to this one but foreshortened, with the bottle in the foreground and just a hint of color, more subdued, in the objects around it.
Eugenio Riccòmini

26
Giorgio Morandi. 1890-1964
Paesaggio
1961

Giorgio Morandi, *La strada bianca*, 1933

Oil on canvas, 45 x 45 cm.
Signed on the back: «Morandi».
Provenance: Galleria del Milione, Milan.
Bibliography: L. Vitali, *Morandi, catalogo generale*, Milan, 1977, no. 1245, b/w ill.

From the years 1960 to 1963, having resumed his old habit of passing the summer in Grizzana, Morandi intensified his painting of landscapes. In four years he painted thirty-nine of them. They make up a group of such sublime poetry, so difficult to define and of a form so independent and different from the painting styles around it, that it still has not found, if it ever will, a writer capable of adequately describing and interpreting it. Some changes had taken place: the tendency to abolish or reduce the spatial depth was accentuated so that everything — houses, sky, hills, trees — was brought to almost a single surface, and yet the sense of natural giving way became even more intense. A uniform light, almost without, or with very little, hindrance from shade, extends fully over the entire painting, unifying every point. The subject matter continued on its course towards the essential, reaching, in the last year, a slight and intense rarefaction. Michael Semff states that these landscapes «form a lofty peak within all his work» and that with them «Morandi reached the highest point on the scale of landscape painting in the twentieth century.» And finally, «observing the landscapes painted in those last years of his life, it is not specious to affirm that, because of their extreme audacity [...] they take their place above the still lifes.»[1]

This landscape, painted in 1961, is one of the most resplendent and successful of the group, and represents the reappearance of a subject, which under the title of *La strada bianca* had its origins, its first example, in an etching from 1933 (Vitali, *L'opera grafica*, no. 104). Four paintings with the same title followed it, one in 1939 (Vitali no. 248) and three in 1941 (Vitali nos. 339, 340, 341). In this work, the perspective point is removed to the other side of the street and moved up slightly, almost in front of the houses. The real subject is the group of Case del Campiaro in Grizzana, but there is a great

distance between these and the pictorial image. In reality, the Case del Campiaro are edifices of spontaneous beauty as we can see from the photograph (in R. Renzi, *La città di Morandi*, Bologna, 1983, p. 188, fig. 202). They are of a perfectly harmonic structure, built of stone, a noble material which becomes much more attractive with age, when time has weathered and colored it, immersed within the changing hues of the grass and the tall, yet simple and modest, trees along the road. The Case del Campiaro in Morandi's work are an immensely different image. They appear subtly gold- or rose-colored, united, without windows or details, without depth, matter without matter, of a hue which is established between them, inundated with light spread evenly on the walls, roofs, trees, street and sky. They are noonday ghosts and natural truth, imaginary figures and poetic essence. That is the real landscape, but the metamorphosis is enormous. Morandi succeeds in having us feel the recognizability of the town and the extraneousness of the transfiguration. The work has its own eternal existence, but cannot be completely uprooted from the reality which generated it. Between these two entities, the real «Case del Campiaro» and the painted «Case del Campiaro,» there not only exists the distance created between nature and painting, but also another additional one, a different metamorphosis, undescribable and impenetrable, which Morandi's work consists of.

In this *Paesaggio* the street is no longer the protagonist, the title is no longer that of the five paintings with a similar subject which preceded it since the light does not violently illuminate the wide, triangular strip that wedges itself between the fields, but spreads itself evenly with uniform value, extended without shade in a noonday inertia, whitewashing every aspect. The white and pink prevail against the macerated green of the edge and the transparent blue of the sky: white the narrow strip of road, white the foliage of the slender trees, white the patches without real equivalent on the grass and against the side of the first house; pink the field, the trunks of the saplings, the earth, the walls of the houses, the roofs. As if a

Spring of improvised and light colors and moods, drenched with clear light, delicate and pleasing, had descended on that tract of the Apennines to catch for eternity that timeless moment. But the lines on a narrow door, on the edge of a house and along the edges of the roofs — a slightly grey shadow — engrave thin veins of mystery, a torn and melancholy ribbon, in such a faint light.
Roberto Tassi

1. M. Semff, «Gli ultimi paesaggi di Morandi» in *Giorgio Morandi 1890-1990, Mostra del Centenario*, exh. cat., Milan, 1990, pp. 51-52.

Giorgio Morandi, *La strada bianca*, 1941

Giorgio Morandi, *Paesaggio*, 1961

Filippo de Pisis, *Pan*, 1930

Oil on canvas, 130 x 110 cm.
Signed and dated on bottom right: «Pisis 35».

Already appearing in the works of de Pisis from the years 1915-25 are those effeminate figures inspired by mythological characters which a little later would become the protagonists of many of his paintings. Many stories and anecdotes, often lurid, are known about where and how de Pisis encountered the young models who posed for him in his studio even if sometimes, as in this case, he painted them immersed in vague, unreal landscapes.

Forerunners of this work are undoubtedly a *Pan* from 1930 and other figures of youths depicted as Mercury, as in a painting from 1931 (General Catalogue, no. 101) and in one from 1937 with a layout very similar to the one here (*Mercurio che dipinge*, General Catalogue no. 25).

The character here is most likely portrayed as Pan playing a flute in which the mythological reference serves to suggest the Depisisian dream of a return to an innocently pagan sensuality. The figure, executed with his customary painterly lightness and rapidity, is portrayed in a plane so close as to establish a curious expansion of the character which, seated on an almost invisible chair, together with an enormous cabbage, looms somewhere between the fairytale-esque and the metaphysical in a curious landscape in which small, distant structures and a sapling coexist with a frog, an apple and a shell. A unifying pictorial element, the sky brings to mind Venetian paintings of the 1700s and, although in it numerous, thick clouds alternate with the blue, it filters an extremely intense light that pours out onto the objects.

In this period, de Pisis, in his presentation of the catalogue of the second Rome Quadriennale in which he exhibited nineteen works in a room dedicated to him, defended himself against what could appear superficial in his painting, putting the accent on his own painterly individuality that originated from his observation of what was real, but through the use of sincere emotion and wanted to arrive at a lyrical painting style.

Observing this work, it is clear how this type of misunderstanding that the artist had to defend himself against could arise since at an initial, superficial glance, certain details, above all the houses on the right, could seem naive. But it is exactly in the unity and stylistic and lyrical coherence of the whole and also, perhaps, in an almost imperceptible irony of Metaphysical origin, that it completely redeems itself.

Certain famous paintings of de Pisis come to mind, like *Le cipolle di Socrate*, in which two reddish onions in the foreground were, as the cabbage, frog and other everyday things are here, estranged elements which suggest a Metaphysical interpretation of the painting. A Metaphysical outlook, that of de Pisis, certainly indebted to de Chirico but which becomes completely original, above all stylistically, in his airy, unquestionably Impressionistic style that also exists in this work.

In this regard, de Pisis wrote to Vitali in 1938 about the typicality of his metaphysical art: «It remains clear, it seems to us, that for those of good faith, the Metaphysicality (poetry, in other words) that emanates from a work of art does not only refer to the more or less abstract forms of which it is composed, but to the spirit which gives it form. Truly lovely painting (and it cannot be so if it does not have a minimum of intrinsic nobility) always trespasses towards the afterlife. Metaphysics is more often made up of simplicity, clarity, sonority and throbbing, than of research or sterility.»[1]
Simona Pizzetti

Filippo de Pisis, *Mercurio*, 1931

1. In *Mostra dell'opera pittorica e grafica di Filippo de Pisis*, Verona, 1969.

Filippo de Pisis, *Mercurio che dipinge*, 1937

28
Filippo de Pisis. 1896-1956
Il Lussemburgo
1937

Oil on canvas, 91 x 72 cm.
Signed and dated on bottom right: «Pisis 37».
Bibliography: *Pittura e scultura del XX secolo 1910-1980*, Parma, 1982, col. pl., p. 50; Briganti, *De Pisis catalogo generale*, vol. I, Milan, Electa, 1991, no. 7, b/w pl., p. 400.

De Pisis lived in Paris for fourteen years from 1925 to 1939, years which certainly were among the happiest of his painting career. The atmosphere in Paris was very rich with stimuli for the painter who perhaps could have been influenced by the Impressionists as well as Utrillo, Marquet, Soutine and Matisse, but who fundamentally, in this environment as well, was a recluse always remaining to himself. It is no accident, for example, that in 1937, the year this work is dated, the World Exhibition was held in Paris in which were displayed the «Maîtres de l'art indipendant,» and de Pisis was not among them.

In an essay from 1946, Pallucchini clarified de Pisis' approach to French Impressionism: «There is no question but that de Pisis esteemed Manet as well as Sisley and Pizzarro and, from among the followers of this tradition, Utrillo. He immersed himself in it only as much as was necessary to stimulate his particular painterly expression that shattered appearance in the light and atmosphere. De Pisis revived the premises of Impressionism with an ease and ingeniousness completely Venetian in nature. He leaned upon them in order to learn from them a lesson on freshness, immediacy and sincerity of expression. And so it was that lightening his palette, he refined his use of color, rendering it with touches, and discovered a completely new luminousness for the spatial framework of the scene, recreating an extremely mobile aerial perspective of the type invented in Venice two centuries earlier by Francesco Guardi.»[1]

Like the Impressionists, he often painted *en plein-air* and in the 1930s made quite a few *vedute* of Paris. It is well-known that while he painted he liked to make himself noticed by passers-by with his famous rapidity and skill in rendering with a few strokes the perspective and characteristics of each *veduta*. He himself wrote: «I would certainly find it unbearable to write a poem with someone standing over me reading each word. But perhaps because of the open air, manual and pictorial work neutralize the unpleasant impression of an onlooker. It is certainly true that if I could not paint with bystanders over my shoulder, I would have to give up working *en plein-air* which for me is absolutely indispensable for accomplishing good things. In fact, except in special cases, I do not make a single stroke without having life in front of me. I am a bit of the opinion of Cézanne who recommended his followers to «Paint what you see!» I must say that I am so completely used to having onlookers that I almost do not notice them. Sometimes I even have fun staging a little play [...] A phrase that I repeat (that of a great Parisian critic) is: 'Here are the youths, the people, who become part of history without even knowing it: you see painting one of the greatest artistic talents that has ever existed.' I also say: 'It is not the season that allows for it, but the perfect agreement between the soul and the light: between the inner light and the surroundings'.»[2]

De Pisis himself underscored the fact that the result of his work was very much linked to his emotional state and therefore, represents the lyrical-emotional transpositions of reality. It was precisely this way of understanding painting that allowed him to get past the lesson, otherwise fundamental, of the Impressionists. His linking of the act of painting to precise emotional states also makes his painting technically different, and in it we find his typically circular brushstrokes, those very rapid and agitated touches and the many tonal outbursts. In 1932 de Pisis had painted, as here, a *veduta* of *Parigi dai giardini del Lussemburgo* which framed the upper part of the Tour Eiffel seen from the west side of the park. In this painting from 1937, on the other hand, the description of the interior of the gardens predominates, swarming with barely-sketched figures and statues represented with a few strokes of white, while two rows of trees create a deep sense of perspective at the end of which appear far-away architectural elements just barely sketched out.

As in many of his other *vedute* of Paris, the trees, with their very dense and intricate tangle of strokes, constitute a dominating element in the landscape, allowing him to make the entire view more turbulent, while, in the uncertain time of day, the almost-menacing sky and an equally vivid and typically Nordic light allow de Pisis to build the painting around three, very muted, dominant colors: ochre, brown, sky-blue and touches of white here and there that accentuate the painting's luminism, all of it reaching a chromatic synthesis which, as always in de Pisis, is perfect.
Simona Pizzetti

1. R. Pallucchini, «Posizione di de Pisis» in *Lettere e arti*, Venice, 1946.
2. In G. Raimondi, *Filippo de Pisis*, Florence, Vallecchi, 1952, pp. 47-48.

29
Chaïm Soutine. 1893-1943
Le printemps à Champigny
(1942)

Oil on canvas, 100 x 73 cm.
Provenance: Madeleine and Marcellin Castaing Collection.
Expositions: Paris, *Soutine*, Orangerie des Tuilleries, April 27-September 17, 1973, no. 93, p. 95 (the reproduction on p. 73 corresponding to that catalogue number is incorrect, it refers, instead, to the very similar work of the Jacques Guérin Collection, Paris, here reproduced in b/w); Milan, *Chaïm Soutine*, Galleria Bergamini, March-April 1987, no. 14, col. ill.; Chartres, *Soutine*, Musée, June 29-October 30, 1989, no. 74, col. ill., p. 316.
Bibliography: J. Leymarie, Introduction to the exhibition at the Orangerie, Paris, 1973, p. 9.

This is one of the most beautiful of all the numerous works belonging to Madelaine and Marcellin Castaing. The friendship which was destined to become very close between the Castaings and Soutine following an initial meeting in 1920 just seven years following his arrival in Paris, began to become more intense at the end of the 1920s and continued throughout the remaining fifteen years of the painter's life. Therefore, it is worthwhile mentioning some aspects of the history of this friendship.

In 1928 Soutine painted Madeleine Castaing's portrait (Metropolitan Museum of Art, New York). Starting in 1930 he was invited by the Castaings and was received in their large villa surrounded by a lovely park in Léves, near Chartres. Soutine stayed there for long periods almost every year during the summer, during which time he painted many of his masterpieces, among which, in 1936, were two versions of *La route des Grans Prés à Chartres*, which can be considered forerunners of this painting and are among the first examples, following the group of works on *L'arbre de Vence* from 1929, of Soutine's interest in large, powerful and age-old trees. Already in these two works small figures appear on the street, in one a farmer with a cow, and in the other two children. This human presence in the landscapes serves, among other things, to give the sense of the colossal dimensions of the trees along the street, and the union between the minuscule human presence and the grandeur of the trunks will reappear in all his paintings of trees, increasingly numerous, until this painting done in the last year of his life. In the meantime, Zborowski had died in 1932 and the Castaings had taken over the financial assistance which, for awhile, the businessman had assured Soutine.

In 1939, at the outbreak of the war, Soutine was in Civerny, a small town near Avallon, with his friend Gerda Groth, a German woman who had fled Germany at the beginning of Nazism. Soutine painted *Jour de vent à Auxerre (Civry)*, and at least three versions of *Les Peupliers*, works in which the subject is the large trees, blown by the wind of the stormy day, but also by the internal gusts which seethed without interruption in Soutine's soul and which he poured out, using the paintbrush, altering them, imbuing the forms and *matière* in his works with their life, drama and poetry. In 1939 he also painted *Le retour de l'école après l'orage*, in which the great trees are missing, placed far away on the horizon, and in the foreground are the figures which earlier were flattened by their looming presence, those two children hand-in-hand, tender, moving, spirits.

But history intervened. The villa in Lèves was requisitioned by the Germans. Gerda Groth was arrested at the Vélodrome d'Hiver. At the beginning of 1941, Soutine left Civry and returned to Paris. He changed his address often; in the police files he was identified as a Jew. He met Marie-Berthe Amanche who had been the wife of Max Ernst. He lived with her and was forced to go into hiding along with her, then, during the summer, he left Paris. He went to live at Champigny-sur-Veuldre. He still had a rapport with the Castaings who continued to buy his paintings. In 1942 he painted a series of large trees: *Paysage au bord de l'eau, Champigny, Arbre dans le vent*, and *Le grand arbre*, plus a group of three similar paintings, *L'automne à Champigny*, previously in the Castaing collection, *Paysage d'automne à Champigny* from the Jacques Guérin Collection, Paris, and this *Le printemps à Champigny*, the largest of the three.

Marcellin Castaing who, along with his wife as has been seen, played a leading role in a very lovely and intense story in the rapport with Soutine, offering him friendship, admiration, acceptance and help such that he dedicated himself almost exclusively to him and his painting, understood what a genius he was and how his work sat at the summit of European art of the entire century. In those years he was a privileged observer and it is worthwhile listening to what he said in this excerpt: «Il voulait connaître le secret du paysage, de la nature morte, de la personne et il détruisait lorsque le miracle ne se produisait pas. Peintre uniquement d'inspiration il l'attendait passant d'une période de paresse incoercible à cet état second dont parle Balzac qui l'emportait dans l'audace de toutes tentatives. Il allait par sa nature même jusqu'au bout de son effort et sans peur du déchaînement total et sans concessions il atteignait souvent cette confusion de la vie avec la matière qui est la grande tentation et le grand espoir de tous les initiés.»[1]

Soutine was truly a great initiate of painting. The profound sense and ineluctability of the *matière*, so dense, so violated, luminous and rich with spirit, probably has no paragon in any other painter, with perhaps the exceptions of Rembrandt and Courbet. He was a wanderer, delicate and wild, hopelessly immersed in the fate of painting. The distortion of the images sprung from such dark recesses and such necessary impulses within himself that often he went against his very reason and will. He was not able to control it, it was the sign of his dramatic destiny. However, in the last two years of his life, from mid-1941 to mid-1943, a more extended lyricism entered into his painting. His great agitation, that furious struggle and the violence, sometimes so pure, of color, was a bit calmer. This appeared in the portraits which were more melancholy than tragic, in the stroll of children down a country road returning from school, and above all in the landscapes dominated by a spring-like green and blue, or by a few autumn yellows.

But more than the landscape overall, the protagonists of these extremely beautiful paintings are the great trees as moving figures, airy against the breeze of the sky, bent, open to the light. Soutine

Chaïm Soutine,
L'automne à Champigny, 1942

had a horror of motionlessness, of order, of the straight line. As Francesco Porzio wrote in publishing *Le printemps à Champigny*: «In his last years, Soutine gave his best in the lyrical abandon of the landscapes, portraits of great trees shaken by the wind in which man has taken on a fragile, barely evoked, dimension.»[2] And Jean Leymarie, in referring to this and all the other landscapes of the period wrote: «Mais c'est surtout dans la campagne, autour de Civry et de Champigny, que se multiplient, durant les derniers mois, d'incomparables paysages d'arbres sous lesquels circulent des figurines d'animaux et des personnages rustiques. Irradié dans l'espace et d'âge immémorial, l'arbre est l'image par excellence du système cosmique et le symbole inépuisable de la vie renouvelée. Il participe de tous les éléments, rythme le cours des saisons, vibre aux moindres inflexions de l'atmosphère. Soutine représente tantôt des géants isolés, déployant leurs vastes couronnes où s'engouffre le tumulte des vents, tantôt des massifs élancés qui tressent de flexibles réseaux sur un ciel tendre et laiteux. Son lyrisme éperdu se décante et s'amplifie en épousant, dans ces ultimes chefs d'oeuvre, les ondulations de l'espace et de la lumière, en nuançant, selon la saison, l'heure et le vent, les variations infinies de cette chair végétative soustraite aux passions humaines mais parcourue, ces racines à la cîme, par le flux universel.»[3]
Roberto Tassi

1. «He wanted to know the secret of landscapes, of still lifes, of the human being, and destroyed the painting when the miracle did not happen. A painter of inspiration, he waited for it passing from a period of insuperable laziness to that state which Balzac spoke of that dragged him into the audacity of every attempt. By nature he went to the extremes of his energy, and without fear of a total outburst and without making concessions, often reached that mixture of life with matter which is the great temptation and the great hope of all initiates.» M. Castaing in *Cent tableux de Soutine*, Galerie Charpentier, Paris, 1959.
2. F. Porzio, *Soutine*, cat., Galleria Bergamini, Milan, 1987, pages unnumbered.
3. «But above all, it is in the countryside of Civry and

Champigny that there multiplied the incomparable landscapes of trees under which small figures of animals and farmers move. The tree, radiant in the space and dating from time immemorial, is the image par excellence of the cosmic system and the endless symbol of life which renews itself. Involved with every element, it marks the course of the seasons and vibrates with the least movement of the atmosphere. Sometimes Soutine portrays isolated giants who spread their vast crowns, plunging into the tumult of the wind, and at other times slender cortins which interweave flexible latticework against a soft, milky sky. His lost lyricism exalted and amplified, joining, in these last masterpieces, the undulations of space and light, blending, according to the seasons, the time of day and the wind, the infinite variations of this plant flesh removed from human passion but imbued with the flow of the universe from its roots to its very top.» J. Leymarie, Introduction to the catalogue of the Soutine exhibit at the Orangerie, Paris, 1973, pp. 8-9.

Chaïm Soutine, *Paysage d'automne à Champigny*, 1942

Oil on canvas, 70 x 100 cm.
Signed on bottom left: «Permeke».
Provenance: Beatty Permeke Collection, Audenaarde; Bruno Sargentini Collection, Rome Exhibition: Rome, Galleria L'Attico, October-November 1963, no. 22, b/w ill.

Born in Antwerp, Permeke lived in a region in which the rapport with the sea or with the waters of the rivers and canals was constant and often a necessity of life. For at least two years as a child, his home was a boat on the Escaut, the only house his father in that period. From 1892 to 1930 he lived in Ostend in close contact with the sea, sailors and fishermen. He started painting seascapes in 1912, almost from the beginning of his activity as a painter, continuing throughout the Ostend period and, with less frequency, even after, with moments in which the paintings with this subject were more numerous, around 1924 and, above all, in 1927 and 1928. In fact, it seems that in 1928 a collector commissioned one hundred seascapes and he executed them all.

This seascape could be part of that group or the result of activity later that same year. But with Permeke, precise dating is very difficult since he rarely dated his works and kept no register or catalogue of them. On the other hand, his style underwent little change, and what little there was took place slowly over the years. It is a painting style of substance, of a Nordic spirit and Expressionist nature. In the landscapes he painted following his move to Jabbeke and in the Ostend seascapes, the structure is almost always the same: dense land or sea, thick, darkened, damp and muddy, as if the sod, the fields and the water were all made of the same substance. Skies that are overcast with intense light, filtered, diffuse or in places dazzling because of extensive haze or roving clouds, and which are also white, grey, brown, sometimes golden or even green, but never blue.

The precedents for this are located in the entire tradition of Flemish and Dutch landscape painting, and closer to him, in particular, the seascape painter Louis Artan, as well as in the seascapes painted

31
Constant Permeke. 1886-1952
Winderlandschaft
(1935)

in the mid-19th century by Courbet at Palavas and Etretat. The same solitude, the same vastness, the same content — high skies, dense earth, dark waters. This is what Francesco Arcangeli meant when he wrote in 1965: «His painting [...] seems to relaunch in our century in a way that is not at all slavish, the immense gravitation of Courbet.»[1]

That «immense gravitation» is renewed in this seascape in which the water is still dark with nocturnal shadows, revealing itself only in the breaking of the waves against the shore, even if in the sky the great light of dawn extends unexpectedly, in which the shore and the dunes or rocks which occupy it, are shown in strong chiaroscuro and, in the vast and monotonic symphony of brown, gives us in such a simple and profound way, the unlimited sense of nature, powerful and dramatic.
Roberto Tassi

1. F. Arcangeli, «Constant Permeke» in cat. exh., Galleria San Luca, Bologna, 1965; reprinted in *Dal Romanticismo all'Informale*, vol. I, Turin, 1977, p. 243.

Oil on canvas, 50 x 70 cm.
Provenance: John Permeke Collection, Cape Town; Bruno Sargentini Collection, Rome.
Exhibition: Rome, Galleria L'Attico, October-November 1963, no. 12, col. ill.

In 1930, Permeke, who had built a house inland in Jabbeke, abandoned Ostend and the sea and went to live in his new town where the plain with its meadows, fields and marshes stretch into infinity, strewn with villages, barns, haylofts and trees, and no longer sterile and wild like the expanse of the sea. But the skies are the same, white at dawn, yellow at midday, always thick and speckled with muddy, overhanging, turbid nimbus clouds. The light and colors change with the seasons: snowy winters, summers of a slightly-forlorn gold, springs fogged-over with a green light. Even more so than in the seascapes, the horizon is low and far-away, as it was in the seventeenth century Dutch Masters. Here Permeke was an earthly genius, and the group of landscapes he painted between 1930 and approximately 1938 when the subject of female nudes took over as protagonists in his work, forms another marvel of naturalistic painting in our century.

Permeke's style was always violent, powerful and solid, above all in the paintings with human figures and episodes which belong to the history of Northern Expressionism. But in the landscapes, that power and distortion it demands are somewhat alleviated by his profound passion for natural phenomenon with the light which changes and enfolds the entire countryside, the lack of clear-cut outlines and the indistinctness of the substance and space, almost anticipating an Informal nature painting. In this Permeke seems to find himself in the midst of a process of handing down or a great current that could have its start in the seascapes and landscapes, with their more contorted subject matter, of Courbet, touched peripherally by Soutine, and arrive, with the generation which came after him, at de Staël and Morlotti.

This *Winderlandschaft* sits well midway in that decade at Jabbeke so fertile with landscapes, as one

of the many masterpieces that enriched it. The air which still seems snowy and the snow which weighs down the trees and covers the earth, enclose in their fused harmony of light greys, dull whites and luminous mother-of-pearl, a unique, immense and silent space. There are no human beings, houses or birds; everything is pure, essential, transformed and also very true, very poetically natural. Merging in this painting are happiness and desolation, solitude and light. Writing about a work whose craftsmanship and poetry are very similar to this one and in which only the season changes, the *Autumn* of 1934, Arcangeli said: «This is the simple solitude, grey, pathos-laden and restrained, of *Autumn*: a low-lying, brown line of earth, a grey and immensely uniform sky, an isolated flight of crows. A simplicity which gives proof to the variety of sentiments in this apparently monochord individual.»[1]
In this *Winderlandschaft*, everything is even more pressed to its essence, the pitch darkness of the trees and the earth, the white of the snow spread with the knife and the ever-more delicate and more intense variation in the grey.
Roberto Tassi

1. F. Arcangeli, «Constant Permeke» in cat. exh., Galleria San Luca, Bologna, 1965; reprinted in *Dal Romanticismo all'Informale*, vol. I, Turin, 1977, p. 242.

Constant Permeke, *Autumn*, 1934

32
Nicolas de Staël. 1914-1955
Ciel à Honfleur
1952

Gustave Courbet, *La mer à Palavas*, 1857

Oil on canvas, 89 x 130 cm.
Signed on bottom left: «Staël».
Provenance: M. Knoedler & Co., Inc., New York; Gimpel Hanover Galerie, Zurich; Galerie Krugier, Geneva.
Exhibitions: New York, M. Knoedler & Co., Inc., March 1953, no. 17; Hanover, Kestner-Gesellschaft, December 1, 1959-January 24, 1960, no. 53; Hamburg, Kunstverein, February 7-March 13, 1960, no. 53; London, Crane Kalman Gallery, *The Sea*, June-August 1962, no. 39, col. pl. no. 19; Turin, Galleria d'Arte Moderna, May 3-June 12, 1960, no. 69, b/w ill.; Zurich, Gimpel & Hanover Galerie, April 19-May 18, 1963, no. 22, col. ill.; London, Gimpel Fils Gallery, June-October 1963, no. 22; Saint-Paul de Vence, Maeght Foundation, July-August 1972, no. 40, b/w ill.; Paris, Galeries Nationales du Grand Palais, May 22-August 24, 1981, no. 54, b/w ill.; London, Tate Gallery, September-November 1981, no. 54; Edinburgh, Scottish National Gallery of Modern Art, *Creation*, August 15-October 14, 1984, no. 14.
Bibliography: F. Russoli, «Percorso di Nicolas de Staël» in de Staël exh. cat., Turin, 1960, p. 21; D. Cooper, *Nicolas de Staël*, New York, W.W. Norton, 1961, p. 52; Italian ed., Istitute Arti Grafiche, Bergamo, 1967, p. 61; A. Chastel, J. Dubourg, F. de Staël, G. Viatte, *Nicolas de Staël, Catalogue raisonné des peintures*, Paris, Les Editions du Temps, 1968, no. 365, b/w ill., p. 184; C. Brandi, *La Mostra di de Staël*, Il Punto, Rome, May 28, 1960, b/w ill., p. 8; R. Tassi, «La 'maggior chiarezza' di Nicolas de Staël» in *Paragone*, Nov. 1965, reprinted in *L'atelier di Monet*, Milan, 1989, p. 249.

In the spring of 1951, Nicolas de Staël visited, at the Musée des Monuments Français, an exhibition dedicated to the mosaics in Ravenna in which Gino Severini had collaborated. In 1937, during his vagabond years, he had been to Ravenna and was already acquainted with these mosaics. But here, although faced with copies of them, they made such a strong impression on him that he saved the catalogue as a collection of useful images for his work. In fact, the juxtaposition of the colored tiles according to relationships or contrasts that contributed to creating the space, seemed to resolve his study of the spatial function of color. One can only believe that he was profoundly influenced by them since from that moment, almost unexpectedly, his works up until the end of 1951, approximately thirty-seven paintings, are based on a kind of checkerboard, a pattern of square tiles, placed very freely and with variety, but always grouped according to chromatic relationships and spatial necessity, almost mosaic weaving without rules and obvious figurations. Cesare Brandi gave a good formal description of these works: «The colored tile is never a tile; it is frayed on the edges, torn in the middle, reveals some red if it is green, blue if it is yellow, and also reveals other colors as well as extremely soft, almost invisible contrasting backgrounds, but enough to guarantee the area of color, the tile, an exigency and a spatial halo.»[1]

These tiles acquire force and vitality above all in the coloring of the edges which are vivid, not clear-cut, and establish a subtle harmony, not a boundary or break, with the surrounding ones, thus creating a unified fabric which is harmonic, profound, spatial and poetic. In a 1950 letter to Roger von Guindertaël de Staël wrote: «... Je crois à l'âme des contours tu le sais, si du moins je crois à l'âme quelque part c'est dans les contours.»[2]

But in January 1952 de Staël painted in the lower part of a very large canvas the usual tiled structure, extremely irregular with some very large and other small tiles, and then unexpectedly he erected above it a vast, homogeneous, grey, surface of sky and entitled it *Les toits*. This painting, in addition to being one of his masterpieces, is a pivotal work, a work which resolved one crisis and marked the start of a new period, a new rapport with reality. Germaine Viatte notes in a comment that chronologically follows the entirety of de Staël's work: «Nicolas de Staël avait bien le sentiment en cette fin d'année 1951 d'être en un point critique de son évolution.»[3]. And de Staël himself in November 1951 wrote in a letter to Denys Sutton: «Hess a dû vous dire que je pense pouvoir évoluer Dieu sait comment vers plus de clarté en peinture et que cela me met dans un état désagréable de trouble permanent.»[4] Almost all critics of de Staël date this new period, this different rapport with reality, as the consequence of an impression he gleaned during a nighttime soccer match between France and Sweden played at the Parc des Princes on March 26, 1952 and which he described in a letter to René Char. But it is a commonly-held belief in fact born out by that letter and by the fact that de Staël, starting the day after that match, began to do paintings of *footballeurs* in which the figures of the players emerged with the reds and blues of their jerseys strongly intensified in hue by the violent light, and he painted almost thirty of them without let-up in April and the beginning of May. But *Les toits*, with its chromatic beauty in which the greys, blues and blacks fluctuate, with its large space, its overcast sky, its incongruous and extremely poetic union between a solid tiled structure and free surface of the air, with that creation of a horizon line, is the work which indicates a new way of seeing and painting reality. Following this work, in January and February of the next year, are paintings of bottles, apples and some landscapes. Thus, in his personal show which opened in London at the Mathiessen Gallery on February 21, 1952, out of twenty-six paintings presented, seven belong to this new vision, and can be called «figurative.» G. Viatte commented: «These first bottles, apples and landscapes seemed to be an inconceivable anachronism.»[5].

It was the moment in which abstract painting exploded in the post-war period, from *action painting* and *tachisme* to *abstraction lyrique*, and reached its greatest diffusion and repute. De Staël, who had given the impression of being part of it, now seemed to be a deserter or traitor. In fact, the show was not very successful; the critics were skeptical. Only John Russel, in the *Sunday Times* of February 24, 1952, called him «the most interesting new painter of the last four or five years,» writing a phrase which de Staël found so correct that he included it in a letter to his daughter, Anna: «Je t'envoi le catalogue et tu diras à ta tante Olga que Dimanche un jeune critique a fini son article

Constant Permeke, *Seascape*, 1912

Constant Permeke, *Fields after the Storm*, 1937

Nicolas de Staël, *Ciel à Honfleur*, 1952

comme cela: 'There are paintings in which the painter risks everything: it is for us to risk and enhance an hour of irrevocable life by going to see them. [...]'»[6]

On his return from London where he had gone for the opening, de Staël began to paint landscapes. This time, he needed to leave his studio and work with the subject. He left at dawn and stopped in small towns not far from Paris — Fontenay, Gentilly, Chevreuse. He followed the Seine, arriving at Mantes, and once as far as its mouth at Honfleur. His friend Jean Bauret whom de Staël went to visit often since he lived in a house near Mantes, wrote: «[...] il a pris l'habitude de prendre exemple sur les formes picturales de la nature au lieu de prendre leçon dans les Cahiers d'Arts.»[7]

On April 26, 1952, de Staël wrote to René Char: «Je fais pour toi des petits paysages des environs de Paris pour t'apporter un peu de mes ciels d'ici...»[8] In March and April he continued to paint many landscapes, mostly of small format and on cardboard along with, occasionally, some larger paintings. He painted with a knife using quite dense material, homogeneous surfaces, some square tiles and long, horizontal streaks. He was immersed in color. Everything was patches, streaks or surfaces of color, and the space was born of their overlapping. The color was not too-violent or dazzling, but pure and taut, and the light, instead of bringing it out and making it incandescent as it would just a little while later, impregnated it, softened it. Standing out from among the landscapes painted during these two months is *Ciel à Honfleur*, the largest and most poetic of them all, and almost seems to be a summation of the entire period as if placed right in the middle of his entire work and of its changes and variations.

In de Staël's work, one can, in fact, identify two decisive shifts which come at different moments and involve two different factors. The first was described at the beginning of this essay and takes place within the framework of the subject, the rapport with reality or the natural image. The second within the framework of the *matière*, the primary element on which he bases his painting. Thus there

are formed four zones, periods or groups, in pairs not coinciding with each other. In relation to the subject, there is a first group in which it is not recognizable and about which, rather than abstraction, it is better to speak of a distancing from reality and the natural image. The titles of the works in this group are abstract, almost all the same, *Composition*, or sometimes symbolic, metaphorical and suggestive of a mood. In the second group, the relationship with the natural image is closer, the subject recognizable, the assumption of reality more direct, and correspondingly the titles become pertinent to the image, indicating the subject or the place. The shift between these two groups took place at the beginning of 1952 and can be established in January with the work, *Les toits*. This division of his work has given rise to much discussion. On one side it has been stated that it is a definite «return to the figurative» style, on the other it is said that the contrasting terms of abstract/figurative so much debated during those years cannot be applied to it. It is unquestionable that an unbroken continuity, both in the sense of its vital involvement as well as its structure, language and beauty of its poetry, exists throughout the ten-year period from 1945 to 1955. But that such a change exists in its subject, its vision and, in part, its spirit is equally unquestionable. The ambiguity in various of de Staël's declarations, in addition to showing that the problem was not of much interest to him, also confirms, however, that this shift existed but involved the same volition, the same destiny to just paint, the same love and the same poetry. In 1950 he said: «Toujours il y a toujours un sujet, toujours.»[9]; and in 1951: «Il n'y a pas de sujet [...] Les choses communiquent constamment avec l'artiste pendant qu'il peint, c'est tout ce que j'en sais.»[10] In 1952, regarding the contrast between abstraction and figuration, he said: «Je n'oppose pas la peinture abstraite à la peinture figurative. Une peinture devrait être à la fois abstraite et figurative. Abstraite en tant que mur, figurative en tant que représentation d'un espace.»[11]

As for the second shift, or change, that took place with the *matière*, there is a first group in which the

matière is thick, solid, pasty. It corresponds to a spiritual and psychological state, to the need for compromise, for violence, for vitality. In the second group, the work is made up of a *matière* that is thinner, more delicate, tauter, light, sometimes even transparent and veil-like, as if the violence of the impulse had lessened, making room for meditation, and the anguish or sadness had become more internal. The passage between the two parts is not clear-cut but gradual. It had its inception in some paintings done towards the end of 1953 and was made clear at the beginning of 1954.

Ciel à Honfleur is a work which is involved with the different and opposing characteristics of the four periods: the lack of any «figure,» the unblemished simplicity of the composition and the homogeneous and limitless surface make it seem abstract. But at the same time, its direct relationship with reality is clear, its subject seems simple, recognizable, completely open to a natural vision. The work falls within the period in which the *matière* is expressive in relation to its depth. *Ciel à Honfleur* is also a work of *matière*, but the paint is less thick than usual, lighter, almost airy, so much so that, above all in the upper part of the painting where the sky becomes distant and immense, it could appear as a pre-intuition of the last period when the *matière* is illuminated, lightened and becomes calm. Thus, *Ciel à Honfleur* seems to contain and unify all the moments of a varied language, fused into poetry. It corresponds to what de Staël wrote in a letter to Douglas Cooper: «[...] la peinture, la vraie, tend toujours à tous les aspects, c'est-à-dire à l'impossible addition de l'instant présent, du passé et de l'avenir.»[12]

Because of this, *Ciel à Honfleur* is a miraculous work. In his article that has been already quoted and which was written for the Turin exhibition in 1960 Cesare Brandi said: «There is that *Ciel à Honfleur* from '53 [sic] that will remain, we believe, one of the greatest paintings of this century, and of which one cannot even speak about the subtlety of its painting style and overall energy.»[13] It is as if de Staël had achieved in it, for a moment, that «plus de clarté en peinture» that he posed as his objective in a letter written in November 1951. In it, with minimal means he accomplished a great painting in every sense: for the expansion of its space, its concentrated poetry, its intense spirit, its completely internal, variable quality diffused with airy waves and light. Above the thin and dark base of earth, there rise an immense, impending space marked with various light-blue stripes and, depending on the light the color absorbs, becomes pale touching on the milky pearls of dawn, more intense — a sky-blue drenched with luminous haze — or barely gusting with air. It is all sky, light, cheerful, infinite, cloudless, of a blue which seems to absorb the reflections of the sea. *Ciel à Honfleur* expresses vastness, solitude, silence, light, music, poetry. In it de Staël brought together the many contrasting elements of his difficult and very pure nature: its expressive force and refined color, the violence of the impulse and the delicateness of the spirit, trauma and meditation. In June of 1952 he wrote to Dubourg: «Et vous savez cette histoire: deux choses important, l'intensité de la frappe et celle de la méditation.» [14]

But a work so outside the rules and customs of painting in those years did not spring from nothing. During his boyhood and adolescence in Belgium, de Staël had become acquainted with Flemish, and above all, Dutch landscape painting. He was probably fascinated by the skies of Konincks, Ruysdael and Hobbema. Perhaps he also came to know Constant Permeke, who was closer to him in time, and his material painting, his skies, dense, overcast and vast over the sea or the plain. On September 8, 1951, a few months before painting *Ciel à Honfleur*, he had written to René Char: «Tu m'as fait retrouver d'emblée la passion que j'avais enfant pour les grands ciels.» [15]. That vastness, pure in Ruysdael, impure in Permeke, is not extraneous to the inspiration from which *Ciel à Honfleur* was born.

There is another painter who, even more than the Flemish and Dutch, influenced de Staël and this painting in particular: Gustave Courbet. *Ciel à Honfleur* seems to derive, almost directly, from the seascapes he painted between 1854 and 1865. For example, *La mer à Palavas* of 1857, in which the

similar elements are the lack of «figures,» the vastness of the space, the meagerness of its means, the homogeneous structure, the diffusion of the light, the coexistence of delicateness and strength. De Staël, who had travelled throughout Europe and had an extremely rich art culture, almost certainly knew this seascape. And how much he loved Courbet is shown in a letter written on November 6, 1954 to Dubourg after having seen his exhibition in Lyons: «C'est un immense bonhomme, on mettra encore quelques siècles à le reconnaître. Je dis immense parce que sans esthétique, sans pompierisme, sans préambule, il descend à jet continu des tableaux uniques, avec la même sureté qu'un fleuve qui coule verse la mer dense, radiant à larges sonorités et toujours sobre. Cézanne est un gamin à côté [...] C'est un titan, Courbet.» [16]

While he was still painting the group of landscapes to which *Ciel à Honfleur* belongs, on March 26, 1952, as was previously mentioned, de Staël attended the nighttime soccer match during which he experienced the revelation regarding the great intensity colors take on when they are hit by a very bright light. A little later, in May, he left for the south and went to live in Bornes-les-Pins and Le Lavandou, and he experienced even more violently this revelation of burning, explosive light that reinforces and transforms color. «Me voilà près de cette lumière vorace que tu connais. Quelle histoire la méditerranée!», [17] as he wrote to René Char. From that moment his colors took on a dazzle which lasted for some time. But in *Ciel à Honfleur* it is still the light of the north which envelops, subdues and imbues it with spirit, that impregnates the colors from within without burning or transforming them, and radiates in the homogeneity of the space its restrained and melancholy splendor.
Claudio Zambianchi

1. Brandi 1960.
2. «I believe in the soul of the edges, as you know. At least, if there is a soul somewhere, I believe it is in the edges.» Chastel 1968, p. 32.
3. «Nicolas de Staël, at the end of 1951, had the sense that he was at a critical point in his evolution.» Chastel 1968, p. 170.

4. «Hess will have told you that I think I am evolving, God knows how, towards a greater sense of clarity in painting and that this puts me in an unpleasant state of continual turmoil.» Chastel 1968, p. 170.
5. *Ibid.*, p. 176.
6. *Ibid.*, p. 182.
7. «[...] he is accustomed to taking as his model the pictorial forms from nature rather than taking lessons from the Cahiers d'Arte.» Chastel 1968, p. 188.
8. «I am in the process of doing small landscapes of the environs of Paris for you, so that I can send you some of my skies.» Chastel 1968, p. 188.
9. «There is always a subject, always.» Chastel 1968, p. 176.
10. «The subject does not exist [...] The things are in constant communication with the artist while he paints; that's all I know.» Chastel 1968, p. 150.
11. «I do not place abstract and figurative painting in opposition to each other. Painting must be abstract and figurative at the same time. Abstract in terms of a barrier, figurative as a depiction of a space.» *Nicolas de Staël*, exh. cat., Paris, 1981, p. 15.
12. «[...] painting, true painting, always tends to encompass all aspects, i.e., the impossible summation of the present, past, and future moment.» Chastel 1968, p. 382.
13. Brandi 1960. The error in the date derives from the catalogue in which the painting, erroneously, bears the date of 1953. The reproduction of the painting that accompanies the article removes any doubt.
14. «You know this story: only two things matter, the intensity of the trauma and the intensity of the meditation.» Chastel 1968, p. 218.
15. «You made me rediscover unexpectedly the passion I had as a boy for large skies.» Chastel 1968, p. 166.
16. «He is an immense individual. Several centuries will still be needed to recognize him. I say immense because without esthetic, without overstatement, without any pretense, he continuously produces unique paintings with the same confidence with which a river flows to the sea, dense, radiant with wide sonorities and always sober. Next to him Cézanne is a mere child... Courbet is a titan.» Chastel 1968, p. 354.
17. «Here I am near this voracious light you know. What history, the Mediterranean!» Chastel 1968, p. 218.

33
Ennio Morlotti. 1910-1992
Paesaggio sul fiume (Adda)
1955

Oil on canvas, 55 x 80 cm.
Signed and dated on the back: «Morlotti 55».
Note: on the back are labels from the La Bussola, Gissi and Saletta la Cornice galleries in Turin.

«At that time I was a Picassoian and I couldn't shake it, I cursed Picasso and all his petty rhetoric; I clearly understood the limits and falsity of that world, but if I looked at a figure or a bottle, what came out was Picasso. Until one day, on the River Adda, I had that revelation. Confronted with that landscape I understood that there could be something real and I said to myself, 'This summer I'm coming here [...]'. And there I had a sense of my destiny: first of all, the roots sunk in nature and thus my nature, my roots. Finally a completely different principle, I didn't think about the «vision» or the «landscape,» but I looked at a strip of grass which yielded another strip of grass, the apple tree which yielded the apples. It was the emotion of this fact which I translated into painting.»[1] This is the way Morlotti remembered the moment in 1952 in which, propelled by the urgency to renew contact with nature, he passed from an artistic style strongly-tinged by Picasso — a style he had practiced in the fifteen years between 1947 and 1952 — to a completely different way of painting, with implications deeply-rooted in the landscape on the banks of the Adda. Even before his Picasso phase, towards the middle of the 1940s, Morlotti was challenged by the subject of nature and the Lombardy landscape. Yet, in the «Adda» series which this *Paesaggio sul fiume* is part of, things seem radically different: the *matière* assumes a new consistency, becoming dense and thick and is unexpectedly lit up with very bright colors. The composition rejects any descriptive aspiration, the perspective point moves closer and the subject carves out a piece of the landscape parallel to the direction of the painting. Through the use of these elements, nature takes on the «wall-like» aspect which critics like Roberto Tassi hold to be one of Morlotti's key advancements in the creation of the modern landscape. «With respect to the more measured growth of the previous landscapes, here

there is a sudden frenzy that runs through the painting and pours out color in an explosion of yellows, reds, lilacs and purples. So, redoubled by the reflection from the water, the edges of the wall of vegetation even begin to lose their definition and broaden, expanding along the polyphonic scale of chromatic taches in a spatial 'continuum', absorbing the entire surface, and the view completely sinks into the painting and penetrates it beyond the threshold of vision, in the process of becoming the body of the *matière*.»[2]

In the «Adda» series, for the first time the *matière* becomes analogous, very closely analogous, to the natural material, in its «birth, growth, culmination and decay.»[3] It is in this moment that Morlotti, as Giovanni Testori first intuited, passes from a «naturalism of observation» to a «naturalism of participation.»[4] What dominates is a sensuous conception of nature, of living it from within, which would bring Morlotti just a step away from completely merging with it. In this phase of Morlotti's output, the tendency towards Eros prevailed, between the two opposite poles of «Eros and erosion,» love and death, within which, as the artist himself explicitly admitted, his work moves.[5] Right from their first appearance, these «Adda» paintings led the critics, especially those closest to Morlotti, to pose the question of the «modernity» of his way of understanding nature whose sources of inspiration are recognized in a succession reaching from Courbet to de Staël. Both Arcangeli as well as Testori (with greater determination) defend Morlotti from the possible accusation of nineteenth century-ism: «if these *vedute* of the river on the banks of which he was born evoke in many the usual 'nineteenth century' suspicions and such, I think that, even if they are not their favorite works, those who have their wits about them, must accept them as a sign, perhaps an even too-explicit one, of the existential authenticity, the 'here and now', of Morlotti's art.»[6]

Testori, for his part, states that «it is an error in interpretation to divide Morlotti's work into, on one side, a phase of nineteenth century persistence and, on the other, a phase of dramatic modernity. The truth about his work, involved as it is in many

directions not permitting — even from a technical standpoint — any attempt to divide it up, is that in him the pressure of age-old natural truths is realized in a search for the moments in which those truths, from time to time, become reality, i.e., history.»[7]
Claudio Zambianchi

1. P.G. Castagnoli in Bordighera, Palazzo del Parco, *Morlotti. Pastelli e disegni 1954-1978*, exh. cat., December 15, 1978-January 15, 1979.
2. P.G. Castagnoli, *Ennio Morlotti*, Ravenna, Agenzia Editoriale Essegi, 1983 (published on occasion of the Ravenna exhibition, Loggetta Lombardesca, *Ennio Morlotti*, April 23-June 5, 1983), p. 24.
3. F. Arcangeli, «Gli Ultimi naturalisti,» *Paragone*, 59, November 1954; published in idem, *Dal romanticismo all'informale*, vol. 2, *Il secondo dopoguerra*, Turin, Einaudi, 1977, in particular, pp. 317-19.
4. G. Testori, from the catalogue of his personal exhibition at the Galleria del Milione in Milan, anthologized in M. Valsecchi, *Morlotti*, Milan, Vangelista Editore, 1972, p. 66.
5. See R. Tassi, «La realtà di Morlotti,» *Paragone*, 233, July 1969, p. 63.
6. F. Arcangeli, *Ennio Morlotti*, Milan, Edizioni del Milione, 1962, p. xl.
7. G. Testori, *Morlotti*, Ivrea: Centro Culturale Olivetti, 1957 (publ. on occasion of his personal exhibition at the Centro Culturale Olivetti), p. 26.

34
Ennio Morlotti. 1910-1992
Paesaggio (Brianza)
1958

Oil on canvas, 73 x 82 cm.
Signed on bottom right: «Morlotti»; signed and dated on back: «Morlotti 58».
Provenance: Galleria del Milione, Milan; Ponti-Loren Collection (just as the one in description no. 37, this painting temporarily remained in storage at the Galleria Comunale d'Arte at the Villa Manzoni in Lecco, was then returned to its original owners and finally sold).
Exhibitions: Turin, Palazzo delle Arti, *Peintres d'aujourd'hui France-Italie/Pittori d'oggi Francia-Italia. VI Mostra*, September 1959, no. 42; Rome, Palazzo Barberini, *Morlotti*, January 28-March 15, 1966, no. 29, (b/w pl. no. 29 in cat.); Darmstadt, Kunsthalle, *Ennio Morlotti*, December 10, 1966-March 15, 1967, no. 19, (b/w pl. no. 19 in cat.); Basel, Kunsthalle, *Ennio Morlotti*, January 28-March 5, 1967, no. 29; Milan, Palazzo Reale, *Ennio Morlotti, Mostra antologica*, G. Bruno, curator, October 9-November 29, 1987, no. 57 (cat. Milan, Giorgio Mondadori, col. ill., p. 93); Bologna, Galleria d'arte Villa delle Rose (later, Milan, Galleria Bergamini, *Morlotti. Dipinti 1954-1964*), November 10, 1991-January 12, 1992 (cat. Bologna, Alfa Editoriale, col. ill. p. 63).
Bibliography: L. Bortolon, *Ennio Morlotti*, Milan, Istituto d'Arte Mondadori, 1974, no. 12, p. 44; Lecco, Musei Civici di Lecco, Galleria Comunale d'Arte, Villa Manzoni, *Opere del patrimonio comunale*, 1983, no. 83, p. 89, col. pl., no. 83, p. 92.

Starting in 1957, Morlotti's artistic eye took another step towards the subject of nature, hence the emergence of landscapes such as this one. The horizon lifted, the motif became the dense seething of nature on a reduced scale. The «organic feeling» Morlotti spoke of[1] became radicalized and the painter felt «like an insect inside things,»[2] almost as if swallowed up by them. «The distance is slowly consumed in the progressive sinking until the perspective is abolished and the viewer, to the same degree as the painter, is drawn into the green swelling of the vegetation.»[3]
It was a brief moment lasting approximately three years, from 1957 to 1959, and marked the peak of Morlotti's involvement with this theme. «I felt myself attracted to a romantic impulse; I wanted to become involved with nature rather than stand there looking at it and painting it from the outside,» Morlotti stated to Marco Valsecchi in 1964.[4] It is the period in which Morlotti's painterly *matière* thickened into clots that tend to emerge from the surface of the canvas: the thick impasto «became [...] in his work the condition by which the physical thickness, the sense of weight, of depth, of the dark density of the walls of the world, transformed itself into a dramatic image, organized itself according to a structure of internal forces and condensed itself into Eros.»[5]
In this phase, the painter was just a step away from losing himself in nature and therefore abandoning any point of reference with visual reality, a step which, fundamentally, he did not feel able to make since in his paintings there is always an implied tension between a dissolution and recomposition of the form that keeps the artist from dissolving them in an indistinct disarray. In other words, as a great number of critics have pointed out, it is as if in the process of disintegration the form is subjected to, there was also an implicit principle of reintegration in a process analogous to the life cycle in nature. Crispolti speaks of a «sinking into the deepest roots of the state of existence *sub specie naturae*.»[6] Thus, one can make out a further layer in the web of analogies tied into the complex stratification in Morlotti's painting.
The density of meaning in his «naturalism» explains the difficulty in interpreting it, particularly evident in the 1950s in the opposing viewpoints of Arcangeli and Testori. These two critics, as was said in the previous description, were both convinced of Morlotti's modernity, but while Arcangeli made Morlotti the champion of «latter-day naturalism» and saw his contribution linked to local roots in Lombardy,[7] Testori holds that this position «evades» the historical questions posed by Morlotti's painting[8] and rather he «claims European prominence and inspiration in the experimentation» of this painter.[9]
Claudio Zambianchi

1. P.G. Castagnoli, *Ennio Morlotti*, Ravenna, Agenzia Editoriale Essegi, 1983 (published for the Ravenna exhibition, Loggetta Lombardesca, *Ennio Morlotti*, April 23-June 5, 1983), p. 28.
2. Morlotti, quoted by G. Marchiori in his presentation at Cortina d'Ampezzo, Galleria Hausamann, *12 dipinti di Ennio Morlotti*, exh. cat., August 23, 1965.
3. M. Valsecchi, *Ennio Morlotti*, Milan, All'insegna del pesce d'oro, 1968, p. 22.
4. M. Valsecchi, «Vorrei dipingere un nudo come Giorgione,» *Tempo*, February 22, 1964, reprinted in Castagnoli 1983, p. 87.
5. R. Tassi, presentation in Milan, Galleria del Milione, *Morandi, Morlotti*, December 12, 1970-January 12, 1971.
6. E. Crispolti, introductory essay in *Burri, Cagli, Fontana, Guttuso, Moreni, Morlotti, sei pittori italiani dagli Quaranta ad oggi*, cat. exh., A. Del Guercio and E. Crispolti eds., Arezzo, Galleria Comunale d'arte contemporanea, cat. exh., May 6-June 11, 1967; printed in A.C. Quintavalle, *Morlotti, Struttura e storia*, Milan, Gruppo Editoriale Fabbri, 1982, p. 39.
7. F. Arcangeli, «Gli Ultimi naturalisti,» *Paragone*, 59, November 1954; published in idem, *Dal romanticismo all'informale*, vol. 2, *Il secondo dopoguerra*, Turin, Einaudi, 1977, see in part. p. 313.
8. G. Testori, *Morlotti*, Ivrea, Centro Culturale Olivetti, 1957 (publ. on occasion of the personal exhibition at the Centro Culturale Olivetti), pp. 24-25.
9. Quintavalle 1982, p. 94.

35
Ennio Morlotti. 1910-1992
Fiori su fondo viola
1958

36
Ennio Morlotti. 1910-1992
Autunno
1958

Oil on canvas, 100 x 80 cm.
Signed and dated on bottom right: «Morlotti/58»;
signed and dated on back: «Morlotti 58».
Provenance: Galleria Bergamini, Milan; Private Collection, Turin Exhibitions: Lecco, Azienda Autonoma Soggiorno e Turismo, *Mostra antologica di Ennio Morlotti*, May 18-June 16, 1963; Rome, Palazzo Barberini, *Morlotti*, January 28-March 15, 1966, no. 37 (cat., col. ill. pl. 37); Darmstadt, Kunsthalle, *Ennio Morlotti*, December 10, 1966-March 15, 1967, no. 24 (cat., col. ill. pl. 24, cover); Basel, Kunsthalle, *Ennio Morlotti*, January 28-March 5, 1967, no. 36; Bologna, Galleria d'Arte Forni, *Maestri contemporanei italiani e stranieri*, February 23-March 16, 1991, col. ill. p. 41.
Bibliography: C. Volpe, *Ennio Morlotti*, Rome, Edizioni Galleria Odyssia, 1963 (personal exhibition in Lecco, 1963), col. ill. pl. 37.

Flowers, along with landscapes and bathers, constitute one of the dominant themes in Morlotti's output during the last three years of the 1950s and characterize the period closest to that of an Informal style in his painting. As can be seen in the two examples chosen here, the floral compositions differentiate themselves from the bathers (see no. 37) and the landscapes (no. 33) in that they are characterized by a coagulation of the *matière* and the image at the center of the painting. The emphasis is placed on a nucleus of maximum density which gradually spreads outwards towards the edges of the painting. This approach gives the painting a vortical rhythm and a sense of vibration that very much remind one of certain results of American action painting or the way Wols's images present themselves: «I think that for my generation,» Morlotti stated, «the only way to save oneself is to risk everything. Wols, Pollock, de Staël and Gorky painted their truth until they burned themselves out. I unquestionably feel myself closer to them than to our great fathers Braque, Picasso and Matisse who were only driven by formal considerations.»[1] In his floral paintings, it is as if Morlotti were referring back to the most profound meanings the still life theme has assumed in the course

of the history of painting starting with the Baroque: the still life as an allusion to the frailty of beauty and life, a meaning which Morlotti refers to not in the spirit of a learned painter citing the art of the past, but in order to analyze in depth its eternal theme which Arcangeli defined as «the life-death alternative.»[2]. It is perhaps exactly because of these references, that in these paintings the metaphoric potential of the painterly *matière* is developed more fully from the standpoint of the «Eros and erosion» dichotomy: «The antagonism of these two concurrent impulses forms the most personal nucleus in Morlotti's pictorial vision and is at the root of that confused tangle of gestures and stratification of *matière* within which are revealed, expressed and debated, the feeling of an existence that simultaneously flowers and withers, develops and dies.»[4]. In this painting one could also cite another dichotomy which, according to Franco Russoli, is part of Morlotti's feeling for the painting material. It is the «duality between the 'organic' and 'crystallized' materials, between color made up of earth, flesh, water, grass and sky, and color that is a set gemstone, veined marble, a sheet of beaten gold.»[5] It reveals a «miraculous» sense of the material which Russoli links up with the great medieval tradition of Lombardy goldsmiths.[6]
Claudio Zambianchi

1. E. Morlotti, film on Ennio Morlotti by the RAI, March 10, 1970 dir. by P.P. Ruggerini; in R. Modesti, «Commento iconografico» in F. Biamonti, *Ennio Morlotti*, Milan, Club Amici dell'Arte, 1972, p. 34.
2. F. Arcangeli, film on Ennio Morlotti by the RAI, March 10, 1970, dir. by P.P. Ruggerini, published in Acqui Terme, Palazzo «Liceo Sarracco,» *Ennio Morlotti*, exh. cat., February 2-24, 1972.
3. M. Calvesi, «L'Informale in Italia» in Livorno, *Aspetti della ricerca informale in Italia fino al 1957*, exh. cat., March 1963; published in idem, *Le due avanguardie*, vol. 2, Bari, Laterza, 1975, second ed., p. 264.
4. P.G. Castagnoli, «Ennio Morlotti. Le Rocce» in Modena, Galleria Civica, *Ennio Morlotti. Le Rocce: 1975-1984*, exh. cat., May 4-June 11, 1985, Modena, Edizioni Panini, p. 13.
5. F. Russoli in Rome, 1966, p. 31.
6. *Ibid.*

Oil on canvas, 108 x 78 cm.
Signed and dated on bottom right: «Morlotti 58»;
signed and dated on back: «Morlotti 58».
Exhibition: Lyons, Musée de Beaux-Arts, *Peintres et sculpteurs italiens du futurisme à nos jours*, 1959 (travelling exhibit), no. 64.
Bibliography: G. Cavazzini, P. Consigli, R. Tassi, eds., *Pittura e scultura del XX secolo 1910-1980*, Parma, Banca Emiliana, 1982, p. 123, col. ill. p. 123.

«At times Morlotti turns the brush around against the painting and dips it in the soft and yielding paint, furrowing it with convoluted, sadistic grooves, complicated and irascible graffiti which are as rabid and precise as barbed wire. He often uses graffito-work on his flowers and nothing is less floral than Morlotti's flowers.»[1] The gestural violence identified by Cesare Garboli appears in this *Autunno* perhaps even more than in *Fiori su fondo viola*. It almost seems as if the marks scoring the material cut grooves which remain open, revealing depths that are throbbing and still alive.
And yet, as Roberto Tassi observes, Morlotti's is an «elaborated violence, it is violence within the work and not against the work, it is a violence that passes from the spirit to the painting, like that of Rimbaud.»[2]

In the analysis of *Fiori su fondo viola* (see no. 35), the emphasis was placed on the similarity between Morlotti's floral paintings that have the pictorial spaces of Pollock and Wols thanks to the presence of a swirling and pulsating central nucleus. This *Autunno* points out the difference in emphasis between Morlotti's painting and such extreme examples of the American and European Informal style. If the frantic rhythm with which Pollock constructs his space captures the viewer and forces him to move to the brink of a bottomless and dizzying depth, Morlotti replaces the emptiness with a *matière* that grows organically. The tension remains strong, but in the final analysis it is composed.

Luigi Carluccio acutely grasped this aspect in introducing a group of Morlotti's works in the exhibition *Pittori d'oggi Francia-Italia*, in which were

37
Ennio Morlotti. 1910-1992
Studio per bagnanti n. 2
1959

shown, among others, *Brianza* (no. 34) and a painting of flowers very similar to this one in its size and compositional structure: «Morlotti's vocabulary,» the critic wrote, «is willingly violent if one speaks of its intent, it develops with the inflections of its painting, is perfumed with sanguineous clots as well as aromatic herbs, and almost by analogy realistically reconstructs the resistance that divides the things. That is, he lays aside the afflicted and arcane flexing which attracts him from deep within and rejects him [...]. I know of no other conception of nature equally as animated and populated, that implies sensuousness and modesty, harshness and tenderness, and becomes the warm presence of a living substance aware of its organic limitations as much as is implied in Morlotti's concept.»[3]
Claudio Zambianchi

1. C. Garboli in La Versiliana, Marina di Pietrasanta, Fabbrica di pinoli, *Ennio Morlotti, Antologica,* exh. cat., July 28, 1990, Bologna, Grafis Edizioni.
2. R. Tassi in Parma, Palazzo della Pilotta, *Morlotti, Figure 1942/1975,* exh. cat., March 8-April 13, 1975, p. 11.
3. L. Carluccio, «Ennio Morlotti» in Turin, Palazzo delle Arti, *Peintres d'aujourd'hui France-Italie/Pittori d'oggi Francia-Italia, VI mostra,* exh. cat., September 1959.

Oil on canvas, 151 x 129.5 cm.
Signed on bottom right: «Morlotti»; signed and dated on back: «Morlotti 59».
Provenance: O. Skouras Collection; Ponti-Loren Collection (as no. 34 this painting was temporarily in storage at the Galleria Comunale d'Arte of the Villa Manzoni in Lecco, was then returned to its original owners and finally sold).
Exhibitions: San Paolo, Museo d'Arte Moderna, *V Biennale del Museo d'Arte Moderna. Artistas Italianos de Hoje,* September-December 1959, no. 92; Rome, Palazzo Barberini, *Morlotti,* January 28-March 15, 1966, no. 49 (col. pl. no. 49 in cat.); Darmstadt, Kunsthalle, *Ennio Morlotti,* December 10, 1966-March 3, 1967, no. 31 (col. pl. no. 31 in cat.); Basel, Kunsthalle, *Ennio Morlotti,* January 28-March 5, 1967, no. 46; San Gimignano, Palazzo del Podestà, *Morlotti. Mostra Antologica,* October 1972, no. 9; Parma, Palazzo della Pilotta, *Morlotti. Figure 1942/1975,* R. Tassi, curator, March 8-April 13, 1975, no. 27 (cat. Milano, Electa; b/w pl. no. 27); Milan, Palazzo Reale, *Ennio Morlotti. Mostra antologica,* G. Bruno, curator, October 9-November 29, 1987, no. 63 (cat. Milan, Giorgio Mondadori; col. pl. no. 62, p. 98); Bologna, Galleria d'Arte Villa delle Rose (later Milan, Galleria Bergamini), *Morlotti. Dipinti 1954-1964,* November 10, 1991-January 12, 1992 (cat. Bologna, Alfa Editoriale; col. ill. p. 73).
Bibliography: M. Valsecchi, *Morlotti,* Milan, Vangelista Editore, 1972 (published on the occasion of his personal exhibition in San Gimignano, 1972), col. pl. no. 9, p. 25 and fourth cover); Lecco, Musei Civici di Lecco, Galleria Comunale d'Arte, Villa Manzoni, *Opere del patrimonio comunale,* 1983, no. 86, p. 89, col. pl. no. 86, p. 94.

Beginning in 1952, the subject of the female nude within the landscape is constant in Morlotti's work, and ends only with his cessation to work and death. In fact, his last group of paintings, done just a few months before he died, is all «bathers» and is like a mysterious jolt of youth and colorful happiness (one of the loveliest examples is found in the Barilla Collection, see no. 39). In the ostensible (even if a bit forced) division between «figures» and «landscape,» this subject, because it unites the two modes of expression, is like a summation of landscape and figure painting fused together.

The origin of and reason for this subject as well as its pre-eminence in the rest of his work, can be found in something Morlotti said: «My life is the life of a man who loves nature, the landscape, who would like to possess it, like love. Like possessing a woman.» Morlotti is a painter who lived on impressions and passions, and these two things were provoked by nature and woman. In *Studio per bagnanti n. 2,* the two elements are so fused and confused that one cannot be distinguished from the other. Therefore, it is necessary to know the precedents leading up to it in order to understand its profound implications and to be able to see it as a culminating point of all his work. In fact, Morlotti himself wrote to the current owners of the painting: «I learned of your purchase of my red painting of the Bathers. I want to tell you that I am very pleased, it was one of the two paintings I loved best,» the other being its companion work from the same year and with the same theme, *Studio per bagnanti n. 1.*

The external element which, along with the internal ones, is operant in Morlotti's painting and leads to *Studio per bagnanti n. 2,* is the Informal poetic. Morlotti began to accept it, a bit cautiously and in an indirect fashion, between 1953 and 1954, even though a sense of it had enhanced his previous landscapes from 1942 and 1944. The series of works, almost all bearing the title «bathers,» in which the female nude appears as a kind of breaking down within the landscape, started in 1955 with two paintings in which the figure — head, thighs, breasts — is still not very distinct within the red, yellow and green weave of the *matière.* Two paintings followed in 1956, two in 1957, one in 1958 and three in 1959. The progression towards a completely Informal style is constant, as is the progression towards a prevalence of red, until the two elements reach their culmination in *Studio per bagnanti n. 2,* the largest, most extreme and, in my view, loveliest of the entire group.

38
Ennio Morlotti. 1910-1992
Rocce
1982

In Morlotti's work, 1959 is the year of red, as if a dramatic flame, intense and limitless, was burning the space, the *matière*, the bodies and nature, along with the painter's spirit and desire. It is not only the sense of the female flesh and human passion which spreads; the landscapes from this same year are also burning with a red that ignites the earth, the dry twigs, the branches, the banks and not the sky (it is not the red of sunset), as happened in his other masterpiece, *Colline in Brianza* owned by Mario Lavagetto of Parma. In this landscape, and in a few others like it from the same year, the earth, almost coagulated blood, also manifests itself as a woman's body. The visionary violence of that red, excited and mysterious and completely pertinent to the *matière*, is one of the strongest and most real fantasies of «natural» painting. In *Studio per bagnanti n. 2*, in an even more marked fashion, there is the same fusion of bodies and earth, sky, water, and grass, all made up of this red-hot *matière*. In my view, even at its peak — Pollock and de Staël having just recently died — there is nothing in that year in European and American Informal painting that can stand up to this work.
Roberto Tassi

Oil on canvas, 110 x 120 cm.
Signed on bottom right: «Morlotti/x».
Provenance: Galleria Bergamini Diarte s.r.l., Milan.
Exhibitions: Ravenna, Loggetta Lombardesca, *Ennio Morlotti*, April 23-June 5, 1983, no. 27 (see below, Castagnoli); Turin, Gissi Galleria d'Arte, *Morlotti*, November 1983, no. 19 (col. ill. in cat.); Modena, Galleria Civica, *Ennio Morlotti. Le Rocce: 1975-1984*, P.G. Castagnoli, curator, May 4-June 11, 1985, no. 23 (cat. Modena, Edizioni Panini, col. pl. no. 23); Venice, *43rd Venice Biennale of Art*, 1988, no. 3 (Morlotti section); La Versiliana, Marina di Pietrasanta, Fabbrica di pinoli, *Ennio Morlotti, Antologica*, from July 28, 1990, no. 40 (cat. Bologna, Grafis Edizioni, col. pl. no. 40); Parma, La Sanseverina, *Ennio Morlotti. Opere 1982-1990*, R. Tassi, curator, October 13-December 14, 1990, no. 1 (col. ill. in cat., p. 10).
Bibliography: P.G. Castagnoli, *Ennio Morlotti*, Ravenna, Agenzia Editoriale Essegi, 1983 (published on the occasion of the Ravenna exhibition, 1983, b/w pl. no. 27, p. 75).

Morlotti held that, within the history of his painting, the rock series had an importance not less than that of the paintings dedicated to the Adda. The inner drive must have had an intensity equal to the discovery of feeling himself «like an insect within nature» which characterized his rediscovery of the Lombardy landscape in the early 1950s. But the rocks took a very different, perhaps even antithetical direction. In any case, they verified, along with the «Skulls» series which had come just before, the abandoning of the sense of the «organic» in favor of a painting style with a more philosophical and meditative meaning that was dominated by a sense of death: «Suddenly,» as Morlotti said in 1983, «I felt myself close to death and so I began to feel other needs, I experienced all this as a hallucination and from that moment I tried to give an image to this hallucination, to this blinding. It is this blinding sense I am trying to portray today with the «Rocks» paintings.»[1]
    Their proximity to the skulls, not just chronologically but also in terms of content, is remarkable.

Pier Giovanni Castagnoli pertinently observes that «the rock is like the skeleton of the natural organic matter.»[2] What are the formal indications of this profound change? First of all, a clear variation in the chromatic range; from the greens and violets which dominated the Ligurian landscapes one passes to a range based on ochre-hues, whites and blues: «the anxiety, of an overflowing and very beautiful poetic sense, was that of letting one take away one's own memorabilia of the greens, one's memorabilia of the earth tones.»[3] The «distance» of the subject also changed. While in the previous years Morlotti painted as if he saw things from close up, in the Rocks he chose a reference point quite a bit farther away. This preference implies a change in the «psychic distance» of the object «and consequently — within this kind of projection of detachment onto the contemplative screen of consciousness — the configuration of the picture takes on new modalities.»[4] This «distancing» from the subject goes hand-in-hand with a new monumental sense in the composition that should perhaps be put in relation with the likeness Morlotti created between his rocks and Romanesque cathedrals.[5] On the other hand, Morlotti did not give the idea of «landscape as a wall»[6] which had characterized all of his previous output starting from the beginning of the 1950s. Yet, the emphasis on the horizontal line that divides the painting in two clearly distinct zones is a new acquisition.[7] This way, as Fabrizio D'Amico noted, the horizon becomes the «cornerstone of his vision.»[8] This, within the context of the Rocks series, became even more evident in 1982, the year in which this painting was made.
    In the Rocks dating from that year, as Tassi says, «the sky has taken on [...] a lightness that spreads very finely and deeply, almost as if it were really a silk sail made of air and light, material without material, and yet, in its rigorous frontal aspect, space without boundaries, the tension of that material towards the infinite, or, more appropriately, towards the limitless. The rocks below, although issuing forth from the light are also parched, wounded and blinded by it [...and...] take on, instead, a relevance, a weight, a space which again

39
Ennio Morlotti. 1910-1992
Tre bagnanti
1992

clash against, in the opposite sense, the frontal manner in which it is painted. Thus, in a more evident and dramatic way than usual, there is born between the two zones and the two spaces, a contrast lending power and richness to the painting that is located somewhere between turmoil and calm, irruption and flow, age-old earthquakes and age-old inertia and between the tragic sense of death and acceptance of it.»[9]
Claudio Zambianchi

1. Castagnoli 1983, p. 83.
2. P.G. Castagnoli in Bordighera, Palazzo del Parco, *Morlotti. Pastelli e disegni 1954-1978*, exh. cat., December 15, 1978-January 15, 1979.
3. G. Testori in Lucca, Galleria Barsotti dei F.lli Poleschi, *Morlotti. «Rocce«*, cat. exh., November-December 1980.
4. G. Bruno, «L''interminabile tensione' di Morlotti» in Milan, Palazzo Reale, *Ennio Morlotti. Mostra antologica*, G. Bruno, curator, exh. cat., October 9-November 29, 1987, Milan, Giorgio Mondadori, p. 27.
5. E. Morlotti, «Nota» in V. Sereni, *Morlotti. Rocce*, Busto Arsizio, Edizioni Bambaia, 1982.
6. R. Tassi, «Il paesaggio di Morlotti» in Locarno, Casa Rusca, *Il paesaggio di Morlotti*, exh. cat., May 30-July 19, 1987, Milan, Mazzotta, p. 14.
7. See R. Tassi in Milan, Galleria Bergamini Diarte s.r.l., *Ennio Morlotti. Le Rocce 1975-1982*, cat. exh., March-April 1982, and P.G. Castagnoli in Modena, 1985, p. 14.
8. F. d'Amico, «Morlotti. Ancora Rocce» in Sant'Andrea in Percussina, Casa del Machiavelli, *Morlotti*, exh. cat., 1974, p. 26; quoted in Castagnoli 1985, p. 14.
9. Tassi 1982.

Oil on canvas, 150 x 170 cm.
Signed on bottom right: «Morlotti».
Provenance: Galleria Ruggerini e Zonca, Milan; Galleria La Sanseverina, Parma.
Exhibitions: Milan, Ruggerini and Zonca, *Morlotti. Variazioni sopra un canto. Bagnanti 1991-1992*, February-April 1992, col. ill. in cat.; Parma, La Sanseverina, *Morlotti. Bagnanti 1991-1992*, December 12, 1992-January 31, 1993, col. ill. in cat.

The series this painting is part of was inaugurated with two paintings of bathers exhibited at the 1988 Venice Biennale and chronologically constitutes Morlotti's last travail. These nudes come from the *Rocce* and convey the same kind of sublimation of the subject, that is, an analogous shifting of level from sensuousness to «hallucination.» Such a change of perspective, not only visual but also poetic, allows the painter to gain a sense of distance from what he is painting and, in the case of this last group, a new sense of habitability[1] and atmospheric feel in the space which until this point had been unusual, or at least left implicit and undeveloped. To Filippo Abbiati who interviewed him in 1987 about his return to the subject of the bathers in terms so different from the late 1950s and after, Morlotti said: «They are landscape nudes. I would like to do large landscapes and large nudes, just as Cézanne did. Large paintings with nudes in the air, screened, which are part of the elements like a plant, a fragment of the landscape, almost destroyed by the air, the environment, the light.»[2]

The name Cézanne is the one that appears most in the critical writings dedicated to these last works.[3] Renato Barilli sees them connected to Cézanne's first nudes[4]. But their most important precedent can most likely be discovered in the late Philadelphia *Bathers* of Cézanne which Morlotti had the opportunity of seeing in Paris in 1937, the same time he saw *Guernica*, and was strongly moved by them. Starting in 1964, Morlotti stated that he was involved in an inquiry that had its fundamental precedents in Cézanne's painting: «I would like to do my own *Bathers* or *Déjeuner sur*

l'herbe as Giorgione, Manet and Cézanne did. I would like to do a summary of my experiences. In Cézanne, for example, there is the sacredness of the light that glorifies everything; I would like to do the sacredness of the flesh.»[5] With these late *Bathers*, Morlotti seems to have succeeded in both of his intentions, to do «the summary of his own experiences» and reach the «sacredness of the flesh.» His summary is very selective, but includes, as Roberto Tassi has noted, the three influences which, pruning away the rest, are the essential ones in Morlotti's work: Courbet and Cézanne on one side and the Romanesque on the other. The latter goes with his «desire for always greater spoliation and always more limited simplicity in order to arrive at the almost religious essence of things.»[6] As for the «sacredness of the flesh,» Morlotti seems to have attained it at the end of a journey which leads him to the lowering of the sensual temperature and the consequent sublimation of erotic impulses. This allows Morlotti to regain a more organized sense of the pictorial space.
Claudio Zambianchi

1. C. Garboli in La Versiliana, Marina di Pietrasanta, Fabbrica di pinoli, *Ennio Morlotti, Antologica*, exh. cat., starting July 28, 1990, Bologna, Grafis Edizioni.
2. F. Abbiati, «Sono stanco di rocce. Adesso dipingo nudi,» *Arte*, 174, May 1987, p. 86.
3. Garboli 1990.
4. R. Barilli in Milan, Galleria Bergamini Diarte s.r.l., *Ennio Morlotti «figure nel paesaggio»*, I, *I dipinti a olio*, exh. cat., February 22-April 12, 1990.
5. M. Valsecchi, «Vorrei dipingere un nudo come Giorgione,» *Tempo*, February 22, 1964, reprinted in P.G. Castagnoli, *Ennio Morlotti*, Ravenna, Agenzia Editoriale Essegi, 1983, p. 90.
6. R. Tassi, «Bagnanti e paesaggio» from idem, *Bagnanti 1987-1992*, Bagnara di Romagna, Erreti, 1992 in Parma, 1992.

40
Alberto Burri. 1915
Combustione F
1960

Paper, acrylic, glue on paper, 100 x 70 cm.
Provenance: Galerie de France, Paris; Galleria Gissi, Turin, no. 3468.
Exhibitions: Cologne, 1960, no. 20; Turin, 1968, no. 3.
Bibliography: Gueguen, 1961, p. 24, ill. (Combustione F60); Brandi, *Burri*, Rome, Editalia, 1963, b/w pl. no. 84; *Burri, contributi al catalogo sistematico*, no. 1918, p. 446, b/w pl.

The first *Combustioni* date back to 1956 and represent a coherent development of the discussion, begun with the *Sacchi*, towards greater autonomy of the *matière*, and also, therefore, of the work. In fact, along with the *Sacchi*, they represent one of the major themes Burri returns to and taken together they can probably be considered the two fundamental matrices from which all the others derive.

At the end of the 1950s, Burri was undoubtedly already an artist who ranked as one of the great innovators and also exerted a strong influence even on an international level. In 1958 he was photographed as he shot at a beer can which, riddled with holes, was placed on a support and offered as a sculpture. This sequence was published in the American magazine *Horizon* in January 1959 under the title «Birth of a New Art Form.» For Burri, as Calvesi said, it was just a gesture, for Niki de Sain-Phalle it suggested a career, not to mention Yves Klein who started his *peintures de feu* which repeat to the letter Burri's *Combustioni*.[1]

In fact, a *Combustione* accompanies the 1959 text by Argan in which the critic writes that it is exactly at the end of the destructive gesture of burning, in the extreme of such degradation, that the material is returned to the organic state with a not-a priori geometric progression, but in its embryonic state; in short, the seeds of a guaranteed rebirth.[2]

More than ever playing a fundamental dialectical role in the *Combustioni*, is the chromatic relationship between red and black. In these abrasions caused by fire, the result of a destructive power, the red appears as a vital element. What is created,

even if *a posteriori* as the result of a procedure and artistic creation that are completely independent, is an antithesis between life and death. No less important are the black sections ranging from shiny to opaque, underscoring the basic function the color also has as *matière*. Despite the direct action of the flame, we find ourselves faced with results in which the sublimation of the *matière* remains more evident, or even surpasses, its own dramatization. Burri's approach, even in the light of subsequent solutions, seems increasingly distant from Expressionist matrices and, on one hand, not that remote from the poly-materialism of the Futurists, but on the other, because of the use of color as a «signal,» not removed from a certain Suprematist sensibility, all of this reinvented with absolute originality of style and independence of spirit.

In his 1963 monograph, Brandi had previously written: «Burri arrives at the oxyhydrogen flame by steps, gradually as he realizes that his materials should be the least brutish possible, even if displayed in a brutal way. Only in this way, in the act itself of calling up the most personal and turbulent associations, could there be produced the blow by which everything would be silenced, or, better, placed in a pentrough, in a fixed and insuperable channel. The *matière* in and of itself, without active elaboration, is a transitory diversion or insignificant horror. The sack had tears, stains, stitching, patches; here the plastic and wood have spasmodic contortions, fissures, seething [...]»[3]

More than ever these *Combustioni* from the 1960s, characterized by interrelationships between shiny and opaque black surfaces, between different archetypical circular shapes and a *matière* which, compared with many earlier works is sharpened and embellished, bring out the Apollonian component in Burri's output that also theoretically exists even in those works in which it is less-easily identified.

Simona Pizzetti

1. M. Calvesi, *Burri*, Milan, Fabbri Editori, 1971.
2. G. C. Argan, *Burri*, Brussels, 1959.
3. C. Brandi, *Burri*, 1963.

41
Alberto Burri. 1915
Rosso plastica 3
1961

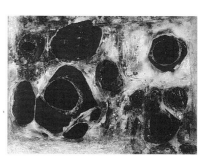

Plastic, acrylic, combustion on canvas, 75 x 100 cm.
Exhibitions: Rome, 1962-1963, ill. p. 17; New York, 1964, no. 1; Sao Paulo, 1965, no. 22; Lisbon, 1966, no. 6.
Bibliography: Brandi, *Burri*, 1962, p. 17, col. pl.; Marlborough, Rome; Brandi, *Burri*, 1963, no. 331, ill.; Wittet, 1963, p. 246, ill.; *Pittura e scultura del XX secolo, 1910-1980*, 1982, p. 101, col. pl.; *Burri, contributi al catalogo sistematico*, 1990, no. 710, p. 168, col. pl.

This work appeared in the 1962 exhibition at the Marlborough Gallery in Rome in which Brandi presented this substantially new cycle, even if there were some technical antecedents in works dating from 1957-58 (see, for example, *Burri*, 1990, no. 443). In his introduction to this catalogue, Brandi noted that in a period in which other artists were also choosing to draw their inspiration and materials from the world of industry, Burri elected to use fire on these shiny and unpleasant coverings, but took on their transparency and wasteful destination in imagery, reviving it in intangible figurative situations and underscoring the destructive act of the fire caught in a charred form and the stratigraphy of the *matière* as the structure of the figuration in this «drapery emptied of bodies and yet full of imagery.»[1]

When Burri began to use plastic — a material that by its very nature is commonplace and can be placed in a historical context but yet does not bear allusions to the life it has led like sacking or other organic materials which lend themselves better to more dramatic and existential interpretations — it was clear to all critics that preponderant in Burri is an extremely rigorous sense of planning that has always aimed at completely independent results, both formally and semantically, in a work of art, in which the *matière* is both the cause and effect of the painting, and this gives the work its own life independent of any analogic form. The organic growth suggested in certain of Burri's works does not refer to anything but a style of painting which is a true life form that tends to expand and become three-dimensional in a continuous evolution in

which the medium thus defined, as if crystallized and completely coherent with the form, still seems capable of further evolution.

In the *Sacchi*, the tears and seams appear to be interventions external to the *matière*. Here, on the other hand, the use of plastic substances in this process in which the transformations in the material also come from within, has the artist make yet another step along this coherent journey of increasing independence in his work. In addition, in Burri, everything, in spite of the fact that it is so calculated, seems to be absolutely spontaneous.

Despite all this, one cannot negate the existential and dramatic matrix of works such as this, but it is their intrinsic authenticity that makes us burden them with our human problems and not vice versa.

In 1955, in his first monograph on Burri, Sweeney wrote: «That which for the Cubists would have been reduced to the partial intensification of a painted composition, to a protest for the Dadaists, an illustrative fantasy for the Surrealists, and a *Merzbild* for Kurt Schwitters, for Burri became a living organism: flesh and blood.»[2] This as long as it is clear, as Argan pointed out, that in Burri it is not the painting that feigns reality, but reality which feigns painting.

In these *Plastiche*, an internal movement predominates that seems to construct craters of *matière*, previously represented by Burri in some of his early works, but from this point his discourse unmistakably takes off, standing out even more in the *Ferri* towards the prevalence of formal considerations in works increasingly asemantic and aniconologic.

These *Plastiche*, like the *Sacchi* before them, were also received very critically and, paradoxically, if the *Sacchi* provoked scandal for the use of such plain and debased materials, the *Plastiche* were taken to task for an excessively pleasing aesthetic sense and inordinate elegance. What was taken for superficial elegance was the imaginative continuous regeneration of the material which, in transforming itself, was sublimated in formal perfection. Burri himself stated that the value of the material is secondary and that his interest is only

aimed at the pictorial result.

There are also those, like Enrico Crispolti, who primarily locate Burri's experience in a raw existential state: «Material not sublimated in imagery, but rather completely observed in its own ineluctable, yet meaningful, existentiality [...] material not exempt from the effects of human contact, but rather, the trace, symptom and tracks of a direction, a rejection, of a human event: the charrings are truly the flotsam and jetsam and the imprints of a flame that destroyed and killed.»
Simona Pizzetti

1. C. Brandi, *Burri*, 1962, Marlborough, Rome.
2. J. J. Sweeney, *Burri*, 1955, L'Obelisco, Rome.

Water-base paint on canvas, 100 x 84 cm.
Signed and titled on the back: «Lucio Fontana/ Concetto Spaziale/Attese/1+1-XXYA3».
Provenance: McRoberts & Tunnard, London; Galleria Angolare, Milan; Private Collection, Pavia.
Exhibitions: Amsterdam, Stedelijk Museum, *Lucio Fontana. Concetti Spaziali*, March 23-May 7, 1967 (later Eindhoven, Stedelijk van Abbenmuseum, May 12-June 18, 1967), no. 41 (b/w ill. in cat.); Humleblaek, Louisiana Museum, *Lucio Fontana, Ideen om Rummet*, January-February 1967, no. 38 (cat. in «Louisiana Revy» 8/2, November 1967, b/w ill., p. 15); Stockholm, Moderna Museet, *Fontana: Idéer om Rymden*, August 26-October 1, 1967, no. 38; Hanover, Kestner-Gesellschaft, *Lucio Fontana*, January 25-February 25, 1968, no. 38 (b/w ill. in cat. p. 49).
Bibliography: Archivio Lucio Fontana, Milan, *Lucio Fontana*, Brussels, La Connaissance, 1974, vol. I (E. Crispolti, *Traccia per l'opera di Lucio Fontana*), p. 136; vol. II (*Catalogue raisonné des peintures, sculptures et environnements spatiaux rédigé par E. Crispolti*), p. 126, no. 61, b/w pl. no. 28; G. Cavazzini, I. Consigli, R. Tassi, eds., *Pittura e Scultura del XX secolo. 1910-1980*, Parma, Banca Emiliana Parma, 1982, p. 94, col. ill., p. 94; E. Crispolti, ed., *Fontana, Catalogo Generale*, Milan, Electa, 1986, 2, p. 428, no. 61, b/w pl. no. 28.

«With the cut I have invented a formula I do not think I can improve upon. Using this formula, I have succeeded in giving the viewer an impression of spatial calm, of cosmic rigor, of infinite serenity,» declared Lucio Fontana in an interview with Giorgio Bocca on the occasion of his personal room at the 1966 Venice Biennale.[1] Fontana arrived at the «cuts» — in a certain way a definitive point in his experimentation — in 1959. The cuts elaborate that severing of the pictorial surface already present in the «holes» begun in 1949. Fontana's is a progressive development towards the essential, made up of «continuous sacrifices that allow 'the internal space' to be reached.»[2] The cuts reside in an essentially mental dimension in which the idea prevails over the *matière* and the execution: «Art is eternal, but it

43
Afro (Basaldella). 1912-1976
Sagra delle Ciliegie
1960

cannot be immortal,» declared the artist in his manifesto, *Spaziali I* (end of 1947, beginning of 1948). «[...]It could live a year or thousands of years, but the hour of its material destruction will always arrive. It will remain eternal as a gesture, but die materially. [...] We are not interested if a gesture, once made, survives for an instant or a millennium, because we are truly convinced that, having done it, it is eternal.»[3]

Therefore, the gesture with which Fontana cuts the canvas has nothing which is visceral or violent. Fontana «will never stop taking Pollock to task for [...] the symbolism of a gesture of individual, vain rebellion.»[4] His act is premeditated and endowed with a specific purpose that has nothing of the arbitrariness of the Informal: «There are no arbitrary gestures in Fontana's art, just acts. And acts are always imbued with a sense of finality. Gestures ramble. Acts know where they are going, even when that knowledge does not fit our discursive moulds.»[5]

It is, therefore, a constructive act which opens up a new spatial dimension: «Everyone believed I wanted to destroy, but this is not true. I constructed, I did not destroy, the thing is there. [...] The cut [...] the hole [...] was not the destruction of the painting, the Informal gesture [...] went a dimension beyond the painting, the freedom to conceive of art through whatever means, through whatever form.»[6] What Fontana intends, therefore, is to «break [...] dimensional limitations» of traditional pictorial surfaces in order to create something different.[7] The cuts appear in various ways: in this case they have «multiple opposing directions»[8] against a white background, «the purest, least complicated» color.[9] As for its title, *Concetto spaziale. Attese*, Crispolti notes that the meaning is purposely left ambiguous: The primary meaning of «Attese» is that of «futuristic hypothesis,» but it also «opens up towards a contemplative, almost metaphysical, intent, arriving at a sexual implication, even if it is erotic symbolism purified almost to the point of abstraction.»[10]
Claudio Zambianchi

1. G. Bocca, «Incontro con Lucio Fontana, il vincitore a Venezia. Il taglio è taglio,» *Il Giorno*, July 6, 1966; quoted in Crispolti 1986, vol. I, p. 31, fn. 87.
2. B. Blistène, «L'heliotrope,» in Paris, Centre Georges Pompidou, Musée National d'Art Moderne, *Lucio Fontana*, exh. cat., October 13, 1987-January 11, 1988, p. 11.
3. *Manifesto Spaziali (Spaziali I)*; quoted in G. Joppolo, «Pour une lecture des manifestes et écrit théoretiques du spatialisme,» in Paris, 1987-88, p. 283.
4. D. Zacharopulos, «Eloge de Lucio Fontana,» in Paris, 1987-88, p. 33.
5. P. Rouve, introd. cat. London, McRoberts & Tunnard, 1962; reprinted in the catalogue of the 1967 Amsterdam exhibition.
6. C. Lonzi, *Autoritratto*, Bari, De Donato, 1969, pp. 170-71 and 322.
7. Statement by L. Fontana in *Artecasa* (1965); quoted in Van der Marck, introd. cat. of the Fontana exhibition, Minneapolis, Walker Art Center, quoted in Amsterdam 1967.
8. Crispolti 1974, vol. I, p. 136.
9. Lonzi 1969, p. 177.
10. Crispolti 1986, vol. 1, p. 24.

Mixed technique on canvas, 73 x 100 cm.
Signed and dated on bottom right: «Afro. 60».
Provenance: Galleria Toninelli, Milan; Private Collection, Rome.
Exhibitions: New York, Catherine Viviano Gallery, *Afro*, March 8-April 2, 1960, no. 19; Milan, Toninelli Arte Moderna, *Afro*, February-March 1968.
Bibliography: C. Brandi, *Afro*, critical essay by V. Rubio included in the general catalogue ed. by V. Gramiccia, Rome, Editalia, 1977, p. 186, no. 141 (b/w ill. no. 141, p. 186).
Note: On the back appears the inscription: «Opera originale e autentica di Afro/Roma 26/XI/71» [«Original and authentic work by Afro/Rome 26/XI/71»] and an illegible signature.

In Afro's development, the *Sagra delle ciliegie* comes two years following a justly famous declaration of his poetic style, written for the book, *Pittori Italiani d'oggi* by Lionello Venturi and published in 1958. «For some time,» Afro wrote, «I had been feeling somewhat uncomfortable with my work: I was outside the painting I was creating, as if it did not respond to a development, to an inner need that became ever more urgent and precise.» Afro ascribed this crisis to an increasing disinterest in the use of «certain representative symbols which had seemed to me to lend order to and in a certain sense stabilize the connection with reality» and which instead, at that moment, were nothing more than «screens between me and the painting, obstacles to new discoveries.» In other words, «it was not enough for me to depict a reality of fantasy, dreams or memory beyond the painting and for which the painting was a mirror or intermediary, instead I wanted that reality to identify itself with the painting style and for that style to become the reality itself of the feeling, not its representation. The painting does not allude to, but rather puts forwards its existence, secret and indelible like everything dreamed of and regretted.»[1]

This is a declaration of extraordinary emotional intensity which constitutes the approach Afro took in his art between the second half of the 1950s and the beginning of the 1960s. This approach, as

44
Jean Dubuffet. 1901-1985
Cérémonie végétale
1959

Enrico Crispolti says, was one of «burning [...] the distance of memory»[2] and to render the pictorial surface not a projection screen for internal images, but a plane on which, with a gesture, an emotion would be caught in the act. It was along this route that Afro's search radically approached that of Informal art,[3] particularly in its American form.[4] Afro knew American Abstract-Expressionism from 1950, but it was only at this moment in his life that he developed its most radical implications, approaching, in other works contemporaneous with this one which played with the dramatic contrast between white and black, De Kooning and Kline. On this basis, he found agreement in Italy in the painting of Toti Scialoja.[5] In the paintings done between the end of the '50s and the beginning of the '60s, stroke and color arrange themselves into a new synthesis, is a more agitated, nervous and dynamic rhythm. The group of works to which the *Sagra delle ciliegie* belongs is, according to Francesco Tedeschi, that of «form-color» in which its specific nature is made up of the «constructive function taken on by the color, utilized as a unique element in the composition of the form.»[6] In this work, what should be noted is the dramatic concentration of the central nucleus of the painting from which the strong black brushstrokes seem to radiate towards the outside of the composition.
Claudio Zambianchi

1. Quoted in F. d'Amico, «Afro e New York: la sua pittura negli anni Cinquanta. Dalla memoria, alla vita della forma,» in Verona, Galleria dello Scudo, *Afro. L'itinerario astratto. Opere 1948-1975*, L. Caramel, ed., exh. cat., October 7-November 19, 1989, Milan, Mazzotta, pp. 32-33.
2. E. Crispolti, *I Basaldella. Dino, Mirko, Afro*, Udine, Casamassima Editore 1984, p. 262.
3. *Ibid.*, p. 263.
4. D'Amico, p. 31; and L. Caramel, «La pittura come realtà del sentimento,» in Milan, Palazzo Reale, Sala delle Cariatidi, *Afro, Dipinti 1931-1975*, L. Caramel, ed., exh. cat., September 24-November 8, 1992, Milan, Silvana Editoriale, p. 36.
5. D'Amico, p. 31.
6. F. Tedeschi ed., «Catalogo delle opere,» in Verona, 1989, p. 71.

Burdock, 90 x 70 cm.
Provenance: Arthur Tooth Collection, London; Galleria Toninelli, Milan Exhibition: London, Arthur Tooth and Sons, *Jean Dubuffet, Eléments Botaniques (Août-Décembre 1959)*, May 31-June 18, 1960, no. 34 (b/w ill. in cat.).
Bibliography: M. Loreau, ed., *Catalogue des Travaux de Jean Dubuffet*, Fascicule XVII: *Matériologies*, Lausanne, Weber, 1969, p. 41, no. 41 (b/w ill. p. 41).

This is one of the *Eléments Botaniques* Dubuffet produced in Vence starting in August 1959 up until the end of that same year. Dubuffet had already experimented with compositions of vegetable elements the year before in a painting, *Jardin au sol*, in which vegetable fragments are «stapled to the bottom of a butterfly box.»[1] From this Dubuffet realized something: «Leaves are skillful logographers; they have the writing of their veins, nervous and branching out to infinity, and equally dark and richly narrative.»[2] He thus decided to develop the idea in a *suite*[3] and called his friend Philippe Dereux to his aid. He «came to help him during his vacation, made the presses in which to dry the leaves and went up into the hills around Vence to hunt for trees (just as he had the butterflies), gathering more than were needed. The grasshopper could fiddle all winter.»[4]

The second half of 1959 was a «frenetic» period for Dubuffet, occupied with the «final *Topographies* [...] oil paintings variously inspired by 'beards', 'rocks' and 'some imaginary figures'.»[5] An intense work which foreshadowed the «Matériologies.»[6]

Forty *Eléments Botaniques*, this among them, were presented in a show at the Arthur Tooth and Sons Gallery in London in May of the following year as laid out in a letter to André Pieyre de Mandiargues written on November 17, 1959.[7] It was a group of «assemblages of dried leaves, tree bark, flowers and roots with very beautiful, warm hues, rich with unusual shapes and veining of great decorative effect [...] glued onto paper or wooden panels.»[8]

Cérémonie végétal is made of burdock, a plant which in the London catalogue is identified as «a common species of compositae which is often found by roadsides in Europe and Asia.»[9] Dubuffet did not limited himself to taking the lovely, mature plant, even if, at first glance, this is the most unsettling aspect of the work. Instead, he elaborates the image in such a way as to bring to mind other aspects of the world of nature — gardens or landscapes — and highlight, at the same time, the attributes of weaving. «Although it is true that his forms in the *Eléments Botaniques* are determined largely by the materials he employs [...] it is just as obvious that the end products are the results of an *idée fixe* which runs throughout his work [...]. He pastes down the leaves in such a way that, although they form a landscape, their textures and patterns are sharply revealed and call attention to their specific structure. Moreover, they closely resemble his painted landscapes with their high horizons or overall expanse, or they look like his 'tables' or his 'stones' in their rough, monotonous surfaces. One could say that Dubuffet starts with tangible nature in the strictest sense and then transforms it with his mind and hands, arriving at a new, personal and very singular image of nature itself.»[10]

This image, as Gaëtan Picon noted, implies a profound change from the point of view traditionally adopted by artists in taking on natural scenery. It represents the desire to «become the mole in the ground, the ant on the pavement, the mushroom on the tree.»[11] And yet, despite the radical novelty implicit in this change in outlook, Lawrence Alloway, in introducing the London show, saw in these works the results of a «pastoral» lineage in its artistic style. Dubuffet would therefore be connected to an iconographic motif with a long tradition: «Dubuffet takes his pastoral from the forest floor. It is the multilayered deposit of seasons, into which some forms are settling and from which others are starting.»[12]
Claudio Zambianchi

45
Jean Paul Riopelle. 1923
Composition
1955

1. M. Loreau, «Présentation,» in Loreau, 1969, p. 7.
2. *Ibid.*
3. *Ibid.*
4. *Ibid.*
5. L. Trucchi, *Jean Dubuffet*, Rome, De Luca, 1965, p. 256.
6. *Ibid.*
7. J. Dubuffet to A. Pieyre de Mandiargues, November 17, 1959; published in J. Dubuffet, *Prospectus et tous écrits suivants*, H. Damisch, ed., vol. II, Paris, Gallimard, 1967, p. 324.
8. Trucchi 1965, p. 256.
9. London 1960.
10. P. Seltz, *The Work of Jean Dubuffet*, New York, The Museum of Modern Art, 1962 (published on the occasion of the retrospective at the MOMA, 1962), pp. 154-56.
11. G. Picon, «Préface,» in Paris, Musée des Arts Décoratifs, Palais du Louvre-Pavillon de Marsan, *Jean Dubuffet 1942-1960*, exh. cat., December 16, 1960-February 25, 1961, p. 19.
12. L. Alloway, «Dubuffet as pastoral,» in London, 1960.

Oil on canvas, 72.5 x 114.5 cm.
Signed and dated on the back: «Riopelle 55».

In the decade between 1950 and 1960, Riopelle's *matière*, «worked with the palette-knife, was organized in a fragmented, vibrant and mosaic-style surface, animated by long and vigorous streaks, a kind of chromatically-contrasting tracks.»[1] The primary inspiration of Riopelle's painting is nature with which the artist professes to have a very intense relationship: «For me, nature is the only reference point. That is the only place in which freedom exists, and at the same time, the greatest constraint. A tree can only grow one way. There is no way in which a tree can be tragic, elegiac or cheerful. There is just the right way.»[2]

Nonetheless, as in all Informal painting, of which Canadian painter Riopelle is one of the major exponents, the rapport with nature has changed compared with art of the past: «The image is not composed according to rules of representation, but according to that which makes it organic to nature.»[3] In other words, it is as if the artist did not intend to depict what he sees, but rather create an analogy with nature's rhythms. As Pierre Schneider says: «Riopelle is a force of nature. More precisely, he is inhabited by the force of nature.»[4]

The spontaneous impulse to create a relationship with nature is filtered through a series of references to previous art. Riopelle's search, Franco Russoli observes, is a «linguistic» search, and thus the artist must choose for himself «his companions in illusion» whom Russoli identifies in the «late-Classical mosaicists,» «Medieval New Testament covers,» the «the Titian-hued fringes and fingerprints,» as well as in Rembrandt, Cézanne and Van Gogh.[5] Other critics make reference to late Monet.[6] But once again it is Russoli who defines two aspects that place Riopelle within the painting of his own day: «the suture» the artist makes «between Courbet and Cézanne,» and the «encounter» brought about «between Cubism and the Informal.»[7] The reference to Courbet and Cézanne allows the sources of Riopelle's conception of space to be identified. It is a space experienced as «primary

fullness of material uniformly laid out and resistant in every part of the painting which has neither center nor edges,» thus placing Riopelle in a different sphere from that of Pollock.[8]
Claudio Zambianchi

1. S. Blottière, in Rennes, Musée des Beaux-Arts, *Riopelle. Autour d'une oeuvre*, exh. cat., November 26, 1987-February 29, 1988.
2. Quoted in P. Schneider, «Préface,» in Paris, Musée National d'Art Moderne, Centre Georges Pompidou (later at the Musée du Québec and Montréal Musée de l'Art Contemporain), *Jean Paul Riopelle. Peintures 1946-1977*, exh. cat., September 30-November 16, 1981.
3. F. Russoli, «Jean-Paul Riopelle,» in Venice, *XXXI Esposizione biennale internazionale d'arte. Personale di Jean-Paul Riopelle*, exh. cat., 1962.
4. Quoted in C. Lonzi, in Turin, Notizie. Associazione Arti Figurative, *Dipinti di Riopelle*, exh. cat., opened December 2, 1960.
5. F. Russoli, in Milan, Galleria d'Arte Borgogna, *Riopelle*, exh. cat., November 9, 1970.
6. For example, M. Valsecchi, «La mostra. Grandine pittorica di rossi e di neri,» *Il Giorno*, March 18, 1971, p. 8.
7. Russoli 1970.
8. Lonzi 1960, p. 2.

46
Sam Francis. 1923
Painting
1957

47
Graham Sutherland. 1903-1980
Standing Form
1950

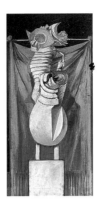

Watercolor on paper, 114 x 155 cm.
Provenance: Anthony Denney Collection; Galleria dell'Ariete, Milan.

«What we want is to make something that fills utterly the sight and can't be used to make life only bearable; if the painting till now was a way of making bearable the sight of the unbearable, the visible sumptuous, then let's now strip away [...] all of that.»[1] In this extract from a letter written in 1957 (the same year *Painting* was executed), Sam Francis states that his painting strives to be a total experience, something akin to a formative journey. He continues: «You can't interpret the dream of the canvas for this dream is at the end of the hunt on the heavenly mountain — where nothing remains but the phoenix caught in the midst of lovely blueness.»[2]

Sharing with the artist the experience of the painting means to take on, along with him, the basic meanings given to the forms and colors. Francis's abstraction is anything but a formalistic exercise in itself. Thus we let it lead us into a reality «which breaks with the three-dimensional representational world and offers us a two-dimensional space in which the temporality of the vision takes the place of the third dimension that has disappeared, a temporality that is simultaneously full and instantaneous into which not a single narrative characteristic enters.»[3]

The temporality implied in Francis's paintings is primarily defined in relation to the color: «Since white is the expression of all colors, for me it loses its immediacy and places itself beyond time, while blue and red, for example, appear to me just as moments.»[4] From a spatial standpoint, white is empty space: «I feel,» says Francis, «that white is equivalent to the space that extends between things.»[5] Thus, the colors serve to make visible this sensation: «Sam Francis uses brushmarks only to the extent they are necessary to bring out the space.»[6]

Michel Waldberg says that «in the paintings from 1957-58, the appearance of form provokes a gap in space, presents space as an *opening* between things

but also an opening caused by the appearance of things [...]. It is as if things are impatient to appear, to come to light, as if there is a precipitation accompanying the other precipitation; of blood, of humors, of flowing organic fluids.»[7]

In fact, it is during the period between 1956 and 1958 that white takes on an absolutely key role in Francis's painting. Up until that point, white occupied the spaces between the colored forms which uniformly plugged the painting's surface, suggesting an «interstitial depth.»[8] Here, above all in relation to certain vast mural compositions — like the triptych for the Basel Kunsthalle (1956-58), which *Painting* is stylistically extremely close to — white takes on greater weight and the colored forms create «a double movement of concentration and expansion [...] that constitutes the rhythm of Sam Francis's [subsequent] work.»[9] The dynamism these colored forms create on the surface has often been traced back to the late works of Claude Monet whom Francis knew well since he lived in Paris from 1950 to 1957.

Claudio Zambianchi

1. S. Francis, «Unpublished Statement in an Unpublished Letter,» in New York, Museum of Modern Art, eds., *The New American Painting As Shown in Eight European Countries*, exh. cat., travelling exhibit, 1958-59, p. 28.
2. *Ibid.*
3. Y. Michaud, *Sam Francis*, Paris, Editions Daniel Papierski, 1992, p. 14.
4. Quoted in G. Duthuit, «L'image en souffrance,» Paris, 1961; anthol. in Paris, Centre National d'Art Contemporain, *Sam Francis*, cat. exh., December 10, 1968-December 1969, p. 28.
5. *Ibid.*
6. P. Schneider, «Peintures de Sam Francis» in Paris 1968-69, p. 5.
7. M. Waldberg, *Sam Francis, Metaphysics of the Void*, Moos Book Publishing Ltds.
8. Michaud 1992, p. 26.
9. *Ibid.*, p. 29.

Oil on canvas, 149 x 68 cm.
Signed on bottom right: «Sutherland 1950».

«Personally, I believe that one must draw from reality the image of something different; that the mysterious and intangible must be made manifest and tangible. People often ask me, regarding my *Standing Forms* [...]: 'What does it mean?' Obviously they do not mean anything. These forms are based upon the principle of organic growth that has always interested me. For me they are monuments and presences. But why then use these abstract forms and not human figures? Because at the moment, I believe it is necessary to capture the taste, the quality, the essence of the human presence — the mysterious immediacy of a figure upright in a room or against a hedge, its shadow, its consciousness, its thoughts — as if no one else had ever seen it before, by means of substitution. I am aware that, for the moment, this is the best way to render these qualities real in my eyes; and the best intermediaries from this standpoint are organic forms.»[1]

This is the way Sutherland explained his *Standing Forms*, a motif he concentrated on very intensively between 1949 and 1953. These paintings have as their point of departure a motif taken from nature. Sutherland maintained that a large part of his motifs were natural in origin and it is well-known that the painter took long walks in the woods armed with pencil and sketchbook in which he made note of subjects to be developed later in his studio, a habit which he said «helped me to nourish my ideas and keep me on good terms with nature.»[2]

But the attention with which Sutherland looks at this motif of nature implies a very strong level of transformation «in accordance with some private visionary impulse.»[3] From this standpoint, Douglas Cooper, one of the most refined of Sutherland's interpreters, holds that this painter cannot be considered a «landscapist» as Herbert Read would have him, but rather a «nature painter,»[4] recognizing in this aspect the most specifically English characteristic of his art.

48
Graham Sutherland. 1903-1980
Poised Form in a Landscape
1969

Sutherland in his studio with *Standing Form*

Nature in Sutherland is not a welcoming womb. It is described, or better, transformed, in the light of ambivalent feelings in which, mixed in with the «fascination» are «awe» and sometimes «horror.»[5] In other words, it is a sense of nature in which, while maintaining a remote link with perceived reality, develops the metaphoric implications of the theme, understanding metaphor, as Roberto Tassi suggests, in its broadest sense, «almost every image born of the creation of a relationship based on analogy and similitude.»[6]

These *Standing Forms*, inspired by «figures in gardens — half hidden in the shade,» are paraphrased and «recreated» through a series of associations ranging from organic to the human figure in «mechanically inspired shapes.»[7] In this way, Sutherland arrives at «totemic-ancestral»[8] images, mysterious and «polysymbolic»[9] that allude to those «energies of struggle, of contrast, of opposition, the energies of violence and organic growth»[10] he saw moving inside nature.
Claudio Zambianchi

1. G. Sutherland, «Thoughts on Painting,» *The Listener*, September 1951; published in G. Sutherland, *Parafrasi della natura e altre corrispondenze*, R. Tassi, ed., Parma, Pratiche Editrice, 1979, p. 39.
2. G. Sutherland, «Welsh Sketchbook,» letter to Colin Anderson, *Horizon*, April 28, 1942; published as «Quaderno di schizzi gallesi» in *Parafrasi*, p. 53.
3. D. Cooper, *The Work of Graham Sutherland*, London, Lund Humphries, 1961 (reprinted 1962), p. 39.
4. *Ibid.*, p. 3.
5. *Ibid.*, p. 2.
6. R. Tassi, «Preface» to *Parafrasi*, p. 9.
7. J. Hayes, *The Art of Graham Sutherland*, Oxford, Phaidon, 1980, p. 29.
8. F. Arcangeli, *Graham Sutherland*, Milan, Fratelli Fabbri Editori, 1973, p. 12.
9. See, R. Sanesi, *Graham Sutherland*, Centro d'Arte Zarathustra, 1979, p. 16.
10. Tassi p. 13.

Oil on canvas, 117 x 170 cm.
Initialled and dated on bottom right: «G.S. 3/viii/69»; on the back, initials, title and date «G.S./Poised Form in a Landscape/3/VIII/69».
Provenance: Marlborough Gallery, London; Galleria de' Foscherari, Bologna; Private Collection, Milan; Galleria Contini, Cortina d'Ampezzo-Venice.
Exhibition: Cortina d'Ampezzo, Galleria Contini, *Opera prima. Pittura del Novecento in Europa e in America*, December 28, 1991-February 9, 1992 (cat., Milan, Electa, col. ill., p. 65).
Bibliography: F. Arcangeli, *Graham Sutherland*, Milan, Fratelli Fabbri Editori, 1973 (col. pl. no. 184); R. Sanesi, *Graham Sutherland*, Centro d'Arte Zarathustra, 1979, b/w pl. no. 84, p. 125; J. Hayes, *The Art of Graham Sutherland*, Oxford, Phaidon, 1980, b/w ill., fig. 133, p. 159; Locarno, Casa Rusca, *Sutherland*, R. Chiappini ed., exh. cat., April 2-May 29, 1988 (Milan, Mazzotta, b/w ill. p. 88).

In 1967, following a hiatus that had lasted several years, Sutherland decided to return to one of the places which had most inspired him in the past: Wales. His extended absence was due to the fact that «unfortunately» Sutherland was «convinced that he had exhausted everything the landscape could offer [him], both in its 'vocabulary' of forms as well as a source of inspiration.» «I was wrong,» he said in 1976, «and in the last ten years I have made amends for my error.»[1] *Poised Form in a Landscape* derives from his renewed interest in Welsh nature. A photograph taken by Giorgio Soavi of the colossal roots of an oak tree indicates one of the possible sources of inspiration for this painting.[2] As in *Standing Form*, the natural scene is transformed by his imaginative vision, but with the passing of the years, «Sutherland's narrative-symbolic capacity [...] becomes more dazzling as well as simpler.»[3] Again here, as in the previous painting, it is a phenomenon of organic growth, but referring, to a previous moment, that of forms caught in the act of taking shape and emerging from the soil. «The phenomenon of growth fascinates me,» Sutherland said, «the movements of natural forms trying to

liberate themselves from the earth.»[4] Another characteristic aspect of the forms in the foreground is their likeness to mechanical elements. In fact, Sutherland asserted that he was struck by the «correspondence between natural forms — animals, man, geologic or botanic forms — and machines, the things built by man.»[5] The reduced scale of the human figure in the background to the right with the sun, emerging from black clouds looming overhead, contributes to the scene's unsettling effect.
Claudio Zambianchi

1. G. Sutherland, *La raccolta del castello di Picton* in London, Graham Sutherland Gallery, *Sutherland in Wales*, exh. cat., 1976; publ. in G. Sutherland, *Parafrasi della natura e altre corrispondenze*, R. Tassi, ed., Parma, Pratiche Editrice, 1979, p. 54.
3. See Hayes, p. 40.
3. Sanesi, p. 19.
4. *Interview with Graham Sutherland* in Turin, Galleria d'Arte Narciso, *Graham Sutherland*, exh. cat., 1976; published as «Conversazione con Paul Nicholls» in *Parafrasi*, pp. 99-100.
5. *Ibid.*

Sutherland's studio with
Poised Form in a Landscape
and, on the left, the
Portrait of Giorgio Soavi

49
Francis Bacon. 1909-1992
Two Americans
1954

Oil on canvas, 68 x 74.5 cm.
Provenance: Lucian Freud, London; Beaux Arts Gallery, London; Mr. and Mrs. James W. Alsdorf Collection, Winnetka; Richard Feigen Gallery, Chicago; Mr. and Mrs. Harold X. Weinstein Collection, Chicago; Galleria Toninelli, Milan; Galleria Galatea, Turin.
Exhibitions: Chicago, Richard L. Feigen & Co., Inc., *Francis Bacon, 12 Paintings 1947-1958*, July 6-August 1, 1959, no. 7; Los Angeles, The Art Galleries, University of California at Los Angeles, *Francis Bacon – Hyman Bloom*, October 30-December 11, 1960, no. 6; London, Tate Gallery, *Francis Bacon*, May 24-July 1, 1962, no. 48 (b/w ill. in cat.); Milan, Galleria Toninelli, *La figura*, March 30-April 30, 1966, no. 1; Turin, Galleria Galatea, *Selezione 8*, May 19-June 10, 1967, no. 3 (b/w ill. in cat.); Turin, Galleria Galatea, *Selezione 9*, June 10-July 12, 1969.
Bibliography: *Francis Bacon*, introd. by J. Rothenstein, annotated catalogue and documentation by R. Alley, London, Thames and Hudson, 1964, p. 91, no. 91 (b/w pl. no. 91).

«I would like my pictures to look as if a human being had passed between them, like a snail, leaving a trail of the human presence and memory trace of past events as the snail leaves its slime.»[1] In this case, the two human beings who left their imprints on the painting are two Americans Bacon «had seen a number of times from the window of his hotel in Rome.»[2] The painting was done in Ostia[3] during his several-week stay in Italy in the autumn of 1954. As an aside, during his Italian visit, the artist did not go to see Velazquez's *Innocenzo X* – which he had reinterpreted more than once – nor did he go to the Venice Biennale where a group of his paintings were on exhibit.[4]
Bacon considered this painting «unfinished.»[5] His suspension of work on it probably derives from a fear the artist expressed on more than one occasion: «Very often in working, one loses the best moments of a painting in trying to take it further.»[6] This painting contains all the elements of Bacon's works during the decade between 1945 and 1955.

The figures are situated against a very dark background painted before the figures are. Only later would Bacon start to paint first the figures and then the background.[7] The space in the painting is crossed by «laser beams which stand sometimes for plain walls and sometimes for a more elaborate but still ghostly architecture.»[8] Regarding this Bacon said: «I cut down the scale of the canvas by drawing in these rectangles which concentrate the image down. Just to see it better.»[9]
Another characteristically Baconian trademark appearing in this painting is the half-opened mouth with teeth displayed in the figure on the left. More than the dying governess in *The Battleship Potemkin* or the figure in the *Slaughter of the Innocents* done in 1630-31 by Poussin – the declared sources for the wide-open mouths in Bacon – this motif seems to draw on some x-rays published in the book *Positioning in Radiography*, the importance of which to his painting Bacon acknowledges.[10]
According to Bacon, the portrait has substituted historical painting as the apex in the hierarchy of artistic genres.[11] Demonstrating this is the fact that, for him, to register an image means, in the majority of cases, restoring the features of a human figure. With a warning, however. The image must be recreated irrationally so that it contains not only the appearance, but also «all the areas of feeling which you yourself have apprehension of.»[12] This route, which implies coming «as closely to one's own nervous system as one possible can,» is the only one possible for the modern artist «outside a tradition.»[13] In this sense, Lorenza Trucchi detects a close affinity between Bacon and Samuel Beckett when the latter wrote: «The only possibility for renewal lies in opening one's eyes and seeing the current collapse: a collapse one cannot understand, but which must be allowed to enter because it is the truth.»[14]
Claudio Zambianchi

1. F. Bacon, «Artist's Statement,» in J. Russell, *Francis Bacon*, London, Methuen, 1964.
2. Alley 1964, p. 91.
3. *Ibid.*
4. *Ibid.*, p. 277.
5. *Ibid.*, p. 91.
6. D. Sylvester, *The Brutality of Fact. Interviews with Francis Bacon*, 3rd enlarged ed., London, Thames and Hudson, 1987 (reprinted 1990), p. 158.
7. Sylvester 1990, p. 195.
8. J. Russell, *Francis Bacon*, London, Thames and Hudson, 1989 (1st ed., 1971; rev. ed. 1979), p. 110.
9. Sylvester 1990, p. 23.
10. *Ibid.*, p. 32.
11. *Ibid.*, p. 63.
12. *Ibid.*, pp. 26-28.
13. *Ibid.*, p. 43.
14. L. Trucchi, *Francis Bacon*, Milan, Fratelli Fabbri Editori, 1975, p. 1.

50
Zoran Music. 1909
Cavallini
1950

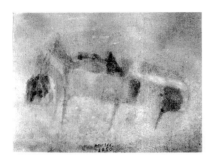

51
Zoran Music. 1909
Point de repère sombre
1963

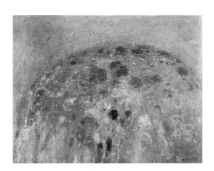

Oil on canvas, 34 x 41 cm.
Signed and dated bottom center: «MUSIC 1950».
Provenance: Artist's studio.

In the 1940s, Music produced his first works with these horses as their subject, without doubt his most famous. He portrays them in Karstic, arid and motionless landscapes, lacking in perspective study, often aligned and far-away. Here the horses are in the foreground, standardized, inscribed within the blue half-sphere of a flattened mountain which so totally takes over the space as to synthesize the imagery of the earth itself, yet another of his, perhaps unconscious, evocations of the Jungian mandalas, i.e., those images which have their origins in dreams and unconscious visions and which make up the religious symbolism of mankind's most ancient religions.

These so essential, slenderly-shaped animals with their hoofless, thin legs, recall pre-historic Neolithic painting. The image, reduced to an archetype, suspended and transient, also expresses the nostalgia for a culture in which man communicated with the soul and nature.

It has often been pointed out that one of the ways Music tried to begin living again, following his tragic concentration camp experience at Dachau, was to have the most distant, ancestral memories emerge from his subconscious, memories that materialized in these primitive and archetypical images. This is possible, but it should be considered just one of the many components of his work which is also so difficult to fit into prevailing critical schemata since Music remains substantially an isolated case. His world, light and veiled, made up of fleeting apparitions, is characterized by a painting style rich with refined transparency and chromaticism, of lyrical affinity between the pale rose and violet, an unnatural blue, and the greys, ochres and some intense touches of orange.

Yet, the simplicity of its means is total and through the pigments of powdered paint, reduced to a minimum, the rough canvas can be glimpsed, incredibly suffused by a light that seems to be the source of the image itself, the First Cause of the apparition. Memory has become light and recollection form. Everything appears to us, as Valery wrote, in that precise moment in which the light begins to clutch at things, to have them stumble over their forms and then their succeeding names.[1] More evident than ever in this work is the intentional ambiguity between the figure and background sought through formal and chromatic relationships. Exemplary of this is the use of the blue which, forming both the background as well as a major part of the bodies of the horses, under close examination, makes the overlaid outlines of the animals uncertain and indistinct. This leads us from a feeling of visual unease to a deeper sense of being lost thanks to imagery so ephemeral and subjective as to call into question its own existence.
Simona Pizzetti

1. Paul Valéry, *Cahiers 1943*, XXVII 539.

Oil on canvas, 80 x 97 cm.
Signed and dated on bottom right: «MUSIC 63».

Music painted many landscapes: the calcareous plateaus of Gorizia, the Siena countryside, Venice, or, as in this case, the outlines of the Cortina mountains, depicted a number of times in the course of the 1960s, starting in 1961 when he began to regularly spend his summers there.

Emanating from it is a series of oils, as well as extremely beautiful pastels and watercolors which, while stylistically akin to the almost-abstract landscapes of Dalmatia and the crumbling landscapes from the end of the 1950s, have a more serene and poetic link with naturalistic terms.

Mazzariol wrote about the Cortina landscapes: «This tangle of simple flowers, colored grass and leaves, unexpectedly emerge once again under the factual gaze of the painter who, in a state of rediscovered expressive necessity, writes some of the most elegant passages of his lyrical diary. In points, the elegance of depiction and soft splendor of the color bring to mind the jewelled vestments of ancient Serbian or Byzantine bishops but seen, or glimpsed, through the ambiguous light of an Art Nouveau window.»[1]

In this landscape, it is not lines, but patches of color distributed on a semicircular surface that suggest the outline and size of the mountain. A large, undulating, overhanging mass occupies the entire painting, nothing indicates the state of the space, its conditions of existence or its inherent anatomy. The image becomes a visual synthesis of many landscapes synthesized in the memory. The result is an almost-abstract form, smooth, regular, a kind of theosophic arabesque.

Chastel, in discussing this landscape and referring to the Byzantine and oriental matrix of its components intrinsic to Music's culture, spoke of «diluted mosaics» in which the allusive and abstract elements perfectly balance each other out.

In order to arrive at this essentiality, Music seems to have eliminated all pictorial artifice: design, perspective, luminism. In truth, light is appropriated from the paint pigments, rendering it

52
Zoran Music. 1909
Collina dalmata
1966

internal to the pictorial matter, while a complete sense of two-dimensionality is overcome by an extremely skillful use of the circular shapes.

The circle and its derivative forms recur too often in Music's work to be just a superficial predilection. In addition to the landscapes, one only need observe the interiors of the cathedrals in which the artist takes delight in studying the relationship between rose windows with their magical play of transparent color, and the outlines of the facades or, even, the series *Non siamo gli ultimi* in which the tragically piled up corpses that taken in their entirety are an almost indistinct rounded mass, reach a sort of visual catharsis and sublimation with the use of the circular form which certainly represents, more or less consciously on Music's part, an archetypical figure, a kind of Jungian mandala. This does not seem daring for Music who has always spoken little about his own work, but who has clearly expressed that its content is always pre-existent in him on an unconscious level.

One can never overstate how little relevance the subject the representation has in Music. His imagery is a completely autonomous creation generated by a spiritual content in complete harmony between «form» and «content,» in which the form identifies itself with the content and the content with the form, to the point of rendering irrelevant the distinction between abstraction and realism, just as Kandinsky so clearly stated during his Bauhaus lectures.
Simona Pizzetti

1. G. Mazzariol, *Music*, Electa, Milan, 1980, p. 12.

Oil on canvas, 81 x 99.5 cm.
Signed and dated on bottom right: «MUSIC 66».

The subject of horses, explored more than once during the '40s and '50s, also returns in the landscapes of the years that followed, like this almost moonlike Dalmatian hillside, probably its umpteenth archetypical citation, this time even more essential and even more ascribable to pure memory. Human beings have disappeared and with them even the most minimal descriptive satisfaction. Gone are the outlines and colors of their clothing and hats and even the summary decorations on their saddles; all that remains is the bare Karst countryside which Music himself has defined «that barren landscape which is life,» life scorched by the sun and beaten by the wind. Everything returns in his work because it is similar, if not identical, to what he has always carried with him, perhaps right from childhood. It is something that every-so-often fades and threatens to leave and then, in order to emerge reinforced and fresh, momentarily requires a new impulse, some help, a new view.[1]

Here the chromatic range is reduced, involving a few shades of ochre punctuated with touches of purple and transparent spots of orange. The pigments of color, present in such minimal quantities as to let the dry weave of the canvas show through, are remarkably still able to absorb the light and reflect it, but its sources are inverted: the sky is opaque, more compact and slightly darker, while the hill, a geometrical semicircular outline, radiates a dusty light in a flowing space without localized points.

Music's poetic sense is based exactly on these silent and serene internal visions that crystallize every dramatic and sentimental impetus, becoming metaphors for the image of the world, an image which comes from the artist's subconscious.

The horses, an undulating strip of colored, surreptitious shadows, an ornament circling the hill, cut across the entire canvas and become symbols of a continuous escape from time, from a time that exists only in the memory, and barely emerge from

the background with which they have a singularly visually ambiguous relationship. This, on a lyrical level, suggests to us exactly that doubt which Music himself has expressed: «The real problem is that we men can never understand how we truly are. We all live in a kind of fog in which everything is, could be, or might even not be. The same could be said for the world which surrounds us: perhaps it exists, or perhaps not.»[2]
Simona Pizzetti

1. P. Levi, *Zoran Music, dialogo con l'autoritratto*, Electa, Milan, 1992, pp. 16-17.
2. *Ibid.*

53
Zoran Music. 1909
Autoritratto
1989

Oil on canvas, 162 x 114 cm.
Signed on bottom right: «MUSIC».
Provenance: Galerie Krugier, Geneva.
Exhibitions: Rome, Accademia di Francia, 1992;
Milan, Palazzo Reale, 1992.
Bibliography: *Zoran Music*, Electa, Milan, 1992,
p. 128, no. 122, col. pl.

In these most recent works, Music, with a lucid examination that starts with himself in order to reach the core of the problems of human existence, definitively clarifies the whole coherent course of his work which is never superficial or descriptive and always aimed towards being more essential.

The relationship between background and figure, always fundamental in Music, has been reduced to that between the bare canvas and the few painted areas. If in his previous works the playing with the ambiguity in this relationship could signify a kind of struggle between being and not-being, here it is a precise indication of a preannounced disappearance. The chromatic range is also reduced to the bare essential, only absolutely necessary pigments remain — white, brown, black.

Behind the figure — larva-like, but at the same time very dignified with its almost monumental bearing accentuated by a full, white, tunic, there remains the semicircular outline so recurrent in all of Music's work, here a dark and indistinct mass, a purely pictorial fact conferring a somber, spatial depth to an image otherwise rigorously two-dimensional.

I do not believe that the self-portraits would have been possible without the experience of *Noi non siamo gli ultimi*. Taking on his extremely painful past liberated the artist not only from all formal conventions, but also from his non-involvement and made it possible in recent years for him to confront himself and arrive at these brutal, definitive confessions.

Music has never wanted to explain his own works, obviously preferring that they explain themselves. But with the self-portraits, he has given some indications which, better than any other analysis, can help in understanding them.

«In truth, the self-portrait probably represents the tormented Music who perhaps does not realize that he is so. Music tormented by painting because only painting could torment him. It is everything that he loves and which still has him live in doubt. The self-portrait was neither a test nor a risk. It is what I have inside me and what I tried to draw out, perhaps with severity. The more one is severe with oneself, the more one can be oneself. For me, being severe means being sincere, I do not spare myself anything, not even those things I would never want to know about myself, let alone see.» He continues: «When I paint a self-portrait, I do not paint it from the mirror, it is born within me. I know myself from inside. If I were to place myself before a mirror, I would only copy the mask of myself.» On colors: «They are colors that bring to mind the desert. I began to use them when I believed I had found myself: I would like them to reveal what is underneath my skin. I would like that they have a profound strength and tension which is not just superficial. It seems to me that they express something more, something which I had never looked for before. They are born from within me, not without pain. This is the power of white and black.»[1]
Simona Pizzetti

1. P. Levi, *Zoran Music, dialogo con l'autoritratto*, Electa, Milan, 1992, p. 54.

54
Zoran Music. 1909
Doppio ritratto
1990

Oil on canvas, 116 x 89 cm.
Signed and dated on bottom right: «MUSIC 90».
Provenance: Galleria Contini, Cortina.
Exhibition: Rome, Accademia di Francia, 1992, no. 139.
Bibliography: *Zoran Music*, 1992, p. 140, no. 139, col. pl.

Since 1989, Music's work has been entirely dedicated to the themes of *self-portrait* and *double portrait*, which obviously stem from the identical set of premises and problems.

Next to the painter is his wife, Ida, also a painter, whom he met in Trieste in 1943 and later encountered again in Venice in 1945 when she was a student at the Accademia and lent Music her own studio; they were married in 1949.

Before the double portraits, Ida, daughter of painter Guido Cadorin thanks to whom Music got to know and love the city of Venice, the incarnation of oriental fascination, was depicted by Music in many portraits in which he simplifies her face into a stylized oval reminiscent of old icons.

In these double portraits, the positions vary slightly and often, as here, the painter depicts himself behind Ida. The larval bodies are faintly hinted at and almost transparent on the canvas, an element with its own precise pictorial value and independent chromaticism, revealing itself in its very nudity.

Standing out from this essentiality, within the rounded black outline in the background, are the faces lined by time and Ida's flaming hair.

With these figures, in which sentiment is not able to conquer the sensation of profound individual solitude, Music represents the dissolution itself of material and spirit and, conferring great nobility on the figures, he wraps them in sacredness. The concise drawing with open lines and the use of few colors in contrast with an increasingly intrusive canvas, give this double portrait the aspect of a sketch that reinforces more than ever the suggestions of these visages that simultaneously reveal existence and its dissolution.
Simona Pizzetti

55
Carlo Mattioli. 1911
Nudo coricato
1961

56
Carlo Mattioli. 1911
Piccola natura morta
1965

Oil on faesite, 33 x 70 cm.
Signed on bottom right: «Mattioli».
Exhibitions: Parma, Galleria della Steccata, *Mattioli*, December 14, 1963-January 3, 1964 (b/w ill. in cat.); Parma, Scuderie della Pilotta, *Mattioli. Mostra antologica 1939-1970*, 1970, no. 30 (col. ill. on cat. cover); Carrara, Accademia di Belle Arti, *Mostra antologica di Carlo Mattioli*, January 29-February 28, 1971 (col. pl. no. III between pp. 12-13 in cat.); Milan, Palazzo Reale, *Carlo Mattioli. Opere 1944-1984*, inaug. May 8, 1984, P.C. Santini, ed., no. 7, col. ill., 7 (col. ill. no. 7 p. 11); Bolzano, Museo d'Arte Moderna, *Carlo Mattioli. Nudi femminili 1944-1974*, April 7-May 28, 1989, P.L. Siena, curator, no. 15 (cat. Milano, Mazzotta; col. ill., p. 39).

Mattioli's nudes comprise the series the artist — born in Modena but resident in Parma — worked the longest on, from 1944 to 1974, with various techniques and numerous stylistic variations. The group painted in 1961 is characterized by a marked stylization of the figure, perfunctorily depicted according to the axes of light, with extreme refinement in the control of the tonal relations. The protagonist in Mattioli's nudes from the early '60s (which, for the generalization of their figures have been compared to his landscapes[1]) is the painterly *matière*. In comparison with his previous studies on this theme «much stronger becomes [...] the need to experience a new expressive force through the relationship between color and *matière*.»[2] «The color [...] becomes a colored paste, a thick layer, an agglomeration.»[3] This mode of using the *matière* brings Mattioli close to experimentation in the Informal realm. Yet, it has been correctly observed that the painter does not follow so much the «*ultimonaturalismo*» of the Po Valley school, as much as approaches derived from abroad (in the nudes, the closest reference point is probably de Staël).[4] Despite these clear references, «Mattioli is not an Informal painter; he is too tied to the visual stimulus of reality to truly be one. He only generically draws from the Informal culture a certain way of handling the material and a broader linguistic free-

dom.»[5] It is not surprising, therefore, that speaking of the sources of these nudes, alongside the names of Post-War European masters, one can also mention that of Benedetto Antelami, with whom Mattioli shares «bare and synthetic anatomies [... and] creating a block of the figure and the background.»[6]
Claudio Zambianchi

1. V. Sgarbi, *Natura e storia in Carlo Mattioli* in Sciacca, Convento di San Francesco, *Carlo Mattioli. Paesaggi 1972-1988*, exh. cat., July 16-August 10, 1988 (Palermo, Edizioni Novecento), p. 12.
2. R. Tassi in Parma 1970, p. 15.
3. P.C. Santini in Milan 1984, p. xviii.
4. V. Strukelj, «La pittura della pittura: Carlo Mattioli,» in Parma, CSAC of the Università di Parma, *Carlo Mattioli*, 1983, p. 43.
5. R. Tassi, «La terra e l'ombra» in Parma, CSAC 1983, p. 25.
6. G.M. Erbesato, «Carlo Mattioli e il nudo» in Bolzano 1989, p. 18.

Oil on panel, 27 x 19 cm.
Signed and dated on bottom right: «Mattioli '65».
In addition to the female nudes, there is another subject of considerable importance in Mattioli's output in the first half of the 1960s: that of the «still lifes.» In this group of works, especially in those done in 1965, the reflection on the relationship between representation, color and material is carried to extreme consequences. In fact, the still lifes from '65 are characterized by very thick material from which the shapes of the objects emerge physically, almost as if in *bas-relief*. And here again, perhaps more so than in any other moment of his creative life, Mattioli is close to Informal art. The name appearing most frequently in the critiques is that of Fautrier,[1] but Burri and Morandi are also mentioned.[2] Yet, not even in the still lifes is his rapport with the Informal such that Mattioli could be defined an artist of that poetic style, but nor, on the other hand, can one speak of figurative painting in these works. Mattioli is moving within a borderline area. As Cesare Garboli said: «There is a paradox in Mattioli. Mattioli is not a figurative painter, but a painter who makes the painterly material become figurative without even wanting to through the contagious power or energy of the material. The painting style manifests itself, makes itself seen, reveals itself, and in this revelation is hidden everything figurative that can be interpreted and deciphered in the painted substance. [...] Mattioli follows a rule: the resistance of the material to the Informal.»[3] The objects in this series undergo a rigorous simplification and the same happens with the color, reduced to «two bands [...] in delicate rapport or sudden contrast.»[4] It is a particular aspect in Mattioli, previously evident in the nudes, «his mode of spoliation, a need to simplify, reduce, 'impoverish', to search for the essence of things.»[5] In this sense, in the still lifes intellectualization seems to prevail over emotion, but, Luigi Carluccio warns, «the emotion [...] is then also sensuously recovered through the character of the pictorial material — tender, with body, absolute — and through the division of the spaces.»[6]
Claudio Zambianchi

57
Carlo Mattioli. 1911
Estate in Versilia
1972-1974

58
Carlo Mattioli. 1911
Aigues Mortes
1979

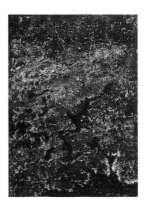

1. V. Strukelj, «La pittura della pittura: Carlo Mattioli» in Parma, CSAC of the Università di Parma, *Carlo Mattioli*, 1983, p. 43.
2. M. Venturoli 1966, quoted in Carrara, Accademia di Belle Arti, *Mostra antologica di Carlo Mattioli*, exh. cat., January 29-February 2, 1971, pp. 10-11.
3. C. Garboli, introduction, *Carlo Mattioli. Paesaggi*, Bologna, Edizioni Galleria Marescalchi, 1990 (from *Falbalas*, Milan, Garzanti, 1990), p. 8.
4. M. Valsecchi 1968, quoted in Carrara 1971, p. 12.
5. Parma, Scuderie della Pilota, *Mattioli. Mostra antologica 1939-1970*, exh. cat., 1970, p. 15.
6. L. Carluccio, «Nature morte 1963-1968 di Carlo Mattioli,» *Compagnia del disegno. Prima collana del Lanzone*, no. 6, Parma 1981; quoted in Parma, CSAC 1983, p. 99.

Oil on cardboard, 94 x 57 cm.
Signed on bottom center: «Mattioli».
Exhibitions: Ferrara, Palazzo dei Diamanti, *Carlo Mattioli. Opere dal 1970 al 1986*, Oct. 26, 1986-Jan. 7, 1987, no. 15 (col. ill.); Sciacca, Convento di San Francesco, *Carlo Mattioli. Paesaggi 1972-1988*, July 16-Aug. 10, 1988 (col. ill.); Milan, Palazzo Reale, *Carlo Mattioli. Opere 1944-1984*, inaug. May 8, 1984, P.C. Santini, ed., no. 65 (col. ill.); Bologna, Galleria Marescalchi, *Carlo Mattioli. Paesaggi*, 1990 (col. ill.).

This painting follows the clearly bipartite horizontal schema of the previous still life and also shares with it the accentuated distinction between the chromatic areas, one of which is very light, the other very dark. The proportions, however, are different: here one notes a considerable unbalance between the painting's two sections caused by the raising of the line which separates them situated near the upper edge of the painting. In this way, Mattioli achieves an upheaval in the surface of the scene accentuating the composition's two-dimensionality. In this painting Mattioli draws his inspiration from «strong visual impressions,»[1] but starts from «a problem of language: nature is in the painting. One must conjugate the latter. In reality, Mattioli has always known that painting is an architectural structure of elements.»[2] Here one of the primary linguistic problems seems to be that of the relationship between material and color. G. Testori observed that in Mattioli's paintings, a polarization between light and shade has become more accentuated over time, «a shade and a light which, not being mimetic but rather magmatic, assign to themselves the ability to realize the theme, and together, to devour it, to highlight it and swallow it up within total dazzle or total night.»[3]
Claudio Zambianchi

1. P. C. Santini in Milan 1984, p. XIX.
2. V. Sgarbi, «Natura e storia in Carlo Mattioli» in Sciacca 1988, pp. 13-14.
3. G. Testori in *12 dipinti di Carlo Mattioli*, Ivrea, Olivetti, 1980; quoted in Bologna 1990, p. 144.

Oil on canvas, 135.5 x 92 cm.
Signed with title and date on back: «Mattioli Aigues Mortes 1979».
Exhibitions: Milan, Palazzo Reale, *Carlo Mattioli. Opere 1944-1984*, inaug. May 8, 1984, P.C. Santini, ed., no. 108 (col. ill. p. 129 in cat.).

The «circumstance» which gave life to Mattioli's cycle of *Aigues Mortes* «happened just like the other time, from brief stays in Versilia. The sea, the beach, the ring of mountains, the pine groves, that even then had entered into Mattioli's eye and soul, this time left no trace. But one day during the summer of 1977 he happened near a canal: a thick carpet of vegetation, changeable in color, set upon shallow stagnant water [...]. Mattioli returned a number of times, and little-by-little that sluggish canal became a universe to be explored, slowly, endlessly. In places the vegetation is interrupted and opens up into bizarre shapes and strange profiles.»[1]

The references called into question for this series of paintings: late Monet of the *Nymphs*, perhaps seen «with the same eyes as Clyfford Still,»[2] the symbolism of Moreau and, above all, of Redon. Mattioli chooses a point of view that looks vertically down upon the water, excluding the banks, concentrating on a limited portion of the surface where «a break had formed, irregular and snaking, that opened up the view into the depths of the water below, like peering into a mystery, a space without definite limits, dizzying.»[3] In other words, symbolic imagery, or better, variations on a single archetype of probably sexual origin and certainly connected with a feeling of the great «unknowable,» of the «gap» also accentuated by the French title which has its origin in a famous Camargue resort.[4] The natural imagery is therefore profoundly transformed and takes on symbolic tones. Moreover, as Vittorio Sgarbi observed regarding the *Aigues Mortes*, «despite the immersion, the cast, the mirroring, Mattioli is no longer a naturalist painter. [...] Like Burri and Tapies, he is clearly an intellectual painter. And he is such in a manner which is more concealed, more ambiguous and

59
Goliardo Padova. 1909-1979
Paesaggio
1967

more tied to the appearance of things. But observing his *matière* from close up, one realizes that, apparently mimetic, it shines in itself, and sometimes does not even shine at all, is dull, opaque, muted and coal-like.»[5]
Claudio Zambianchi

1. P.C. Santini in Rome, Galleria Giulia, *Carlo Mattioli. Aigues Mortes ed altri paesaggi*, exh. cat., inaug. October 18, 1979.
2. V. Strukelj, «La pittura della pittura: Carlo Mattioli» in Parma, CSAC of the Università di Parma, *Carlo Mattioli*, 1983, p. 45.
3. R. Tassi, «Mattioli e un soprassalto della maturità,» no. 9, 1979, publ. in Rome 1979.
4. *Ibid.*
5. V. Sgarbi in Parma, La Sanseverina, *Carlo Mattioli. Aigues Mortes 1976-1980*, exh. cat., January 9-March 12, 1988, p. 6.

Oil on canvas, 70.5 x 59 cm.
Signed on upper left: «Padova».

In the 1930s he had been part of the Lombardy *Chiaristi*. Then came the war, imprisonment and a silence which lasted more than ten years. It was only in 1955 that Goliardo Padova started to paint once again and he concentrated on just a few subjects: farm women, sheaves of grain, oxbow lakes along the Po River, landscapes, and then birds, individually or in flocks. Pietro Del Giudice wrote in 1967: «[...] Padova's birds. The painter's studio is populated, swelled, with them. In the paintings, their flight is over deserted, damp and muddy land where the foggy autumn is about to lose itself in a solitary winter. Going about the countryside there is little sound of clanging metal in the timeless, wintry dairies and stalls of the farmer; it is a long sleep, a vigil of sleep, a torpor that rises and falls again in the flight of the crows, in the stripping away of a passage high among the branches in the seasonal migrations.»[1]

Starting in 1960, two primary sources of inspiration can be seen in Padova's work: «on one side, a line of inquiry having its roots in mid-nineteenth century French Realism that re-elaborates succeeding experiences but is nonetheless closely tied to that matrix, and on the other, a profound link with a so-called 'visionary' aspect, a precise reference [...] to a certain kind of turn-of-the-century symbolism that emerges above all in the 'Uccellacci' series.»[2]

In this flight of birds, which advances almost menacingly over the barren countryside with the earth lit up by unexpected orange and blue flashes, the Symbolist component prevails: in the lower section there seems to be a reference to Segantini, while in the form the birds take in flight, the influence probably comes, as has been observed, from Kubin.[3] The Symbolist influence produces in Padova a nervous and elegant movement of the brush that synthesizes stroke and color, color of strong material consistency, with two results: «the space becomes a trajectory, a graphic continuum»[4] and the painter acquires the possibility of focussing

«on the material, without losing sight of the form.»[5] In this particular context, Padova «draws on those experiences having as the basis of their language the use of the material in an expressive sense [...]. The 'Informal', especially its naturalistic variant in Lombardy, provided him with the stimulus of identifying himself within a figurative culture that has nature and life as the two foci of the ellipse.»[6]
Claudio Zambianchi

1. P. Del Giudice, publ. in «Antologia critica» in Parma, Galleria del Teatro, *Goliardo Padova. Opere dal 1933 al 1967*, exh. cat., March 2-16, 1968.
2. V. Strukelj, *Goliardo Padova*, presentation by A.C. Quintavalle, Parma, CSAC of the Università di Parma, 1987, p. 27.
3. *Ibid.*
4. P. Fossati, «Qualità di Padova» in Parma, Galleria La Sanseverina, *Goliardo Padova. Dipinti e tempere*, exh. cat., March 24-May 10, 1990, p. 7.
5. A. Bertolucci, publ. in «Antologia critica» in Parma 1968.
6. R. Tassi, introduction to Parma 1968.

60
Goliardo Padova. 1909-1979
In un piccolo giardino (Siepe)
(1974-1976)

61
Ottone Rosai. 1895-1957
San Gimignano
1954

Oil on canvas, 72.5 x 72.5 cm.
Signed on upper right «Padova»; on the back, the signature «Padova».

In Padova's painting, there is room for things other than the flight of vaguely menacing birds. «There are also happy moments that are translated into celebrations of color: the silvery cascading of be-jewelled willows and the fragrant perfume of the wisteria in the height of bloom.»[1] In this work, the «secessionist» aspect of Padova's art is elaborated with a decidedly decorative flavor, something which was pointed out by Attilio Bertolucci as well as Paolo Fossati.[2] Bertolucci connects Padova's «ornamental» bent with late Monet, the other oblig-atory reference when faced in this painting with the spatial vibration produced by the dense strips of long, filamentary brushstrokes very similar to the *Iris* or the scenes of the *Japanese Bridge* in the garden at Giverny. Like Monet, in paintings of this genre Padova draws his inspiration from the surroundings which might be humble and banal. One only need consider the title of this painting, *In a Small Garden*. In Padova, there is a deep and affectionate sense of rootedness in the places asso-ciated with his life: «No high-flying tone, nothing heroic or sublime, but neither a humble one; a good dose of reality, correctly in-tune with the painter's ideas and, starting from that firm reality, a loosing of analogies and openings. All told, a 'sim-ple' way of painting in order to reveal an incredible (unexpected and stupefying) richness of paths.»[3]
Claudio Zambianchi

1. P.P. Mendogni in Parma, Galleria La Sanseverina, *Goliardo Padova. Dipinti e tempere*, exh. cat. March 24-May 10, 1990, p. 40.
2. A. Bertolucci, publ. in «Antologia critica» in Parma, Galleria del Teatro, *Goliardo Padova. Opere dal 1933 al 1967*, exh. cat., March 2-16, 1968; P. Fossati, «Qua-lità di Padova» in Parma 1990, p. 7.
3. Fossati 1990, p. 8.

Oil on canvas, 100 x 70 cm.
Signed on bottom right: «O. Rosai».
Exhibitions: Florence, Galleria La Strozzina, *Firenze di Rosai*, June-July 1954; Venice, *28a Esposizione Biennale Internazionale d'Arte*, 1956, Room VI, no. 12 (b/w pl. no. 16 in cat.).
Bibliography: Florence, Palazzo Strozzi, *Mostra dell'opera di Ottone Rosai 1911-1957*, May-June, 1960 (Florence, Vallecchi), p. 86, no. 239; P.C. San-tini, *Ottone Rosai*, Florence, Vallecchi, 1960, p. 218, no. 204; L. Cavallo, *Ottone Rosai*, Milan, Edizioni Galleria il Castello, 1973, pp. 151 and 257, no. 261.

«I will tell you what I have always thought: that the greatest Rosai was the one of architecture [...]. Rosai attended the Accademia from 1909 to 1913 when he left without getting his diploma. But at the end of 1912 he received an honorable mention. In what? In *architecture*. [...] The last great *interven-tion* was when Rosai felt the need to examine the architectural line of San Gimignano and in his city the Palace, the churches from the fourteenth and fifteenth centuries, the Cupola [...]. If you observe Rosai's architecture, you will see that it contains neither *golden section* nor *harmonic proportion*, and yet there is a harmony which surprises and seizes you.»[1] So said Alessandro Parronchi in an interview with Mario Novi in which the critic sang the praises of the last period of Rosai's work. Par-ronchi is not alone in highlighting the remarkable quality of the cityscapes of late-Rosai. Stylistically they are characterized by a simplification of the architectural structures and a considerable brigh-tening up of his palette, which, in the words of poet Mario Luzi, attains results which are «almost *abstracted* [...] with a transparency that dissolves the material into light.»[2]
San Gimignano is not one of the more form-alized cityscapes, but in it one does discover a «revived need for reducing the structural elements in order to attain the clear steadfastness of simple relationships.»[3] This search is clear right from the preparatory stage of the composition: a drawing in which the buildings are depicted almost as if they

were geometrical solids. *San Gimignano* is a theme that recurs a number of times in Rosai's works dur-ing these years. This version could be considered a prototype or at least one of the prototypes of the subject. A smaller version with minimal variations of this composition is well-known,[4] as are other very similar paintings.[5] According to Pier Carlo Santini, this painting constitutes «one of the most valid examples of Rosai's late work.»[6]
Claudio Zambianchi

1. M. Novi, «Intervista ad Alessandro Parronchi» in Rome, Galleria Nazionale d'Arte Moderna, *Ottone Rosai. Opere dal 1911 al 1957*, July 20-September 18, 1983, P.C. Santini, ed., exh. cat. (Florence, Vallecchi), pp. 254-255.
2. P. Tortonese, «Intervista a Mario Luzi» in Rome 1983, p. 248.
3. P.C. Santini, «Nota introduttiva» in Ivrea, Centro Cul-turale Olivetti, *Ottone Rosai*, exh. cat., 1957, p. 41.
4. See, for example, Florence 1960, p. 86, no. 239.
5. See, Cavallo 1973, pl. XLI (facing p. 132), no. 261 and pl. CXIX, no. 277.
6. Santini 1960, p. 218, no. 204.

Ottone Rosai,
Study for *San Gimignano*, 1954

62
Mino Maccari. 1898-1989
Gruppo di personaggi
1974

63
Franco Gentilini. 1909-1981
Washington Bridge
1959

Oil on canvas, 83 x 94 cm.
Signed and dated on bottom right: «Maccari 974».
Provenance: the artist.

This is a painting Maccari did on a direct commission from Pietro Barilla. In it the artist portrayed
some of the personages who appear most frequently in his work: surrounded by women, one
can recognize Mussolini, an Austro-Hungarian
general and the omnipresent Von Stroheim in an
impeccable white uniform. More than the satire in
the costumes — a too dramatic and serious exercise
for someone like Maccari with a witty disposition —
it is a grotesque, tense, world which gives rise to a
smile: «Nothing is more removed from the paintings of Mino Maccari than the role of castigator, at
the most he limits himself to that of someone who
castigates with a laugh, i.e., with the obviousness of
the ridiculous.»[1]

Thus, Maccari's compositions are to be interpreted as the equivalent of a witticism, the play on
words the artist was also famous for. Therefore,
despite the formal affinity with Grosz, as has often
been pointed out, Maccari's tangible connections
with the sharp social criticism of the German artist
are few. In this Gruppo di personaggi, the formal
structure is determined by the graphic structure.
The color, rich with hues, contrast and shading, is
the infinitely variegated territory in which the
drawing singles out — with its limited number of
concise strokes, like those of a cartoonist — the
expressions on the faces and the position of the
figures within the space.
Claudio Zambianchi

1. F. Zeri, Presentation of the volume Addenda. Disegni
   di Mino Maccari, 1926-1984, Florence, Edizioni
   Pananti, 1985; published in Lugano, Villa Malpensata,
   Mino Maccari 1898-1989. Il genio dell'irriverenza,
   exh. cat. (Edizioni Città di Lugano; Florence, Edizioni
   Pananti) 1992, p. 110.

Oil on canvas, 100 x 160 cm.
Signed on bottom center: «Gentilini».
Provenance: Galleria del Naviglio, Milan.
Exhibitions: Lucerne, Kunstmuseum, Italienische
maler der Gegenwart, 1960, no. 104; Rome, Palazzo
Barberini, Gentilini. Antologica, 1965, no. 40;
Venice, XXXIV Esposizione Internazionale d'Arte,
Biennale di Venezia, 1968: exhibition «Linee della
ricerca: dall'informale alle nuove strutture,» no. 40
(b/w pl. no. LXV in cat. «Mostre Speciali»); Ferrara,
Palazzo dei Diamanti (later Faenza, Palazzo delle
Esposizioni), Gentilini. Antologica, exh. cat.,
December 8, 1971-January 1, 1972, no. 77.
Bibliography: Fortune, February 1960 (ill.); Il
Popolo, July 4, 1960; La Fiera Letteraria, Septem-
ber 2, 1965; Pierre Cabanne, «La tematica fantastica di Gentilini,» Panorama delle Arti, March 15-
31, 1971; Alain Bosquet, Franco Gentilini, Bologna,
Edizioni Bora, 1979 (b/w ill. no. 42, p. 26); «Gentilini,» XXe Siècle, year 42, no. 55, March 1980 (entirely dedicated to Gentilini), b/w ill. p. 51; N.
Micieli, Franco Gentilini. I ponti di New York, Pon-
tedera, Edizioni Bandecchi e Vivaldi, 1985, p. 97,
no. X (b/w ill., p. 40, pl. X and p. 97).
Note: A smaller version (50 x 80 cm.) of this painting with some variations exists, no. XVI Micieli,
b/w ill. pp. 46, 100.

On April 29, 1959, Gentilini's personal exhibition
opened at the John Heller Gallery in New York. It
was on the occasion of this show that the American
magazine, Fortune, most likely on the advice of its
art director Leo Lionni, contacted the artist to have
him do a series of paintings based on the theme of
New York bridges. The paintings were to serve as
illustrations for a special issue of Fortune dedicated
to this American city, and was published in February 1960.[1] Gentilini began work, walking 229
miles[2] and making sketches out in the open that he
later used for the final compositions painted in
Rome.[3] There are twelve or thirteen paintings in
all. Nine of them, of which this is one, were reproduced in color in the magazine.[4] For Washington
Bridge, Gentilini did three preparatory drawings
and a smaller format copy. More than New York,

these bridges belong to Gentilinia, as Dino Buzzati
called the imaginary city which was the home of
Gentilini's architectural structures.[5] Certainly the
New York bridges, with their open structures and
steel beams lent themselves to being depicted by a
painter in whose art «the graphic element forms —
as in Klee — the 'poetic' scaffolding [...] developing
itself in an intimate union with the color and in-
tensifying the suggestion of a mural.»[6] Accompanying this insistent predominance of graphic elements is a preference for dense painting material,
obtained by mixing oil paint with sand. Gentilini's
thick material derives from a personal interpretation of some trends in Informal art, particularly in
Fautrier and Dubuffet, whose works the painter
had the opportunity of seeing for the first time in
Paris in 1947, but whose influences would only
produce results a few years later in the early
Fifties.[7] In this regard, Raffaele Carrieri describes
the results Gentilini attained as follows: «Gentilini's
painting material was dried up by a series of in-
tractably hot days. Touching it, one feels the rough
dryness of the sand. Each color is deeply rooted
like minerals in their pure state. In order to reach
an object, you must cross a small desert. When you
have reached it, you cannot remove it because
each form has roots that branch out deeply. The
visible planes on which they rest are just the surface of a number of layers laid down dry.»[8]
Claudio Zambianchi

1. Micieli 1985, p. 13.
2. Editorial in Fortune, February 1960; quoted in «Noti-
   zia» in Franco Gentilini. I ponti di New York, S. Gran-
   dini, ed., Lugano, Editore Giulio Topi, 1985.
3. Micieli 1985, p. 19.
4. Ibid., p. 12.
5. See, for example, A. Jouffroy, Franco Gentilini, Milan,
   Fratelli Fabbri Editori, 1987, p. 29.
6. E. Steingräber, Franco Gentilini, pittore amato non
   soltanto dai letterati, p. 17; in Franco Gentilini, exh.
   cat., touring exhibition 1991-1992, p. 17.
7. See, L. Trucchi, «Traccia per un percorso critico» in
   Rome, Palazzo Venezia, Gentilini 1909-1981, exh. cat.,
   December 21, 1985-February 14, 1986 (Milan-Rome,
   Mondadori-De Luca) p. 16.
8. R. Carrieri, «Gentilini», in Rome 1965.

64
Renato Guttuso. 1911-1987
Il fumatore (Rocco seduto)
1958

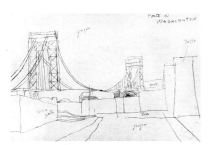

Franco Gentilini, Preparatory drawing
for *Washington Bridge*, 1951

Franco Gentilini, Second version
of *Washington Bridge*, 1959

Oil on canvas, 110 x 87.5 cm.
Signed on bottom right: «Guttuso».
Bibliography: E. Crispolti, *Catalogo Generale dei dipinti di Renato Guttuso*, vol. 2, *1954-1965*, Milan, Giorgio Mondadori e Associati, 1984, pp. xliii and 110, no. 58/20 (b/w ill. p. 110 and col. pl. facing p. 150); E. Crispolti, *Leggere Guttuso*, Milan, Arnoldo Mondadori, 1987, pp. 101, 132-133 and 244 (col. ill. no. 48); Argenta, Chiesa di San Lorenzo, Convento dei Cappuccini, *Guttuso tra segno and colore: Opere 1924-1985*, C. Occhipinti, ed., exh. cat., September-November 1988 (Busto Arsizio, Edizioni Internazionale d'Arte Bandera) p. 253 (col. ill. p. 253); E. Crispolti, *Catalogo Generale dei dipinti di Renato Guttuso*, vol. 4, *1984-86 e Addenda 1924-1983*, Milan, Giorgio Mondadori e Associati, 1989, p. 147, no. 58/20.

This work belongs to a transitional phase in Guttuso's work, when, from a period of «social realism» between the end of the 1940s up to 1956, the painter began to orient himself towards that which Enrico Crispolti designated «existential realism.»[1] At this point in time, Guttuso was particularly attentive to motifs taken from «urban social life in relation to the workplace [...], leisure time» and «typical figures [...] from everyday situations.»[2] The subject of the smoker is one of the most frequent. In this work, Guttuso establishes a new rapport, quite a bit more involved with the painterly material, that takes on more body and is applied with a more-immediate brushstroke that is left very evident and moves along the painting's surface. This way of applying the paint is particularly clear in *Fumatore*, especially in the hands, the tie and the spiral of smoke that merges with his hair.

The painting's freedom of touch and bright chromatic tones bring to mind its Expressionistic ancestry without, however, the «pessimism» of Beckmann and Kokoschka and the latter's «psychological torment,» even if this work has an affinity both in its workmanship and subject with the art of both of these painters.[3] In the treatment of the *matière* in the *Fumatore*, Guttuso, as commonly acknowledged by the critics, also shows himself to be aware of the experimentation of the Informal school. In 1963, on the occasion of the first major Guttuso retrospective in Parma, Franco Russoli mentioned, among others, the names of Pollock and Wols.[4] But Guttuso, as is evident in this painting, never relinquished the confrontation with the external object. A piece written by Guttuso in 1959, the year after he had painted the *Fumatore*, seems particularly explicative, both in the attention given to the Informal, as well as to the distance separating the artist from this form of art: «Let's take the case of Wols since today he is the one who is involved, just as only yesterday [...] it was Pollock, what is the thing they are lacking, the thing they were not able to fish out with their fishing line cast with such rage? Why were they not able to fish out anything but the rage itself that they flung out? Was there really not a single fish in that swamp, no micro-organism, no 'object'? [...] Does consciousness exist if it does not reflect an object, and does consciousness exist without an object?»[5] Nor, on the other hand, are these ordinary «objects,» but things and people with whom Guttuso was deeply involved: in the *Interno dello studio a Velate* (see no. 65), the objects and the setting of his own work, and in the *Fumatore* the portrait of Rocco Catalano, the Sicilian fisherman who had become the painter's assistant.

Claudio Zambianchi

1. Crispolti 1984, p. LXVIII and *passim*.
2. Crispolti 1987, p. 99.
3. See, D. Morosini, «I conflitti del mondo moderno nei nuovi quadri di Guttuso,» *Il Paese*, April 15, 1958; quoted in Crispolti 1984, p. XLIII; and Crispolti 1984, p. XLIII.
4. F. Russoli, «Realtà e cultura nel Guttuso del dopoguerra» in Parma, Soprintendenza alle Gallerie, *Renato Guttuso. Mostra Antologica dal 1931 ad oggi*, exh. cat., December 15, 1963-January 31, 1964, pp. 48-50; quoted in Crispolti 1984, p. LXVII.
5. R. Guttuso, «Le ragioni dei realisti» *Ulisse*, year 12, vol. 4, Summer 1959; quoted in Crispolti 1984, p. LXVIII.

65
Renato Guttuso. 1911-1987
Interno dello studio a Velate
(Grande natura morta)
1961

66
Fabrizio Clerici. 1913
La poltrona di Nonza
1979

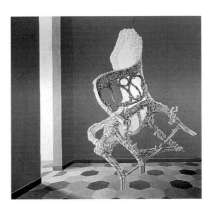

Oil on paper glued to canvas, 182.5 x 230 cm.
Signed and dated on bottom right: «Guttuso '61».
Exhibitions: Seattle, Seattle World's Fair, *Art Since 1950, American and International*, Apr. 21-Oct. 21, 1962, no. 54 (international section); Amsterdam, Stedelijk Museum, *Guttuso*, Nov. 9-Dec. 10, 1962, no. 15; Charleroi, Palais des Beaux-Arts, *Guttuso*, Jan. 12-Feb. 3, 1963, no. 15; Mexico City, Museo de Arte Moderno, *Arte italiano contemporaneo desde 1910*, 1966, no. 2 (Guttuso section, cat. p. 164); Venice, Centro di cultura di Palazzo Grassi, *Guttuso, Opere dal 1931 al 1981*, Apr. 4-June 20, 1982, no. 70 (cat. Florence, Sansoni, b/w ill. p. 168); Milan, Palazzo Reale, *Guttuso, Grandi Opere*, Dec. 12, 1984-Feb. 1985, no. 15 (cat., Milan, Mazzotta, ill. col. pp. 78 and 79, b/w ill. pp. 80, 81).
Bibliography: A. Moravia and F. Grasso, *Guttuso*, Palermo, Edizioni il Punto, 1962, col. ill. p. 162; A.C. Quintavalle, «Guttuso a Charleroy,» *Letteratura*, nos. 62-63, March-June 1963, b/w ill. p. 77; *L'Unità*, Dec. 14, 1963, b/w ill. p. 6; «Debata o Guttusovi,» *Vytvarny Zivot*, Bratislava, Feb. 2, 1965 (trans. «Dibattito su Guttuso,» *Il Contemporaneo*, 7/69, Feb. 1964, pp. 17-55), b/w ill. p. 58; E. Crispolti, *Catalogo Generale dei dipinti di Renato Guttuso, Vol. II: 1954-1965*, Milan, Giorgio Mondadori e Associati, 1984, pp. LXXXII, 217, no. 61/46, b/w ill. p. 217, col. pl. facing p. 215; E. Crispolti, *Leggere Guttuso*, Milan, Arnoldo Mondadori, 1987, pp. 101, 149, 246, ill. col. no. 59, p. 149; C. Occhipinti, «Guttuso del malinteso,» in Argenta, Chiesa di San Lorenzo, Covento dei Cappuccini, *Guttuso tra segno e colore; Opere 1924-1985*, C. Occhipinti, ed., exh. cat., Sept.-Oct. 1988 (Busto Arsizio, Edizioni Internazionale d'Arte Bandera), p. 23; E. Crispolti, *Catalogo Generale dei dipinti di Renato Guttuso, Vol. IV: 1984-1986 e Addenda 1924-1983*, Milan, Giorgio Mondadori e Associati, 1989, p. 164, no. 61/46.

The still life theme using objects from his studio recurs constantly in Guttuso's painting, right from the beginning of the 1940s. Between the end of the '50s and beginning of the '60s, the still life became a privileged subject and in some cases, as here, took on a monumental scope. In its style and workman-

ship, this work resembles the *Fumatore*. Particularly striking in the *Interno dello studio a Velate* is the vivacity of the brushstrokes which matches the painting's compositional structure. Its structure is dynamic and, as Carlo Occhipinti pointed out, elliptical in shape in which the central area «has an infinitely lesser importance with respect to what appears and happens on the edges,» and thus is linked with other large compositions of figures from the same years, like *Boogie-Woogie* (1953-54)[1] or, one could add, *La discussione* (1959-60).

Enrico Crispolti divides the still lifes from this period into two groups: the Roman ones in which the objects are more unusual and specific, and the Velate ones, «filled with objects.» In the latter, the artist cultivates an aspect «of contemporary life [which is] 'collective', 'social', insinuating into the private space the meaning [and] signs of mass-based commercialism.» The number of objects alludes to an «everyday objective of accumulating mass-produced objects, of driven 'consumption'.»[2]

From this standpoint Crispolti agrees with (and quotes) Alberto Moravia's analysis given in a monograph study on Guttuso from 1962 on the relationship between Guttuso and the objects in his still lifes from a sociological perspective: «Guttuso experienced the migration to the city as a phenomenon of alienation, of extraneousness from the old world of the farmer, in a world of mass-produced things which were worthless and would not last.»[3] To this sociological analysis, Moravia added an existential nuance when he pointed out the «fierce attention» with which Guttuso observed his objects. «He contemplated these humble objects in an obsessive manner without really understanding them but yet identifying with them. [...] He is still a poet who when faced with the intimacy and mystery of what is real, is dumbfounded, immersed in deep and basic astonishment.»[4]
Claudio Zambianchi

1. Occhipinti 1988, p. 23.
2. Crispolti 1987, p. 149.
3. Moravia 1962, p. 16.
4. *Ibid.*, p. 25.

Oil on panel, 120 x 120 cm.
Signed on bottom right of the moulding: «F. Clerici».
Provenance: Galleria Forni, Bologna; Galleria Consigli Arte, Parma.
Exhibitions: Paris, Grand Palais, *FIAC*, October 23-29, 1980 (cat. ill. p. 146); Brussels, Galerie Philippe Guimiot, *Fabrizio Clerici*, March 12-April 19, 1981 (cat. ill. p. 51); Cortina d'Ampezzo, Galleria d'Arte Moderna, Ciasa de ra Regoles, *Fabrizio Clerici*, August 1982 (cat. ill. p. 23); Rieti, Palazzo Vescovile, October 24-November 29, 1982; Ferrara, Palazzo dei Diamanti, *Fabrizio Clerici*, October 23, 1983-January 8, 1984 (cat. Casalecchio di Reno, Grafis, b/w ill. p. 177); *L'immagine e il suo doppio. Ricerca della pittura internazionale contemporanea fra realtà fisica e metafisica*, touring exhibition, F. D. Santi curator, 1984 (cat. Casalecchio di Reno, Grafis Edizioni, 1984, ill. col. p. 53); London, Solomon Gallery, *Fabrizio Clerici*, inaug. May 9, 1985 (cat. ill. p. 19); Parma, Consigli Arte, *Fabrizio Clerici*, inaug. May 17, 1986 (cat.).
Bibliography: Genzano di Roma, Galleria Cattoli, *Fabrizio Clerici. Opere grafiche 1941-1983*, exh. cat., 1983, b/w ill. p. 13; Rome, Galleria Nazionale d'Arte Moderna, *Fabrizio Clerici*, B. Mantura, curator, June 20-September 16, 1990 (cat. Rome, De Luca Edizioni d'Arte), no. 77, p. 200 (essay by I. Millesimi).
Note: Two absolutely identical versions of this painting exist, the only difference between them being the position of the signature, here on the bottom right of the moulding, and in the other on the bottom left of the moulding. The painting shown here is the first version. The second, in a private collection in Tokyo, was exhibited in Clerici's personal exhibition at the Forni Gallery in Tokyo which opened on November 12, 1984, and following that in Rome 1990, no. 77.

Nonza is the locale in Corsica where Léonor Fini, the famous Surrealist artist, has a house. Fabrizio Clerici, friend of the painter from 1944, stayed there and, Ines Millesimi says, «was particularly struck by the unusual shapes taken on by the gar-

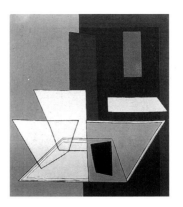

den chairs, stools and armchairs, all made of different materials and now worn-out and falling apart, but yet rearranged with strange assemblages and in a bizarre manner by the painter.»[1]

This was the episode behind the painting which is part of a large group of works Clerici began to paint towards the end of the '70s. These works are characterized by the fact that they take place within an architectural context that «with minimal variations remains practically the same.»[2] Federico Zeri considers these paintings to be «the high point of Clerici's painting.»[3] This scholar interprets them as a series of *Memento mori* in which their completely identical perspective rendering signifies «life, within which, with the lightning-like swiftness of rays, pass the presences that emerge and submerge [...]. These motionless and always identical rooms illuminate the brief parabola of life, that fleeting moment of individualization in space and time which both follows and precedes the void.»[4]

The fictitious reality of the armchair lightly hovered over by some palm trees on a checker-board-floor, is depicted with extraordinary accuracy. In one of his written pieces, Clerici spoke of «iron-clad disciplines of the absurd.»[5] And an iron-clad discipline rules the world of Clerici's painting.[6] Born in 1913, the artist only turned to painting in 1947 following long years of activity exclusively in the graphic arts, and here, as in the best 18th- and 19th-century academic tradition, by common critical assent, he draws on its smooth surfaces. The brushmark disappears in favor of the crystalline clearness of the image. What is thus created is an incongruous representation from the standpoint of the phenomenal reality, but which has the same logic, cohesion and structure as the dreamlike image.

Despite the obligatory reference to the reality of dreams, Clerici nonetheless feels himself closer to Metaphysical art than Surrealism.[7] In fact, the Metaphysical school, with which he shares the sense of «contemplative immobility,»[8] has an Italian and Mediterranean origin Clerici does not repudiate, as the use of a light and sunny palette in

this painting demonstrates. Notwithstanding these references and the friendship which tied Clerici to de Chirico and, above all, Savinio, the artist substantially remains an isolated figure in the panorama of Italian art in this century, something of which Clerici is fully aware. «To speak of my painting and the position it occupies in contemporary art is a question I have never asked myself,» he stated in 1967. «When I do a painting, I really do not ask myself if, once it is finished, it will fit into the current circuit or not. I paint for other reasons, one of which is to offer the viewer an unusual image in which latitude and time merge and disappear outside the limits of memory.»[9]
Claudio Zambianchi

1. Millesimi in Rome 1989, no. 77, p. 200.
2. F. Zeri, «Presentazione» in Ferrara 1983-84, p. 11.
3. *Ibid.*
4. *Ibid.*
5. F. Clerici, «Promenade de Chimeres,» *Galleria*, 38/2, May-August 1988, p. 134 (issue dedicated to *Scritti di Fabrizio Clerici*, I. Millesimi ed.).
6. B. Mantura, «Pittura 'in distanza'» in Rome 1990, p. 12.
7. C. Costantini, «Il magnifico visionario,» interview with Clerici, *Il Messaggero*, April 3, 1990.
8. V. Zurlini in Rome, Il Gabbiano art gallery, *Fabrizio Clerici «Latitudine Böcklin»*, exh. cat., December 18, 1975-January 20, 1976.
9. F. Clerici in exh. cat. *Premio Gaetano Marzotto per la pittura. La pittura figurativa in Europa*, Valdagno, 1967; quoted in M. Quesada, «Cronologia» in Rome 1990, p. 241.

Oil on canvas, 55 x 46 cm.
Provenance: Sinisgalli Collection, Rome; Private Collection, Rome.
Exhibitions: Todi, Palazzo Comunali, Associazione Piazza Maggiore, *Atanasio Soldati. Mostra Antologica 1930-1953*, L. Caramel, curator, October 5-November 9, 1986, no. 7 (b/w ill. no. 7, p. 24).
Note: The following inscription appears on the back, on the left side of the canvas frame (the handwriting seems to be that of Maria Soldati): «Questo quadro fu dato in dono a Milano, prima della guerra del '40, dal pittore Atanasio Soldati a L. Sinigalli per ringraziarlo della prefazione alla piccola monografia stampata da 'Campo Grafico'.»

Carlo Belli relates that in the early years of the Milione when he got together with his artist friends at the Caffé Craja in Milan, Soldati always saved him a seat «since in those years I was his daemon, the one who incited him to abandon a part-Metaphysical, part-Cubist figurative world and enter completely into the 'abstract'.»[1] It was probably due to Belli's stimulus that for a short period around the middle of the 1930s Soldati approached total abstraction, as seen in a group of compositions painted on canvas and panels, similar to this one. His closeness to Belli, including Belli's theories, in this phase of his work is demonstrated in a piece he wrote in 1935 in which Soldati presents his personal exhibition at the Galleria del Milione: «abstract painting (even if this adjective is not right) loves analysis, order, clarity [...] No reproductions of nature or sensations from life. To express drama, there is no need for knives, corpses, canons or flags, just lines, colors, surfaces, that is, all the means of painting itself without any kind of structures, above literature. [...] For us art is a question of spirit; only the spirit can know the spirit. The end of art is imitating nature.»[2] The year before, two poets, Alfonso Gatto and Leonardo Sinisgalli, had dedicated a small monograph to Soldati. Speaking of Soldati's colors Gatto stated: «Soldati does not believe light is a daytime event, but a deserted and eternal one with infinitely precise colors achieved as a whole,»[3] a comment appropriate to the dark hues of this

68
Atanasio Soldati. 1896-1953
Composizione
1946

69
Domenico Gnoli. 1933-1970
Desk
1968

painting, while Sinisgalli considered him «a Pythagorean painter in search of the golden mean.»[4] It was to thank him for what he had written on this occasion that Soldati gave Sinisgalli this *Composizione*. The painting, which shows the «reduced and essential»[5] color characteristic of this phase, in the use of trapezoidal forms that seem to allude to spatial depth as well as in its rigorous geometrical formulation, finds an important precedent in Malevic's art. In fact, it is Malevic who influenced the «insistent anglings»[6] of this *Composizione*, much more than Mondrian and the neo-plastic movement in general, which Soldati nonetheless kept in mind both in this period as well as is in his «concretist» phase. Even though the Suprematist-style dynamism was immobilized,[7] it allowed Soldati's abstract style to retain an allusive and suggestive element and to act as an ordering filter which, a few years later, would allow him to return to the world of Metaphysical objects with a much greater compositional rigor than there had been previously [see no. 68]. It is from this standpoint that even this brief phase of maximum tangency between Soldati and the Milanese abstract school around the Milione could be considered one of the high points of his artistic development.
Claudio Zambianchi

1. C. Belli, *Racconto degli anni difficili* in Prato, Palazzo Novellucci, *Anni creativi al «Milione» 1932-1939*, exh. cat., G. Gori ed., June 7-July 20, 1980 (Milan, Silvana Editoriale), p. 15.
2. A. Soldati, «Dichiarazioni di A.A. Soldati,» *Il Milione, no. 37, February 20-March 6, 1935*.
3. A. Gatto in A. Gatto and L. Sinisgalli, *Atanasio Soldati*, Milan, Edizioni di Campo Grafico, 1934; quoted by N. Ponente in Turin, Galleria Civica d'Arte Moderna, *Atanasio Soldati*, November 6, 1969-January 6, 1970.
4. A. Gatto and L. Sinisgalli, *Atanasio Soldati*, quoted in L. Venturi, *Soldati*, Milan, Galleria Bergamini, 1954, p. 15.
5. Ponente 1969, p. 21.
6. P.C. Santini, *Atanasio Soldati*, Milan, Edizioni di Comunità, 1965, p. 24.
7. *Ibid*.

Oil on canvas, 73 x 54 cm.
Signed upper center: «Soldati».
Exhibitions: Parma, Galleria del Teatro, Salone delle Scuderie, Palazzo della Pilotta, *Atanasio Soldati*, March 1-30, 1970 (b/w ill. in cat.).
Note: Stamped on the back: «Opere inventariate di Atanasio Soldati».

Starting in 1939-40, the world of Metaphysical objects once again peeked into Soldati's painting, commencing a phase which would end ten years or so later with his passing over to so-called «arte concreta.» In comparison with the *Composizione* previously belonging to Sinisgalli (see the previous description), here the geometric filter allows Soldati to tighten up the composition's elements and place them according to a predominantly orthogonal rhythm. As Albino Galvano noted, «the levelling out of the effect,» due to the elimination of any hint of volume, «allows the interruptions in perspective to be seen as the outer boundaries of 'abstract' areas', indicating a tendency towards the «concretist solution.»[1] In this way, the antithesis between «figurative and abstract» is overcome in a manner that brings Soldati strikingly near Klee.[2] It is, perhaps, the most intensely lyrical moment in Soldati's work in which an almost childlike world with objects turned into colorful shapes is arrayed in an ironic, playful and happy way, as if on the stage of a very personal little theater: «a funloving-scenographic metaphysic.»[3]
Claudio Zambianchi

1. A. Galvano, «Preliminari a un'analisi di Soldati,» *Letteratura*, nos. 19-20, 1956, p. 112.
2. N. Ponente in Galleria Civica d'Arte Moderna, *Atanasio Soldati*, November 6, 1969-January 6, 1970, p. 13.
3. R. Barletta, «Soldati, la ginnastica dell'intelligenza» in Gallarate, Civica Galleria d'Arte Moderna, *Atanasio e Maria Soldati. Opere inedite*, exh. cat., November 1-29, 1981, p. 11.

Acrylic and sand on canvas, 131 x 162 cm.
Signed and dated on the back: «D. Gnoli 1968 'Desk'» [the inscription is now hidden by Masonite panels but is recorded in Rome, Galleria Nazionale d'Arte Moderna, *Domenico Gnoli. 1933-1970*, exh. cat., Bruno Mantura ed., February 21-April 12, 1987 (Rome-Milan, De Luca-Mondadori), no. 61, p. 29].
Provenance: Private Collection, Rome; Galleria Contini, Venice-Cortina d'Ampezzo.
Exhibitions: New York, Sidney Janis Gallery, *Domenico Gnoli in his First American Exhibition of Paintings & Sculpture*, December 3-27, 1969, no. 11; Rome, Galleria Giulia, *Domenico Gnoli*, April 1981, no. 7 (col. ill. p. 13 in cat.); Verona, Galleria d'Arte Moderna e Contemporanea «Achille Forti,» Palazzo Forti, *Domenico Gnoli. Antologica*, Giorgio Cortenova ed., November 13, 1982-January 20, 1983, no. 24 (cat., Milan, Electa, b/w ill. p. 42); Lausanne, Musée Cantonal des Beaux Arts, *Rétrospective Domenico Gnoli*, 1983; Rome, 1987, no. 61 (col. pl. no. 61 in cat.); Cortina d'Ampezzo, Galleria Contini, *Opera prima. Pittura del Novecento in Europa e in America*, December 28, 1991-February 9, 1992 (cat. Milan, Electa, col. ill. p. 64).
Bibliography: V. Sgarbi, *Gnoli*, foreword by I. Calvino, afterword by C. Spaak, Milan, Franco Maria Ricci, 1983, pp. 104 and 222, no. 182 of ann. cat. (col. ill. p. 143); Madrid, Fundacion Caja de Pensiones, *Domenico Gnoli. Ultimas obras 1963-1969*, exh. cat., January 16-March 4, 1990 (b/w ill. p. 76).

In a very short little comic scene, from those created and sketched out by Domenico Gnoli with a fine and ironic pen, there appears a table under which is hidden a socialist speaker: «If you really love workers,» he tells his audience, «it's the basic frame of the table you should admire, not its pale varnished exterior which is merely a tame piece of sculpture, a decapitated animal, an anemic temple, a house blown in by the wind, a frame of a painting opening on to emptiness.»[1] The idea that the table could correspond to the picture's frame is developed in *Desk* until they become one in the same. Thus, as Luigi Carluccio says, in the works he

70
Alfredo Chighine. 1914-1974
Composizione blu e rosa
1956

created starting in 1964, Gnoli eliminates «the space outside the object [...]; the space corresponds exactly with the pictorial image, completely absorbed by the presence of the object and within its dimension.»[2] In other words, in that moment the painter discovers a new distance between himself and things.[3] Seen from up close, delineated with a rare and detailed technique, the objects take on a different weight than they have in real life. They are decontextualized, not because they are put next to contradictory elements — as in the Metaphysical or Surrealistic schools — but thanks to a change in the subjective perspective of the artist. From this is born that very special effect of the «wrongfooting»[4] of objects in the paintings of Gnoli who therefore seems quite removed from Pop art with which he shares an interest in everyday objects. In Gnoli, objects subtly (and ironically) become allusions to an existential condition, to a discordant relationship with reality. In an interview with German radio the artist stated: «When enlarged, everyday objects fill me with fear, disgust and enchantment.»[5] It is also not an accident, as some critics have noted, that many of his objects are hollow, implying a human presence that is, in fact, lacking: «the empty table, the house without inhabitants, the bed without a dreamer, the shoe without a foot, the glove without a hand.»[6] Desk is one of the clearest examples of such structures and gives the idea of a world in which, as in Guido Morselli's Dissipatio H.G., the human race has suddenly disappeared, leaving in the objects the silent traces of the lives that have been lived.

Desk was painted in 1968 for a personal exhibit given at the end of the following year at Sidney Janis's gallery in New York. About forty recent works were shown, dedicated — according to the dealer's wish which Gnoli shared — to the «common object.»[7] The show was a great success, but four months after it closed the artist died in New York of cancer at the age of thirty-seven.
Claudio Zambianchi

1. Y. Vu, «Rome, 3rd of May 1933 — New York, 17th of April 1970. On Letters and Notes of Domenico Gnoli» in Madrid 1990, pp. 28-83.
2. L. Carluccio, Domenico Gnoli, Milan, Fratelli Fabbri Editori, 1974, pp. 11-12.
3. F.V. Grunfeld, «Devà, Cinquanta anys, cinquanta pintors,» El Dia de Baleares, Mallorca, April 25, 1984, p. 19; quoted by M. Quesada, «Bibliografia. Immagini e documenti» in Spoleto, Palazzo Racani-Arroni, Domenico Gnoli, exh. cat., B. Mantura, ed. (under the auspices of the XXVIII Festival dei Due Mondi), June 25-July 14, 1985 [Milan, Electa], p. 31.
4. F. Menna, «Nuova astrazione e nuova oggettività nelle mostre dei pittori Patelli e Gnoli,» Il Mattino, Naples, January 17, 1967; quoted in Quesada 1985, p. 44.
5. P. Sager, Deutschlandfunk, «Das Feuilleton,» radio broadcast, August 1, 1973, quoted in Sgarbi 1983, p. 94.
6. W. Schmied, «Domenico Gnoli» in Hanover, Kestner Gesellschaft, Domenico Gnoli, exh. cat., 1968; quoted in Quesada 1985, p. 54.
7. Letter from Gnoli to Ted Riley (early February 1969); quoted in Vu 1990, p. 72.

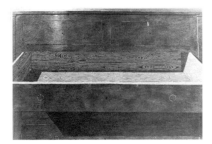

Domenico Gnoli, Open Drawer, 1968

Oil on canvas, 80 x 65 cm.
Signed and dated on bottom right: «Chighine 56».
Provenance: Galleria del Milione, Milan; Molina Collection, Pavia.
Exhibitions: Leverkusen, Städliches Museum Leverkusen, Schloss Morsbroich, Italienische Malerei Heute, 1956, no. 97.
Bibliography: Emilio Tadini, Alfredo Chighine. 12 opere, Milan, Edizioni del Milione, 1958, col. ill. p. 9.
Note: Written on the back of the canvas is «4-1956/ Composizione/Rosa-Blu/Chighine.» Despite this inscription, which should be considered autographal, the title used by Tadini has been preferred to avoid confusion with the Composizione rosa e blu, reproduced in Tadini, p. 11.

The critical questions concerning the interpretation of Alfredo Chighine's art have gone on since the second half of the 1950s, when this work was painted, right up to the present, and have been examined in detail very recently in a well-documented volume by Elisabetta Longari.[1] To what extent Chighine is truly abstract, or to what extent suggestions and stimuli from the natural world persist and are developed in his art, have been, right from the beginning, the central questions raised by the two-sided, or if you will, synthetic, nature of Chighine's images. As the painter himself declared in 1971: «I am not abstract. My paintings are certainly not figurative or realistic. They always have a reference. The reference is a pretext, an opportunity. Like bottles for Morandi.»[2] With this pertinent reference to Morandi, Chighine declares himself to be beyond the contrast between abstract and figurative, making the connection between himself and an artist who undoubtedly had great influence on his painting, Nicolas De Staël.[3]

Composizione blu e rosa belongs to a period of his output during the 1950s in which the compositional organization is particularly evident and makes explicit that «weight,» that «gravitation,» that «immanent sense of things in nature» which Tassi and other interpreters have related to Romanesque culture. In this context it should not be forgotten that Chighine's beginnings were in fact in sculp-

71
Alfredo Chighine. 1914-1974
Rocce di Positano 4
1959

72
Tancredi (Parmeggiani). 1927-1964
Senza titolo
1958

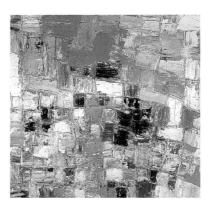

ture. With respect to other episodes in the Italian Informal movement, within which Chighine should be placed, Marco Valsecchi noted how the artist's paintings evaded «a collapse of structural values.»[4] Yet it is not an arrangement that emerges later, a cold reorganization of the memory of a natural event. The proof of this lies in the subtle luminosity of this composition, seemingly belying the depth of the chromatic material,[5] that is, the darting strokes etched in the paint, enlivening the composition with an organic rhythm showing traces of Wols.

Emilio Tadini, who in 1958 published the first small monograph dedicated to Chighine (which included a reproduction of the *Composizione Blu e Rosa*), captures this sense of animation well, saying: «Chighine wants to portray intimate movement, the continuous, unfailing coming into being, existence and immediate decay and re-birth, not of a landscape but of a natural organism. [...] It is no longer a question of reproducing the fixed, definitive culmination of a certain light or certain colors, but rather their 'coming into being'. To catch a color, a light, *in action*.»[6]
Claudio Zambianchi

1. E. Longari, *Alfredo Chighine 1914-1974*, Tenero, Galleria Matasci, 1991.
2. Quoted in Longari 1991, p. 325.
3. M. De Stasio in Milan, Galleria Bergamini Diarte, *Alfredo Chighine. Opere dal 1954 al 1974*, exh. cat., May 24-July 30, 1988.
4. M. Valsecchi in Milan, Galleria delle Ore, *Alfredo Chighine 1966-1967*, exh. cat., December 2-24, 1967.
5. See R. Tassi, «Introduzione all'opera di Chighine» in Milan, Palazzo della Permanente, *Alfredo Chighine*, exh. cat., December 1977-January 1978.
6. Tadini 1958, p. 14.

Oil on canvas, 65 x 81 cm.
Signed and dated on bottom right: «Chighine 59».
Provenance: Galleria del Milione, Milan.

In 1959 Chighine, along with his second wife, Ester Violante, went to Positano, guests of his collector-friend, Carlo Frua De Angeli. This visit inspired a group of paintings which this one belongs to. It is a moment in which that «instinctive need for rational control» that Franco Russoli referred to in introducing Chighine's paintings at the 30th Venice Biennale, is particularly evident.[1] The compositional framework is here structured upon a vertical rhythm of colored forms. Overlaid onto these is a grid of strokes that seems to want to define a «close-up» on the painting's surface in order to give a sense of vibration and depth to the entire work. In a painting such as this, there is a balance between a monumental tendency and a lyric sensitivity. The monumental sense is obtained through the progression of brush strokes extending upwards until they occupy the entire surface of the painting.[2] The lyricism emerges in the fairly complex texture of color that retains a reference to the natural spectacle in a completely internalized key. Chighine's pictorial attitude does not tend first off to express, but rather to delve into, emotion. It is this meditative aspect Luigi Carluccio highlights when speaking of Chighine as an artist who reigns in the hemisphere opposite the one Morlotti dominates, «the other side of the moon, silent and still, because it is immersed in shade: the face in which melancholy does not erupt, nor does it subside [...] or flare up and nature is not living matter to attack in order to have it speak, but rather a still, soft, velvety expanse that it is possible to slip into as into a grave made of water, earth or grass.»[3]
Claudio Zambianchi

1. F. Russoli, «Alfredo Chighine» in Venice, 29th International Biennale of Art, 1960, p. 93.
2. E. Longari, *Alfredo Chighine 1914-1974*, Tenero, Galleria Matasci, 1991, p. 87.
3. L. Carluccio in Acqui Terme, Palazzo «Liceo Sarracco,» *Alfredo Chighine*, exh. cat., Sept. 11-28, 1975.

Oil on canvas, 90 x 90 cm.
Bibliography: G. Cavazzini, I. Consigli, R. Tassi eds., *Pittura e scultura del XX secolo 1910-1980*, Parma, Banca Emiliana Parma, 1982, p. 154.
Note: On the back is painted a Venetian landscape with falling snow. The bottom edge of the canvas bears the inscription in ink: «Questo quadro da me [sic] dipinto a Ve. in S. Stae 1882A nello studio dell'opera Bevilacqua la Masa è dipinto sul retro da (?) Tancredi nel (?) 1958. Alla fine./ In fede, Davide Orler».

«I believe that painting has just been born, that today the material-color is newer than ever and that it has immense possibilities for revealing its very nature, infinitely malleable and marvelous.» So wrote Tancredi in 1959 in the introductory remarks to a personal exhibition held at the Galleria dell'Ariete in Milan that brought together a group of works with Venice as their subject. «I believe it is unlikely that I will do other paintings such as these,» the painter also wrote, «because I have left Venice and a work is always born tied to the place in which it was produced.»[1]
This composition was not included in that show, but is part of the same group of Venetian paintings Tancredi did between 1957 and 1958 when he shared a studio in San Stae with painter Davide Orler. As he had previously done with Giorgio Bellavitis, Tancredi made use of the backs of canvasses painted by Orler in order to paint over them.[2] Tancredi's link with the perceptual reality in Venice, infinitely changeable because of the uninterrupted chromatic vibration, is explicit as the painter's statement quoted above reveals, and was emphasized by the critics. For example, Raffaele De Grada holds that Venice «was for Tancredi the most shining reference point in his whole career [...]. Tancredi tested himself against the extreme luminescences of the pictorial fabric that only a few times in contemporary art have been so sensitive to the color changes in the particles in the space so as to absorb *für ewig*, forever (the precedent for this exists in Monet's «cathedrals») the body of light that becomes form itself, independently of the colora-

73
Carlo Guarienti. 1923
*La sera di Anversa: metamorfosi
dell'angelo e del capitano generale*
1975

tion of an object.»[3] This is the way in which the rapport established in the painting between light and material should be read: the painter's perception chooses the luminous aspect of things and translates it into tiles that are quite thick. His painting takes on a greater physical weight, which Pietro Zampetti speaks of in terms of a «new tactile sense.»[4] The way of proceeding by relatively uniform units of material-color — that characterizes works from the same period such as *Omaggio a Debussy*, for example — brings to mind somewhat the Venetian mosaicists.[5] There also exists in this work, as in other contemporaneous ones by Tancredi, an organizing principle of the image based on orthogons.[6] Yet, this organization of the pictorial space by Tancredi does not conflict with his sensitivity regarding natural phenomenon. «Nature,» the painter wrote in an essay in 1956, «can be divided into forms that can be infinitely multiplied; separating them one discovers their geometry.»[7]

Claudio Zambianchi

1. Tancredi in Milan, Galleria dell'Ariete, *Tancredi*, exh. cat., inaug. June 25, 1959.
2. C. Natto, «Tra poetica e vita» in Milan, Padiglione d'Arte Contemporanea, *Tancredi. Il mio vocabolario è l'universo*, C. Natto, ed., exh. cat. (Milan, Mazzotta), September 13-October 18, 1984, pp. 10 and 12.
3. R. De Grada, «Un Don Chisciotte dell'Informale,» *Corriere della Sera* (Culture section), May 21, 1986, p. 16.
4. P. Zampetti in Venice, Ca' Vendramin Calergi, *Tancredi*, exh. cat., October 25, 1981-January 3, 1982.
5. See G. Ballo in Venice 1967; quoted in Janus, «Tancredi» in Ferrara, Palazzo dei Diamanti, *Tancredi*, exh. cat., October 25, 1981-January 3, 1982.
6. T. Toniato, «L'arte come sogno della verità» in Verona, Palazzo Forti, *Tancredi. 92 opere inedite*, G. Cortenova and T. Toniato eds., exh. cat., March 14-May 16, 1987 (Milan, Mazzotta), p. 20 and D. Marangon, «Tancredi: I colori e le forme di una coscienza europea» in Belluno, Palazzo Crepadona, *Tancredi*, P. Cardazzo and G. Frezzato eds., exh. cat., August 20-September 9, 1990 (Feltre, Edizioni Castaldi), pp. 13-14.
7. Tancredi in Venice, Galleria del Cavallino, *Tancredi*, exh. cat., October 27-November 5, 1956.

Mixed technique on panel, 124 x 127 cm.
Signed on bottom right: «Guarienti».
Provenance: Galleria del Naviglio, Milan.
Exhibitions: Milan, Galleria del Naviglio, *Carlo Guarienti*, January 29-February 16, 1976, b/w ill.
Bibliography: P. Waldberg, *Carlo Guerienti. Il presagio del passato*, Roma, Edizioni della Differenza, 1977 (col. ill. p. 65); V. Sgarbi, *Carlo Guarienti*, Milan, Fabbri Editori, 1985, p. 204.

«Though not a museum fan [...] he actually carries an 'imaginary museum' on his shoulders, and it is obvious that, with a sort of savageness tempered by an apparent gracefulness, he has accumulated it in its 'memory' or rather, to use Bergson's phrase, in his *matière*.»[1] This is how Giancarlo Vigorelli defined the complex relationship between history and *matière*, a question of crucial importance in Carlo Guarienti's work. They are words that seem particularly useful in analyzing the group of paintings (which this one belongs to) Guarienti worked on in 1975. In them, the painter depicts himself in the company of characters from Simone Martini. In *La sera di Anversa o la Madonna e io* (preserved in Antwerp are a number of small panels coming from the polyptych of the Passion by Simone, among which is a famous *Annunciation*), the Virgin is in color but the painter has depicted himself in monochrome. The painting exhibited here is a study for the one previously mentioned and the chromatic range is even more restricted. From this standpoint the painting brings to mind, on one hand — in the absence of an explicit spatial plan and in the apparently incongruous joining of images of a varied nature — a page of sketches drawn by an old master, and on the other — in the rapport between the barely visible stroke and the thick and uneven *matière* — the sinopia of a fresco, laid bare by a quirk of fate. It is well known that Guarienti has a very close and complex relationship with the painting of walls (see no. 76). The sketchbook traditionally contains the most private exercises of an artist's soul, his free associations (here, in particular, the bottle of seltzer has a surrealistic quality),[2] the notes jotted down in haste, the encyc-

lopedia of images to draw on from time to time. The sinopia is, on the other hand, the drawing underneath the fresco, the skeleton of the image destined to be covered by plaster so that the figures and space can take on the brightness of the colors. The reference of the coexistence of the sketchbook page and the sinopia, as well as the autobiographical presence of the painter within his own painting, seem to want to topicize a motif which, in various ways, constantly accompanies Guarienti's work, i.e., the idea that his images are placed in a thin area between finite and not-finite,[3] between revelation and fading away.

Claudio Zambianchi

1. G. Vigorelli, «Il corpo e, 'nel corpo' of Guarienti's graphic works» in *Catalogue of Carlo Guarienti's graphic works 1942-1977*, Milan, Edizioni del Naviglio, 1977.
2. Sgarbi 1985, p. 33.
3. Sgarbi 1985, p. 50.

Portrait of Guarienti in front of *La sera di Anversa: metamorfosi dell'angelo e del capitano generale*, 1975

Carlo Guarienti,
*La sera di Anversa o
La Madonna e io*, 1975

74
Carlo Guarienti. 1923
Natura morta
1990

75
Carlo Guarienti. 1923
Natura morta
1991

Mixed technique on plywood, 69 x 82 cm.
Signed on bottom right: «Guarienti».
Provenance: Galleria Contini, Venice-Cortina.
Exhibition: Venice, Galleria d'Arte Contini, *Carlo Guarienti*, May 8-June 21, 1992 (cat. Milan, Giorgio Mondadori & Associati, col. ill. p. 41).

The still life theme is not new in Carlo Guarienti's work, on the contrary, it has been part of his experience right from the beginning, spanning the '40s and '50s, and we owe it to the re-examination of traditional forms which the painter carried out under the influence of the artist who first recognized the caliber of his work, Gregorio Sciltian. The still lifes executed in recent years mark a significant point in Guarienti's development because they are part of a phase, begun in the second half of the 1970s, in which the painter seems to have abandoned the most openly fantastical and monstrous aspects in his paintings in favor of apparently more everyday subjects.[1] Notwithstanding this, the still lifes from these years have not lost their fantastic potential. The objects manifest themselves within complex surfaces, caught, one could say, in the moment they rise up from the deep abysses and materialize in a spatial context that maintains a very transient reference point in relation to visual perception. It is an ambiguous space the critics describe in terms of contradiction: «apparitions beyond reality but completely contained in reality [...] fantastical happenings of perfectly recognizable things,»[2] wrote Maurizio Fagiolo dell'Arco in 1983. «Fantastical space,»[3] and at the same time, as in the best tradition of modern still life from Cézanne to Morandi, a saturated space with no empty areas in which objects and context overlap without interruption. It is an effect obtained thanks to the use of extremely rich and complex *matière* that acts as the unifying element of the painting. In fact, Guarienti is much more involved with the material in his painting than are the Surrealists to whom he has often been compared because of his visionary tone. It is the potential of the material which suggests the images Guarienti develops, thus renewing the experimentation carried out in the

post-war period by artists such as Tapies and Burri.[4]

In looking at this still life in particular, in which the objects are brought to light with an impalpable lightness within a chromatic range based on a delicate, eighteenth century shade of green, Raffaele Carrieri's description on visiting Guarienti's studio comes to mind: «Leaning against a couch was one of his charming painted screens, an autumnal mood with transparent light green and rose hues like those of Watteau. A friable material, Watteau and Guardi mixed together into a single ambience. The screen seemed to be frosted glass through which outlines of figures could be spied.»[5]
Claudio Zambianchi

1. See G. Briganti, *Guarienti. Disegni e acquerelli*, Oggiono, Edizioni della Seggiola, 1984; quoted in V. Sgarbi, *Carlo Guarienti*, Milan, Fabbri Editori, 1985, p. 48.
2. M. Fagiolo dall'Arco, «Trasformare il veduto in visionario» in Prato, Galleria Metastasio, *Carlo Guarienti*, exh. cat.
3. Tassi, «Il tempo non si ferma» in Venice 1992, p. 8.
4. See, for example, Sgarbi 1985, p. 28.
5. R. Carrieri, «Sguardi indiscreti: Guarienti» in idem, *Il grano non muore*, Milan, Mondadori, 1984; quoted in Sgarbi 1985, p. 37.

Mixed technique on plywood, 122.5 x 132.5 cm.
Provenance: Galleria Contini, Venice-Cortina.
Exhibition: Venice, Galleria d'Arte Contini, *Carlo Guarienti*, May 8-June 21, 1992 (cat. Milan, Giorgio Mondadori & Associati; col. ill. p. 33).

The *Natura morta* from 1991 displays a compact composition based on orthogonal intersection with rare diagonal elements — the pitcher handle, the stick inside the box — which repeat themselves rhythmically. At first glance, some elements in the painting could suggest that it be interpreted as Guarienti's homage to the still lifes of the analytical Cubism of Braque and Picasso: the almost monochromatic coloring, the use of pages from a newspaper, the slightly overturned plane on which the surface objects rest and the consequent interpenetration of the planes that is especially evident in the lower right quadrant. And yet the objects are not scattered but overlapped, almost as if their shape was hinted at through thin and transparent veiled layers from which the outline emerges as a fine, luminous filament. It is, therefore, a space quite removed from the solidity of the Cubists and its ambiguous and fantastical dimension seems reaffirmed by the delicate frieze that traces the perimeter of the painting and breaks off in places, a boundary within an apparently homogeneous structure.
Claudio Zambianchi

76
Carlo Guarienti. 1923
Natura morta
1992

77
Carlo Guarienti. 1923
Natura morta (Omaggio a Villa)
1992

78
Leonardo Cremonini. 1925
Les gouvernantes
1990-1991

Mixed technique, 58 x 62 cm.
Signed on bottom right: «Guarienti».
Provenance: Galleria Contini, Venice-Cortina.
Exhibition: Venice, Galleria d'Arte Contini, *Carlo Guarienti*, May 8-June 21, 1992 (cat. Milan, Giorgio Mondadori & Associati; col. ill. p. 50).

In this work, Guarienti's thinking seems to address Metaphysical painting with which he shares an interest in combining disparate objects — the ball, the cube, the solid in which the ace of clubs is drawn — into an incongruous perspective context in which the three-dimensionality of the space is asserted and negated at the same time. For example, the geometrical elements have their own precise construction, but it is not clear where they rest or how deeply they extend. In contrast with the lightness of the spatial arrangement in which things seem to flutter around like ghosts, is the concreteness and materiality of the picture's support, a heavy piece of synthetic material (the imprint of a piece of road surface) glued to a piece of plywood. It is from this aspect that the comparison to layers of plaster on walls and with frescoes derives, a comparison often repeated by the critics when speaking of Guarienti's work. Moreover, Guarienti studied the techniques of «detaching and removing a fresco.»[1] It should be stated, however, that while the frescoed wall, from the 1400's forward, tends not to stand out as a wall thanks to the effect of the trompe l'oeil perspective, Guarienti, on the other hand, rehabilitates it as an extremely uneven material, laden with history and memories from which the light impressions of the objects emerge.
Claudio Zambianchi

1. V. Sgarbi, *Carlo Guarienti*, Milan, Fabbri Editori, 1985, p. 28.

Mixed technique, 62 x 74 cm.
Signed on bottom right: «Guarienti».
Provenance: Galleria Contini, Venice-Cortina.
Exhibition: Venice, Galleria d'Arte Contini, *Carlo Guarienti*, May 8-June 21, 1992 (cat. Milan, Giorgio Mondadori & Associati; col. ill. p. 49).

The «villa» paid homage to here in the writing appearing in the upper part of the painting is Villa Adriana. This is an explicitly «archaeological» reference, a reference which, according to Roberto Tassi, characterizes the group of recent still lifes in general. Guarienti «started to excavate [...]. 'Les feuilles sont nécessaires', Proust wrote. Fantastical painting always means working among excavations, but these by Guarienti seem to be excavations into the bowels of the earth since the objects that emerge are encrusted, dusty, oxidized and corroded. The letters in the writing which sometimes accompany them seem to be reliefs in marble or stone, like those on ancient monuments.»[1] The «archaeological» reference, the sensation of finding oneself before an ancient bas-relief, is reinforced in this painting by its monochromaticism and the use of a corrugated base with a complex weave which the artist achieves by making a cast of a piece of road pavement. A play with negative-positive impressions reflected in the written lines which appear reversed as if seen reflected in a mirror.
Claudio Zambianchi

1. R. Tassi, «Il tempo non si ferma» in Venice 1992, p. 11.

Diptych, oil on canvas, 114 x 221 cm.
Provenance: the artist.
Exhibitions: FIAC 1991, October 5-13, 1991; Galeria Claude Bernard, October-November 1991; Galleria Forni, *30 anni di libere scelte*, May 1992.
Bibligraphy: H. Haddad, *Leonardo Cremonini ou la nostalgie du Minotaure*, July 1991, Galerie Claude Bernard, exh. cat., p. 18; A. Bosquet, «Cremonini: en ce monde, un autre,» *Le quotidien di Paris*, November 14, 1991, ill.

The painting, *Les gouvernantes*, was started, like so many others, without a precise plan of «where,» «what» and «why.» Its original format was that of the left-hand part of approximately 146 cm. up to the juncture with the section on the right. The beginning was almost *materico*, spatial and luminous, quasi-biological, quasi-psychological. The initial tension was made up of a warm light that devoured or sweated an underlying chlorophyllous space, as in my studio in the summer during the month of August. The images took shape slowly as if with the desire to give form and body to those forgotten memories which when they resurface are no longer orgasms or wounds, but only scars. Thus I only have the suspicion, or the hope, that rigor can coincide with the congealing of passion.
Leonardo Cremonini

79
Gianfranco Ferroni. 1927
Interno - quasi sera
1981-1982

Oil on canvas, 60 x 50 cm.
Signed and dated on upper right: «Ferroni 81-82».
Exhibition: Rome, Il Gabbiano, *Gianfranco Ferroni*, inaug. November 16, 1984, no. 6 (b/w ill. in cat.).

In the early 1970s, in Ferroni's output which up until that point had been filled with references to historical-political events of the day and constructed on the dramatic alternation between agitated filled sections and resonant empty ones, there is a profound change which Luigi Carluccio gave a careful and sensitive summary of in 1974: «Clarity of mind has been fully reached: clarity also in the sense of tranquility, which from the soul and intellect is transmitted to its language and to the objects. In fact, the sentimental charge that bore down on Ferroni's work seems to have been pacified [...]. Ferroni has cancelled the agitation and preoccupation which were the visual signs of his existential anxiety [...]. Ferroni has filled the empty spaces, the pauses; he has unified the compositional grid [...] given life to the strip of neutral connective tissue [...]. Faced with his recent works, one would say that Ferroni has sensed that existence is not only a drama in the tracts where it coincides with the course of dramatic events or with the rationale of an edgy sensitivity. [...] Drama is existence itself, complete. [...] Ferroni's pictorial space now presents itself as a continuum realized with extraordinary technical mastery and incredible delicacy of touch using the points of pencils and brushes. A luminous and dazzling continuum.»[1]

This internalization is also found in a change in the world Ferroni now represents, almost invariably, as the interior of his workshop, «deserted rooms, an artist's or sick person's room.»[2] In this way Ferroni succeeds in painting «emptiness.»[3] The objects and the space they are contained in are minutely described through a fabric of dusty marks of uniform size created with the pen nib.[4] This technical posture, in the synthesis that it succeeds in creating between stroke and light, has more than once led Ferroni's work to be linked to that of Vermeer and Seurat, two artists whom Ferroni cites as sources of his inspiration along with Antonello, Van Eyck and Chardin.[5] The motionlessness and compositional balance have a «classical» flavor but are accompanied, nonetheless, by a sense of unsettling non-involvement, almost as if the infinite and microscopic touches had coagulated, thanks to a mysterious aggregating power, into an image that has a strong presence but also, in the final analysis, the incongruous one of an apparition. Giovanni Testori commented on the mood in paintings such as this: «The painter no longer indicates; one could say that it is he himself who is indicated by an obsession with the finite and perfection that have no illusionist function. [...] We are alone, this is the terrible, basic observation.»[6]
Claudio Zambianchi

1. L. Carluccio in Milan, Galleria il Fante di Spade, *Gianfranco Ferroni*, exh. cat., inaug. March 21, 1974.
2. F. Zeri in Rome 1984.
3. S. Grasso, «Sembra strano, ma io dipingo il vuoto» (interview with Ferroni), *Corriere della Sera* (Culture section), December 27, 1987, p. 4.
4. See D. Micacchi, «La luce della solitudine,» *L'Unità*, June 17, 1989, p. 17.
5. Grasso 1987.
6. G. Testori in Bologna, Forni Galleria d'Arte, *Gianfranco Ferroni*, exh. cat., inaug. March 14, 1981.

80
Alberto Gianquinto. 1929
Luce a Venezia: finestra n. 3
1962

Oil on canvas, 116 x 89 cm.
Signed and dated bottom center: «Gianquinto/1962».
Provenance: Galleria La Nuova Pesa, Rome.
Exhibition: Rome, Galleria d'Arte La Nuova Pesa, *Opere recenti. Gianquinto*, Jan. 8-26, 1963, no. 15.

«To venture out after an experience 'd'après nature', placing oneself with the canvas before the window of one's own room during the precise moment of a specific kind of light, is an act of courage. Gianquinto knows that prolonged contact with a natural phenomenon disarms the modern painter, but he also knows that he can depend on the mastery of modern pictorial language he has acquired in composition through doing paintings.»[1] Thus wrote Ballarin concerning some of Gianquinto's «windows.» The subject of the window displays Gianquinto's desire to maintain in his paintings his rapport with external reality and with the objects, but without forgetting that he is an artist of his own day, on the contrary, he is fully conscious of this both formally and politically. The artistic influences Gianquinto holds in consideration are rich and manifold. This painting reveals above all a reference to Matisse that is even evoked in the delicate range of greys and blues, an influence the painter often combines with that of Picasso, two sources Gianquinto succeeds in integrating despite the fact that other artists consider them «incompatible.»[2] But Gianquinto's culture does not exclude other influences. The way in which the forms are saturated by light in this painting could remind one of Morandi, while the smoothness of the brush stroke combined with the arrangement of flattened forms on the surface recalls Bonnard, another name often raised by Gianquinto's critics.[3] Not forgetting the Venetian influences, going back to Tintoretto whom in 1982 Gianquinto declared to be his favorite painter.[4] Such a tight net of references presupposes quite an indirect rapport with reality, but on the other hand leaves vast room to reinterpret it which in Gianquinto inevitably occurs from a lyrical point of view. As Micacchi pointed out in the introduction to the exhibition where this paint-

81
Paolo Vallorz. 1931
Pioppi siamesi d'inverno alle Ghiaie
1985

ing was shown for the first time, in paintings such as this one «the subject is nothing, but instead the lyrical world is of monumental proportions» revealing the «modern and dialectical power to contradict and stimulate reality, and not just the romantic power to enhance it.»[5] In which framework to place the distance from realism that Gianquinto's painting defines is illustrated by the artist himself in one of his rare statements on poetics: «For some time I have thought that oppositional painting has fulfilled its purpose, the cycle is complete: born before Caravaggio with Tintoretto and equally, but in a different way, with Lorenzo Lotto, it has its great epilogue in Picasso's *Guernica*. Having born witness to the world of murderers, the inhumanity of a society, in 1937 the artist fulfilled the last, great, gesture and opened up alternative painting for the first time in centuries, the value of which lies precisely in the fact that it is an appendage to reality and therefore cannot be called realist.»[6]
Claudio Zambianchi

1. A. Ballarin in Venice, Galleria d'Arte Il Traghetto, *Alberto Gianquinto. Pitture, Sculture del 1966*, exh. cat., September 9-October 1, 1966.
2. D. Morosini, «Il 'maggio' di Gianquinto,» *Paese Sera*, December 2, 1972.
3. R. Tassi, «La Sera, la pittura» in Parma, Galleria Mazzocchi, *Alberto Gianquinto. Opere recenti*, exh. cat., April 22-May 31, 1989, p. 7; F. D'Amico, «Alberto Gianquinto» in Bologna, Galleria Forni Tendenze, *Alberto Gianquinto*, exh. cat., December 1989, p. 4.
4. A. Gianquinto in Busto Arsizio, Bambaia Galleria d'Arte, *Alberto Gianquinto. Dipinti e acquarelli 1981-1982*, exh. cat., October 2-31, 1982.
5. D. Micacchi, «La 'maniera nera' di Alberto Gianquinto» in *LPN*, newsletter of the Galleria d'Arte La Nuova Pesa, no. 12, January 8, 1963 (also exh. cat., Rome 1963).
6. A. Gianquinto, «Appunti per un incontro» in Rome, Galleria Il Fante di Spade, *Per un incontro col pubblico. Per un'esperienza nella storia*, exh. cat., June 9-25, 1964, p. 13.

Oil on canvas, 150 x 90 cm.
Provenance: Galleria Bergamini, Milan.
Exhibition: Milan, Galleria Bergamini, January-February 1986, no. 34, col. ill.

I painted this tree which forks and divides forming two «Siamese poplars» in 1985. It is found in the zone called Le Ghiaie on the banks of the River Noce which runs near my town, Caldés, in the Val di Sole. It is not far from a sawmill where I often went as a boy, so I saw it grow. Then, returning to my town, I saw it get old while on its trunk a woodpecker carved out holes for its nest. We are more or less the same age, but it was only in '85 that I decided to paint it at the point that trees had become the protagonists in my paintings following nudes, portraits, still lifes, animals, landscapes and mountains. I painted it in winter with the blue light of the snow. Is this naturalistic painting? The question does not interest me: when I paint nature, whether men or trees, my only intention is to catch what is essential in the world, in my world. I paint a world which mankind has believed in and lived in, in which one reads the history of man, and thus also my history. I only know that the avantgarde is finished after having created the divorce between man and reality as well as the death of the history of art.

For me, the trunks of the trees I paint are characters with which, right from when I was small, I have had human relationships. They have lived the same life I have, I know them, I am certain that they recognize me, they relate to me the story of life and my own story. When I return to my mountains, I go to say good-bye to them all, one by one, I look at them, I observe them, I hug them, I talk to them, they listen to me, I engage them in conversation and I'm sure that they understand me. We are friends, I paint them more than once each year, their friendship reassures me and calms me. Clearly the same thing happens with them as with my friends: often I also get to know other trees. But with the ones in Caldés the human dialogue is stronger.

As I paint my trees, I get to know them in a deeper way, as happens with a face or a nude, I feel a complete sense of communion between me and them, as if I were a tree and they me. In fact I have given them names, just as my friends, as well as human beings and animals, have names. When I finish painting, I sit at their feet and eat my lunch as our conversation continues. Finally, when I leave to go home, I say good-bye. As I depart, inside I feel a sense of nostalgia like when I leave a friend. Sometimes a tree dies during my absence, or is cut down by man, and when this happens I feel a great emptiness as when one loses a friend forever.

Are these feelings naturalistic? Perhaps, given the fact that everything is *nature*: the world, the sky, plants, animals, human beings, still lifes and natural scenes. After all, in painting man expresses his own nature made up of nature and culture. The important thing is that his culture not kill his nature.
Paolo Vallorz

82
Ruggero Savinio. 1934
La Molla di sera
1992

Oil on canvas, 170 x 140 cm.
Provenance: Galleria Netta Vespignani, Rome.
Exhibitions: Rome, Galleria Netta Vespignani, *Ruggero Savinio*, May-June 1992, col. ill. p. 31; Conegliano, *Savinio opere 1959-1992*, Marco Goldin, curator, October 24-December 8, 1992, col. ill. p. 85.

The setting in which the scene represented here takes place — the painter seated on a windowsill with his bride nearby who is gesturing to him, or to the trees and mountain that can be seen outside, or to the evening which covers the landscape with an ashiness — often like Tuscan farmhouses, has a placename. It is called *La Molla* [*The Spring*]. At the beginning I thought the name indicated the device, and it seemed appropriate to that moment in my life, dedicated to impulsiveness, when I went to live in the house and painted this picture. I then found out that it means «wet» for the coolness of a nearby spring and the water that flows down from the mountain. I no longer live in that house, and if I happen to think about it, or to paint it again, the tonality is that of elegy. If I had to dedicate the painting — or better, offer it, because painting and art are definitely an offering — I would dedicate it to a place, to a time in my life and to the people involved in that period and to a time of day, the most propitious to painting because the discord between light and shade is, if not alleviated, at least suspended. With grateful misty reminiscence I would dedicate it to the evening.
Ruggero Savinio

83
Piero Guccioni. 1935
Spiaggia 91
1991

Oil on canvas, 84.5 x 74 cm.
Provenance: Galleria Il Gabbiano, Rome.
Exhibitions: Chicago Fair, May 1991; Paris, FIAC, October 1991.
Bibliography: *Bailey Guccione Rivers*, Paris, 1991, col. ill.

Spiaggia 91 is one of the few (perhaps four) paintings dedicated to this theme in recent years. The beach is that of Sampieri, a village a few kilometers from Scicli on the southeast coast of Sicily. During the summer, banks of seaweed often form along the shore which are both fairly long and deep and made up of various types that offer strong color contrast in an ambiguous relationship with the surrounding space.

It is this relationship between the black, dense and heavy motionlessness of the substance produced by the squatting seaweed on the bottom, lapped by the variegated and light movement of the water, and the vibrant fixedness of the sky that creates, I believe, the primary movement in these paintings. Of these, *Spiaggia 91* is perhaps the most ethereal, the one that comes close to the rapidity of a note (an impression). Seen and painted through these eyes (in addition to the hand), the heart and «a little bit» with the mind but without the weight and assistance of the whole body, it is, probably, a result subject to what D. H. Lawrence would call «volitional ambition.»
Piero Guccione

84
Jean-Pierre Velly. 1943-1990
La disperazione del pittore
1987

Watercolor on Japanese paper glued to paper, 100 x 70 cm.
Signed and dated on bottom right: «J.P. Velly 87»; title on bottom center «Désespoir du peintre II».
Provenance: Galleria Don Chisciotte, Rome.
Exhibition: Rome, Galleria Don Chisciotte, *Jean-Pierre Velly*, 1988, no. 5 (col. ill. in cat.).

Color appeared relatively late in the work of Breton artist Jean-Pierre Velly who drowned in Lake Bracciano in 1990 at the age of forty-seven. In fact, Velly started as an engraver and as such won the «Premier Grand Prix de Rome» for engraving in 1966, the year in which he definitively moved to Italy, at first working at the Villa Medici which at the time was headed by Balthus (one of the artists Velly most admired), and then by himself in Formello, near Rome.

A hint of his engraver's training shines through in works such as this *La disperazione del pittore*, a title which refers to — as Jean Leymarie observed — the name given to a tree, the stone-break, because of the extreme difficulty artists have in rendering it.[1] The tree's branches, arrayed in a semi-circular fashion in the foreground of the painting, are depicted with extremely fine touches which recall the marks of the engraver's tool. But here, the light values are reversed and from black on white, Velly passes to white on black, transforming the stroke into a delicate filament of transparent and imperceptible light. The effect of spatial depth is obtained by vibration, observant, in this sense, of Pollock's linear refinements.

La disperazione del pittore is part of a group of still lifes in which plants and flowers are placed in the foreground (sometimes marked by a windowsill), foreshadowed in the engravings from the early '70s, like *Fleurs* (1971) or *Arbre et coquillage* (1974).[2] In Velly, «flowers are [...] devices for opening on to visionary backgrounds of coruscant or twilight landscapes, or perhaps stormy sunrises,»[3] says Marisa Volpi, and here the background opens up on a natural setting that loses itself in an unattainable depth and stormy skies in which a sun camouflaged by clouds creates a very clear and

85
Jean-Pierre Velly. 1943-1990
Autoritratto
1988

swirling central area, strongly exhibiting the influence of Turner's most «sublime» works. It is the same golden light of Claude, but captured through a Nordic filter. As critics have often noted, for Velly, German and Flemish art were a constant source of inspiration: «I have the North inside me,» Velly told the director of the French Academy in Rome, Jean-Marie Drot. «I am a Breton and naturally I am attracted by its opposite. It is no accident that Poussin and Claude Lorrain came here and stayed.»[4]
Claudio Zambianchi

1. J. Leymarie, written in 1984, quoted in Rome, Galleria Don Chischiotte, *Omaggio a Jean-Pierre Velly*, exh. cat., October 1991.
2. Respectively nos. 69 and 76 from *Jean-Pierre Velly. L'oeuvre grave. 1961-1980*, annotated cat. by D. Bodart, preface by M. Praz, Rome and Milan, Galleria Don Chisciotte Editore, S. Amadeo, V. Scheiwiller, 1980.
3. M. Volpi in Rome, Galleria Don Chisciotte, *Jean-Pierre Velly*, exh. cat., April-May 1986.
4. «Dialogo tra Jean-Marie Drot e Jean-Pierre Velly» in Rome, Galleria Don Chisciotte, *Omaggio a Jean-Pierre Velly*, exh. cat., October 1991.

Oil on canvas mounted on panel, 97 x 70 cm.
Signed and dated on bottom right: «J.P. Velly 88».
Provenance: Galleria Don Chisciotte, Rome.
Exhibitions: Rome, Galleria Don Chisciotte, *Jean-Pierre Velly*, 1988, no. 17 (col. ill. in cat.); Parma, Galleria La Sanseverina, *Jean-Pierre Velly*, October 21-December 10, 1989, no. 14 (col. ill. in cat., p. 11).
Bibliography: R. Tassi and G. Soavi, *Jean-Pierre Velly*, Milan, Elli e Pagani, 1988 (col. pl. facing title page).

The self-portrait theme has an almost obsessive presence in the last phase of Velly's work. It was first taken on in a series of drawings which bear the traces of the expressive and distorting graphic style of his beloved Grünewald, and then in this oil painting. Vittorio Sgarbi has analyzed the self-portraits from a melancholy viewpoint: one can see behind the artist's almost fleshless features a skull, the harbinger of death,[1] a theme Roberto Tassi also alludes to when he speaks of the «dark shadow» that makes up the hair around the painter's face.[2] For Velly, therefore, the self-portrait is a meditation upon time and the end (it is not accidental that in a previous drawing appear a clock and a skull,[3] both symbols of Vanitas). In describing *La disperazione del pittore* (see no. 84), the transformation of the black stroke in the graphic technique into the luminous one in the watercolor was noted. A similar process can be seen here: the detailed description of the face, the ossification (almost) which characterizes it in the drawings, in the oil painting is translated into the use of a vibrant brushstroke, extremely sensitive to reflections of light, a *matière* that expresses all the complexity of the reverberation of the light and, with different media, can recall the receptiveness of the bronze in Giacometti's sculptures. As in Giacometti — whom, in speaking to Jean-Marie Drot, Velly named as being one of the «great creators of the 20th century»[4] — the feeling for the artistic medium is balanced between optical and symbolic values.
Claudio Zambianchi

1. V. Sgarbi, «Velly oltre Velly ovvero la speranza del niente» in Rome, Galleria Don Chisciotte, *Jean-Pierre Velly*, 1988.
2. R. Tassi in Parma 1989, p. 7.
3. *Ibid.*
4. «Dialogo tra Jean-Marie Drot e Jean-Pierre Velly» in Rome, Galleria Don Chisciotte, *Omaggio a Jean-Pierre Velly*, exh. cat., October 1991.

86
Jean-Pierre Velly. 1943-1990
La quercia
1989

87
Jean-Pierre Velly. 1943-1990
L'ora grande
1989

88
Auguste Rodin. 1840-1917
Mouvement de danse A
1910-1911

Watercolor on paper, 68.5 x 98 cm.
Signed and dated on bottom left: «J.P. Velly — Arbre — 89».
Provenance: Galleria Don Chisciotte, Rome; Galleria La Sanseverina, Parma; Private Collection, Parma; Galleria La Sanseverina, Parma.
Exhibition: Parma, Galleria La Sanseverina, *Jean-Pierre Velly*, October 21-December 10, 1989, no. 28 (col. ill. in cat., p. 25).
Bibliography: G. Soavi, «La luce all'ombra della quercia,» *Il Giornale Nuovo*, May 30, 1990 (reprinted in Rome, Galleria Don Chisciotte, *Omaggio a Jean-Pierre Velly*, exh. cat., October 1991).

«The large oak which shone in his most recent exhibition in Parma, belonged to a villa near Sutri. Velly caught the moment in which shadow and light try to hold on despite the fact that the light of day is already setting [...]. Soon a heavy, humid and dripping darkness would appear, an uncultivated abyss.»[1] The choice of a moment on the brink between light and darkness is reflected in the dramatic alternation in the oak's foliage of light green shades with darker, deeper ones of navy blue or almost black. Strange this Italy of Velly — more nocturnal than solar, more imaginary than real — whose nature seems to be interpreted through the filter of centuries of painting. In this case, for example, the twisted trunk of the big tree brings to mind the gnarled plant shapes of Salvator Rosa, an element which appears throughout the «sublime» landscapes of the 1800s. In this Nordic view of Italy, there is an affinity between Velly and the German painters who worked in Rome in the last century. For this oak in particular, in addition to Ruisdael, Courbet and Théodore Rousseau whom Tassi rightly cites,[2] the name of Arnold Böcklin can unquestionably be added.
Claudio Zambianchi

1. Soavi 1990.
2. Tassi in Parma 1989, p. 8.

Oil on canvas, 234 x 148 cm.
Provenance: Galleria Don Chisciotte, Rome; Galleria La Sanseverina, Parma.
Exhibition: Parma, Galleria La Sanseverina, *Jean-Pierre Velly*, October 21-December 10, 1989, no. 37 (col. ill. on cat. cover).

In this large painting, one notes once again an encounter between the Italian landscape and the fantastical vision of the north. This encounter leads one to cite yet again the name of Arnold Böcklin. The reference to Böcklin seems to be located in the merging of the architecture with the deep green of the landscape in the lower part of the painting. As in the Swiss painter's islands of the dead, the branches of the cypresses stand out against a stormy sky. The rays of sunlight that break through the black, rain-filled clouds, illuminate a landscape seen from a bird's-eye view. In the upper part of the painting is seen a reference to a famous painting by Albrecht Altdorfer, *Battle of Alexander*, one of Velly's favorite works, reflections of which had already clearly appeared in the artist's etchings (for example, *Il massacro degli innocenti*).[1]
Claudio Zambianchi

1. No. 76 in *Jean-Pierre Velly. L'oeuvre gravé. 1961-1980*, annot. cat. by D. Bodart, preface by M. Praz, Rome and Milan, Galleria Don Chisciotte Editore, S. Amadeo, V. Scheiwiller, 1980.

Bronze, 68 cm.
Signed, along the left side of the left foot; the stamp «Georges Rudier» also appears.
Exhibitions: Flint (Michigan), Flint Institute of Art, *Auguste Rodin*, 1980; Washington, National Gallery of Art, *Rodin Rediscovered*, 1981-82; Memphis (Tennessee), Dixon Gallery and Gardens, *The Passion of Rodin: Sculpture from the B. Gerald Cantor Collection*, 1988.
Bibliography: Gassier, *Rodin*, Martigny, Fondation Pierre Gianadda, 1984, col. pl. p. 136; Laurent, *Rodin*, Milab, Fabbri Editori, 1988, b/w ill. p. 142; *Rodin and his Contemporaries*, The Iris & B. Gerald Cantor Collection, 1991, col. pl. p. 89, p. 230.

The dance was a subject which Rodin, who in his works always tried to capture life in movement, found particularly congenial. But not movement per se that could also contradict the meaning and substance of the sculpture itself, but that movement which is resolved in complete harmony with others and therefore does not exceed the bounds of the sculpture.
   Unlike Degas who was so attracted to the rigor and poise of classical dance, Rodin was interested in popular dance because of its spontaneity and basic adherence to nature. It is well-known that, an enthusiast of the Can-Can, starting in 1890 he often had dancers from the Moulin Rouge and the Moulin de la Gallette pose for him, the inspiration of many sketches. From their movements which were anti-classical but frenetic and full of life, he wanted to synthesize first in drawings and then in sculpture the complete balance between all their movements, the marvelous harmony in their relationship, their existence so full of life.
   The works preceding the series *Mouvements de dance* which this sculpture belongs to, are found in two works from 1890, *Iris messenger to the gods* and *Flying figure* in which the portrayal of the two figures at the moment in which their feet leave the ground through a masterful rendering of the rapport between flexing and extension of the limbs, heralds the experimentation Rodin would carry on in the *Dancers* to follow.

89
Henry Moore. 1898-1986
Maquette for «Double Oval»
1966

An important point of inspiration for the creation of this series were the performances given in Paris by some dancers who truly revolutionized dance from the standpoint of a great sense of anti-academicism and naturalness of their movements, dancers such as Loïe Fuller, Isadora Duncan and, above all, Nijinsky who made his Paris debut in 1909 and who later, in 1912, Rodin sculpted in a work in which an examination of movement dominates, rendered through the completely-tensed musculature. In addition, observing these dances, he was able to depict an enormous range of gestures that had never been seen and had always been ignored, and he discovered that the power emanating from them was immense.

In the *Mouvements de dance*, all of which can be dated to the period 1910-1911, Rodin depicts the moments of passage from one movement to another, thus conferring an extraordinarily lively and expressive character to the figure, a sense that is accentuated by an arbitrary distortion of the muscles and limbs that are always excessively elongated.

Evident in this sculpture is a great muscular tension that is released from the body in which every part has the anatomy of the whole and which, when taken together, regains its formal equilibrium in the sinuous continuity of its parts. For Rodin, the human body is only a complete whole when a common action engages all its individual parts and all its energy. Having also conferred on this sculpture many points of view, many finished and precise surfaces, the work, which is not very large, seems to visually exceed the limits of its own size. Also note the rendering of the surfaces, so vibrating and quivering, which on one hand reveals the close relationship always present in Rodin between the work and its surroundings, and on the other his great skill as a sculptor.
Simona Pizzetti

Bronze, 24 cm.
Edition of nine copies.
Provenance: Galleria Kahnweiler, Paris.
Exhibition: Florence, Forte Belvedere, *Mostra di Henry Moore*, G. Carandente, curator, May 20-September 30, 1972, no. 144 (b/w ill. in cat. p. 209).
Bibliography: J. Hedgecoe, ed., *Henry Moore*, London, Thomas Nelson, 1968, p. 516 (col. ill. p. 443); A. Bowness, ed., *Henry Moore, Sculpture and Drawings*, vol. 4: *Sculpture 1964-73*, London, Lund Humphries. Zwemmer, 1977, pp. 11 and 47, no. 558 (b/w ill. p. 46).

«The human figure is what interests me most, but I have discovered principles of form and rhythm through the study of natural objects such as stones, rocks, bone, trees and plants.»[1] The inspiration for *Double Oval* derives from the shape of a bone, duplicated.[2] «The two ovals,» Moore says, «look the same, but they are not. Instead, they are echoes of each other.»[3] This small sculpture in bronze is the starting idea for a piece which was later made larger: there exist a version in marble, 97 cm. wide, and a colossal one in bronze of approximately five and a half meters.[4] Making variations of a sculpture in three such different formats is something that was not unusual in the late works of Henry Moore, as if the object were seen «hand-size, body-size and monument-size.»[5] This is the indication of a change in Moore's creative process. While previously the sculptor started from sketches which he elaborated successively in the three dimensions of the plastic version, beginning at the end of the 1950s his starting point was invariably a small-scale sculpture.[6] Despite the fact that the material chosen for this *bozzetto* (and for the monumental-scale realization of the work) is bronze, Alan Bowness has pointed out how Moore's approach to sculpture is not that of someone who molds «in his hands [...] soft material until a form emerges.»[7] This is particularly evident here in which the formal determining and generating element of the sculpture is the empty space in the innermost nucleus. «The accentuation of empty spaces [...] [takes on] for Moore an importance never seen in the work of any artist before him.»[8] In *Double Oval*, beginning from the central void, the form takes shape little by little, giving the idea of «expansion.» Moore «constructs from the inside, foments the still-imaginary cavity around which the whole of the masses and the tensions put together will grow.»[9] In this, Moore «proceeds as nature does.»[10]
Claudio Zambianchi

1. J. Lassaigne, «Le génie de Henry Moore» in *Hommage à Henry Moore, XXe Siècle*, special number, 1972, p. 3.
2. Bowness 1977, p. 11.
3. Moore in Hedgecoe 1968, p. 516.
4. Bowness 1977, respectively nos. 559 and 560, p. 47.
5. *Ibid.*
6. *Ibid.*
7. *Ibid.*, p. 12.
8. Lassaigne 1972, p. 4.
9. P. Volboudt, «Nature et culture: deux grandes sources» in *Hommage à Henry Moore*, p. 17.
10. *Ibid.*

90
Fausto Melotti. 1901-1986
Tema II con sette variazioni
1969

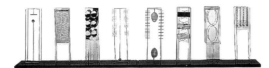

Gold, 30 cm.
Edition of 5 copies (out of 9 planned).
Signed and dated on the little ring at the base of each element: «Melotti 3/9».
Note: This sculpture was realized in three formats: a small one (as the one here); a medium-sized one, 80 cm. high in brass [shown in Turin, Galleria Galatea, *Melotti*, March 2-29, 1971, no. 9 (cat. ill.); Dortmund, Museum am Ostwall, *Fausto Melotti*, October 31-December 19, 1971, no. 43 (cat. b/w ill. p. 28, right half only)], and a large version, 600 cm. high (Giuliano Gori Collection, San Tomato, Pistoia) which was realized in stainless steel in 1981 [shown in Florence, Forte di Belvedere, *Melotti*, April-June 1981 (cat. Florence, Electa, b/w ill. of the model, p. 108) and reproduced in Bollate, Festival di Villa Arconati, *Fausto Melotti, Sequenze d'amore*, G. Celant, ed., exh. cat., June 26-July 28, 1991 (cat. Milan, Mondadori Arte, b/w ill. p. 16 and pl. 48, col. pl. 47 – not shown)].
Bibliography: G. Celant, «La quiete in movimento: le grandi sculture di Fausto Melotti» in Bollate 1991, p. 17. The smaller version exists in a brass version exhibited in Turin, Galleria Civica d'Arte Moderna, *Melotti*, May 26-July 23, 1972, no. 51 (cat. b/w pls. 40-41), bibl. *ibid.*, p. 28); Milan, Palazzo Reale, *Melotti*, May-June 1979, no. 97, a) and b) (cat. Electa, b/w ill., p. 92). There is also this version in gold of which only five copies out of the nine originally planned were made. The work is reproduced in b/w in F. Melotti, *Lo spazio inquieto*, P. Fossati ed., with 48 photographs by U. Mulas, Turin, Einaudi, 1971, pl. 45 and in A. M. Hammacher, *Melotti*, Electa Editrice, 1975, no. 152 (see also no. 152, p. 218).

Melotti's sculptures appear to the observer with unusual features: thin, delicate, light, they move «in a dimension unusual in sculpture: fragility.»[1] They place themselves in an area which grazes that of drawing: «with metal I can draw in space,» Melotti told Giorgio Zampa,[2] and they have a deep affinity with music, a fact the artist never tired of repeating. Music is both fantasy and strict control: «My sculpture is decidedly contrapuntal. It is derived from rules and is not abandoned to every whim which flutters by, or better, this fluttering is connected to geometrical rules.»[3] He returned to this point in a letter to his cousin Carlo Belli (the author of *Kn* and the prophet of the Italian abstract movement during the '30s): «In the musical world, those who come from a chamber music environment have proven that they at least know their trade, and those who ignore this do not have the opportunity of presenting their compositions on concert programs. Exactly because of the affinity between the rules which govern the arts and for the great aid they can lend, above all the basic ones in music, I would like that they form the beginning of the awareness of art. The theories, sterile as they are in themselves, cannot be ignored.»[4] Music, therefore, is a cogent example of the structuring of the imagination: «Music reproached me slowly, disciplining with its rules, distractions and digressions, in a balanced discourse. And so, even while depicting an elementary melodic situation in some of my works, in others I tried to give greater weight to the contrapuntal scansion, making use of canons, imitation and variation which must always appear in exact number and should not be confused, through critical dazzle, with infinite kaleidoscopic possibilities.»[5] Therefore, music is not used by virtue of a vague affinity with non-figurative art, the relationship between the plastic arts and music had been repeatedly affirmed, especially by the leading figures of the avantgarde. But in Melotti this theme is taken on in a new and quite a bit more specific way: «The strength of Melotti's work lies in the concrete way he has of transferring the rhythm of time to space. Not a romantic suggestion of rhythm, but a controlled calculation and a true evaluation of the meaning of the intervals, the empty spaces, the silences: spatial rests.»[6] It is in this «complex metamorphosis that takes place between time and space,» the «transfer» of an art located in time to one located in space, that the radical innovation of «Melottian space» lies. In this world of intangible structures there is no room for «material heaviness.»[8] «Stupid love of the material,» as Melotti says. «Art is not born molded or forged or compressed vacuum-sealed, as Minerva was born from the brain. Many acclaimed works of art are born from a craftsmanlike idea, completely predictable. An insurmountable wall, the wall of poetry, bars the fortress of art. Inside, ideas walk about naked.»[9] This is where the translation into gold of some of his sculpture done in less-precious metals comes from: «It is the transformation of the lowly fragments into sublime material. Gold is the offspring of nature's desires, the perfection of base metals.»[10]
Claudio Zambianchi

1. B. Mantura, «Per Fausto Melotti» in Rome, Galleria Nazionale d'Arte Moderna, *Melotti*, exh. cat., April 28-June 30, 1983, p. 11.
2. G. Zampa, «Nobiltà e indegnità della materia,» *La Stampa*, July 6, 1974; quoted in Mantura 1983, p. 11.
3. Quoted by Z. Birolli in Turin 1972, p. 16.
4. Melotti to C. Belli, ca. 1971, quoted by G. Appella, «Fausto Melotti. Vita, opere, fortuna critica» in Matera, Chiese rupestri Madonna della Virtù and San Nicola dei Greci, Palazzo Lanfranchi, *Fausto Melotti 1901-1986*, exh. cat., June 6-September 15, 1987 (Milan/Rome, Mondadori/De Luca), p. 179.
5. Melotti, acceptance speech at the awarding of the Rembrandt Prize, February 20, 1974, quoted in Appella 1987, p. 181.
6. Hammacher 1975, p. 22.
7. *Ibid.*, p 15.
8. G. Dorfles in Dortmund 1971, p. 6.
9. F. Melotti, *Linee*, Milan, Adelphi, 1981, p. 46.
10. Mantura 1983, p. 11.

91
Marino Marini. 1901-1980
Cavaliere
1945

Polychrome bronze, 103 cm.
Edition of three copies.
Initials «MM» and stamp «Sello Fonderia d'Arte M.A.F.» on the base.
Exhibitions: Münich, Haus der Kunst, *Marino Marini. Skulpturen Zeichnungen*, March 21-May 4, 1952, no. 11 (b/w ill. p. 13 in cat.); Venice, Centro di Cultura di Palazzo Grassi, *Marino Marini. Sculture, Pitture, Disegni dal 1914 al 1977*, May 28-August 15, 1983, p. 55 (cat. Florence, Sansoni Editore Nuova S.p.A.; b/w ill. p. 118); Bologna, Galleria Forni-Scultura, *Marino Marini. Opere dal 1929 al 1960*, October 1990 (col. ill. on cover and p. 21 in cat.).
Bibliography: L. Vitali, *Marini*, Florence, Edizioni U, 1946, b/w ill. of plaster model, pls. 41-42; U. Apollonio, *Marino Marini Scultore*, 3rd rev. ed., Milan, Edizioni del Milione, 1958, p. 38, b/w ill. of plaster model, pl. 69; H. Lederer ed., *Marino Marini*, introd. by E. Trier, Milan, Garzanti, 1961, b/w pls. 18-19; A.M. Hammacher, *Marino Marini. Sculpture, Painting, Drawing*, London, Thames and Hudson, 1970, b/w ill. pp. 97-98; H. Read, P. Waldberg and G. di San Lazzaro, *Marino Marini. L'opera completa*, Milan, Silvana Editoriale d'Arte, 1970, p. 353, no. 209, b/w ill. p. 193; C. Pirovano, *Marino Marini Scultore*, Milan, Electa, no. 212, b/w ill.

«The image of the Rider first appears in Marini's work in 1936/37 [...]. The Rider becomes the parable of his life experience. In 1945, when the war was drawing to a close, Marini saw true-life horsemen! They were the farmers who fled the fires of war on their miserable horses and rose up on their mounts with gestures of desperation but also of new-born hope. The power of this experience transforms the humanistic theme into an image of destiny of great symbolic power — a synthetic, ancient image of man who flees in the face of misery or gloriously asserts himself.»[1]

Summed up in these words of Werner Haftmann are many of the concepts on which critics have based their interpretations of Marino Marini's Riders. First of all, the declaredly anti-heroic treatment of the theme, present right from the beginning, but which gradually became accentuated. (Marino himself declared, «I try to symbolize the final phase of the dissolution of a myth, the myth of the great heroic and victorious figure, the virtuous man of the Humanists.»)[2] In addition, there is the autobiographical value of the Riders which, more than other subjects favored by Marino, embody much more openly the personal sense of the sculptor's life, to the point of being interpreted as a sort of «commedia in the Dantesque sense of the word,» like a «moral self-portrait, that painful and cruel personification, a shining example, historically motivated, point by point.»[3] Therefore, the four riders exhibited also give an idea of Marino's spiritual and artistic evolution, beginning with the slow and calm rhythms of this *Cavaliere* from 1945 and reaching the broken and agitated ones of the 1955 piece. Another aspect mentioned by Haftmann is that of archaism, here particularly evident in the simplification of the forms and the severe compositional structure. Again here, Marino is explicit in his preferences: «I like to go to the source of things; I like a civilization that is beginning; I have always searched for the part that is the nutshell of a civilization, the Etruscans, for example [...]. Of all Greek art, the ancient interests me most.»[4]

Another possible interpretation of Marino's riders is that put forward by Herbert Read who interprets the theme from a psychological standpoint. The rider represents «the man who dominates and guides his own instincts,» the horse «the animalistic side of man and, more specifically, his erotic instincts.»[5] While in this *Cavaliere* these instincts are fully under control, in others, Eros seems to emerge and the horse takes on decidedly phallic connotations[6] (i.e., the rider is depicted in a moment of sexual excitement, as in the famous *Angelo della città* (1949) in bronze from the Peggy Guggenheim Collection in Venice). This creates a context for the famous statement by Cesare Brandi, according to which at the base of Marino's sculpture there is «always» «a formal problem.» «But,» Brandi adds, «this is not adequate to explain it.»[7]

In this case, the «formal problem» is of an essentially architectural nature. Marino works with a stable static form in which any hint of movement has disappeared except the figure's slow turning. For Marino, the period around 1945 was one of rebirth: this *Cavaliere* renews the connection with its predecessors from the 1930s — for example, the *Gentiluomo a Cavallo* (1937) or the *Pellegrino* (1939) — but with a «Classical» variation. Lamberto Vitali wrote in 1946: «The new *Pomona*, the *Giuditta*, the new *Cavalli*, also give us the Marini we knew, and gives us him once again with a certain pomposity and vaguely museum-like scent.»[8] This «Neo-Classical» moment was linked by Alberto Busignani to the end of the war and a brief return of trust on the part of the sculptor.[9] Despite the fact that the primary interest in this work is turned towards the structural aspects of the sculpture, Marino also shows himself to be aware of its chromatic aspect, not just in the chill which runs through certain pieces in the treatment of the surfaces, but also in the explicit intervention of color which was already present in the plaster done by Vitali. It is not a casual or passing use: «That Marino also loved the pictorial factor will remain [...] eternally demonstrated by the works produced in painting right from his first search for an expressive solution, and he continues to refer to this experience not only by still doing today some colored sheets and paintings, but by enriching the plastic subject itself with some chromatic facets.»[10]
Claudio Zambianchi

1. W. Haftmann, «Tragédie de la forme,» *Hommage à Marino Marini, XXe siècle*, special issue, 1974, p. 79.
2. Quoted in W. Haftmann, «Sul contenuto mitico nell'opera di Marino Marini» in Florence, Museo di San Pancrazio, *Marino Marini*, Milan, Electa, 1988, p. 30.
3. Pirovano, p. 84.
4. *Marino Marini*, intro. by L. Papi, Livorno, Graphis Arte, 1979, pp. 17-19; quoted in Mario de Micheli, «Una scultura tra natura e storia» in Venice 1983, p. 16, fn. 3.
5. H. Read, «Introduction» in Read, Waldberg and San Lazzaro 1970, p. 11.
6. P. Waldberg, «Marino Marini» in Read, Waldberg and San Lazzaro 1970, p. 187.

92
Marino Marini. 1901-1980
Cavaliere
1951

7. C. Brandi, «Dal 'Periplo della scultura moderna': Marino Marini,» *L'Immagine*, 2/16, 1951, p. 541.
8. Vitali 1946, p. 28.
9. A. Busignani, «Marino Marini,» *I maestri del Novecento*, I, Florence, Sadea Sansoni, 1968.
10. Apollonio 1958, p. 6.

Bronze, 57.1 cm.
Initialled on the base: «MM».
Edition of six copies.
Exhibitions: Rome, Palazzo Venezia, *Mostra di Marino Marini*, March 10-April 10, 1966, no. 52 (cat., Rome-Milan, De Luca-Toninelli; b/w ill. no. 30); Bologna, Galleria Forni-Scultura, *Marino Marini. Opere dal 1929 al 1960*, October 1990 (col. ill. p. 39 in cat.).
Bibliography: U. Apollonio, *Marino Marini Scultore*, 3rd rev. ed., Milan, Edizioni del Milione, 1958, p. 40, b/w pl. no. 98; «Hommage à Marino Marini,» *XXe siècle*, special issue, 1974, p. 35; A. M. Hammacher, *Marino Marini: Sculpture, Painting, Drawing*, London, Thames and Hudson, 1970, b/w ill. p. 168; H. Read, P. Waldberg and G. di San Lazzaro, *Marino Marini: L'opera completa*, Milan, Silvana Editoriale d'Arte, 1970, p. 365, no. 281, b/w ill. p. 365; C. Pirovano, *Marino Marini Scultore*, Milan, Electa, no. 287, b/w ill.

Marino's trust in history and man's ability to control the world, provoked by the end of the 1945 war, is once again expressed in the two versions of the *Angelo della citta* in which the rider, with his arms spread open and phallus erect, bears witness to his own «energy» and «fecundity,»[1] his dominion over reality. Nonetheless, this «orgastic, almost blasphemous, erotic affirmation, is unambiguously transfixed in a painful expression. Immediately after, in any case, the man-horse configuration, that harmonic interrelationship of stability and dynamic power, would fall forever.»[2] In this *Cavaliere* the beginnings of the impending, lacerating break can be seen: the outstretched arms are «sucked up by the void, [...] reduced to stumps, to the shapeless, monstrous appendages of a fantastical batrachian.»[3] The legs suffer the same fate and the face assumes a pained expression, while the horse, out of control, raises its neck and head with a sense of disturbing vitality. «My statues of riders,» Marino has stated, «are symbols of my preoccupation observing the age I live in. Little by little my horses become increasingly restless and their riders increasingly incapable of dominating them. The catastrophe to which man and animal succumb is equivalent to that which destroyed Pompeii and Sodom.»[4] In other words, «history seems to repeat itself in a troubled manner,»[5] and this sense of tragedy would lead, a few years later, to the images of the horse which falls, dragging its rider along.
Thus this sculpture already contains the germ of pessimism that would become increasingly prominent. And yet, despite the rider's mutilated shape and expression, it makes up a balanced form with the pyramid-shaped trunk. It is the warning light of that philosophical distance from the subject that allows Marino to «recount with clear determination a destiny viewed with an increasingly removed and tragic coldness.»[6]
Claudio Zambianchi

1. M. de Micheli, «Una scultura tra natura e storia» in Venice, Centro di Cultura di Palazzo Grassi, *Marino Marini: Sculture, Pitture, Disegni dal 1914 al 1977*, exh. cat., May 28-August 15, 1983 (Florence, Sansoni Editore Nuova S.p.A.), p. 18.
2. C. Pirovano, *Marino Marini Scultore*, Milan, Electa, p. 11.
3. E. Carli, *Marino Marini*, Milan, Hoepli, 1950; quoted in Pirovano, p. 103.
4. E. Steingräber, «Una grande natura d'artista,» Venice 1983, p. 30.
5. De Micheli, p. 19.
6. C. Pirovano, «Il tema del cavaliere e la poetica mariniana» in *idem*, *Il museo Marino Marini a Firence*, Milan, Electa, 1990; reprinted in the cat., Bologna 1990, p. 5.

Bronze, 115 x 95 x 65 cm.
Edition of five copies.
Exhibitions: Bologna, Galleria Forni, *Maestri contemporanei italiani e stranieri*, February 23-March 16, 1991 (col. ill. in cat. p. 31); Bologna, Galleria Forni-Scultura, *Marino Marini: Opere dal 1929 al 1960*, October 1990 (col. ill. p. 37 in cat.).
Bibliography: U. Apollonio, *Marino Marini Scultore*, 3rd rev. ed., Milan, Edizioni del Milione, 1958, p. 40, b/w ill. of plaster model, plates 99 and 101; «Hommage à Marino Marini,» *XXe siècle*, special issue, 1974, pp. 28 and 62; A. M. Hammacher, *Marino Marini: Sculpture, Painting, Drawing*, London, Thames and Hudson, 1970, b/w ill. of plaster model p. 170; H. Read, P. Waldberg and G. di San Lazzaro, *Marino Marini: L'opera completa*, Milan, Silvana Editoriale d'Arte, 1970, p. 366, no. 287, b/w ill. complete work p. 206 and detail p. 207; C. Pirovano, *Marino Marini Scultore*, Milan, Electa, no. 293, b/w ill.; *Marino Marini*, London, Zwemmer Ltd., 1978, pls. 149 and 150.

«Observing my equestrian statues from these last twelve years one right after the other, one notes that each time the rider is incapable of dominating the horse and that the beast, increasingly wild, becomes more rigid instead of rearing up. I truly believe that we are approaching the end of the world.»[1] This is the way Marino has described the evolution of his riders. In this one, from 1951, the impotence in controlling the animal seems to depend on some unexpected event that surprises the rider along the way. It is not the horse, but the man who rears up and becomes stiff in a backwards-tending diagonal movement, caught, one could say, a second before he falls. The movement of the stunted arms brings to mind shock and an attempt at self-protection. It is a gesture lying somewhere between ecstasy and terror, between Saul's revelation on the road to Damascus and the outspread arms of the victims in *Guernica*, a work which in the early '50s took on increasing importance for Marino.[2] As for the «formal problem» taken on in this statue, one notes in the clear-cut grafting of the diagonal block of the rider onto the

Marino Marini in his studio
while working on *Cavaliere*, 1951

solid structure of the horse, a dialectical rapport between static form and movement, «opening up» the composition. «Each figure,» according to Marino, «has its own space; it is said that for all of them it must be a kind of cage or the infinite.»[3] And it is exactly this theme of movement caught at its peak, of the rider about to be thrown, that would characterize Marino in the years to follow.
Claudio Zambianchi

1. M. Marini, quoted by P. Waldberg, «Marino Marini» in Read, Waldberg and San Lazzaro 1970, p. 187.
2. M. de Micheli, «Una scultura tra natura e storia» in Venice, Centro di Cultura di Palazzo Grassi, *Marino Marini: Sculture, Pitture, Disegni dal 1914 al 1977*, exh. cat., May 28-August 15, 1983 (Florence, Sansoni Editore Nuova S.p.A.) p. 19.
3. Quoted by G. Carandente in Rome, Palazzo Venezia, *Mostra di Marino Marini*, exh. cat., March 10-April 10, 1966 (Rome-Milan, De Luca-Toninelli), p. 19.

Bronze, 59 x 39 x 32 cm.
Edition of six copies, plus two unnumbered.
Exhibition: Bologna, Galleria Forni-Scultura, *Marino Marini: Opere dal 1929 al 1960*, October 1990 (col. ill. p. 35 in cat.).
Bibliography: H. Read, P. Waldberg and G. di San Lazzaro, *Marino Marini: L'opera completa*, Milan, Silvana Editoriale d'Arte, 1970, p. 372, no. 336, b/w ill.p. 373; C. Pirovano, *Marino Marini Scultore*, Milan, Electa, no. 342, b/w ill. no. 342 and p. 120, pl. 130; Florence, Museo di San Pancrazio, *Marino Marini*, Milan, Electa, 1988, p. 229, no. S69, b/w ill. p. 171, pl. 160; *Marino Marini: Impressioni di Lorenzo Pagi*, Priuli e Verlucca Editori.

Along with a version with slight variations,[1] this work constitutes the starting point for a large monument realized three years later in a square at The Hague which Eduard Trier has defined a «powerful synthesis of Abstract Constructivism and Figurative Expressionism.»[2] The equilibrium between horse and rider which had been progressing towards a crisis point, has now been definitively broken and the rider is caught in the moment in which, having been thrown, he is about to collapse onto the ground. In this sculpture, the influence of Picasso's *Guernica* «establishes a stylistic change [...]. The open fissures in the bronze, the shapes increasingly more markedly angular, the greater syntheticism and the determination to bring out more the architectural lines of the structure are not [...] examples of architectural merit per se, but rather deeply rooted within the meaning of the image which must give the impression of life reduced to a skeleton, to rock, to a mineral structure, to a boulder shattered by lightning, to a solitary fossil.»[3]
From this is born a new awareness of the treatment of the bronze surfaces that are rich with imperfections to catch and hold the greatest amount of light. It is as if alongside an impulse towards the geometrical formalization of the figure there was a correspondingly intense demand to render the epidermis of the sculpture as vibrant as possible. This aspect hearkens back directly to

95
Giacomo Manzù. 1908-1991
Filemone e Bauci
1932-1933

Marino's painting activity. In 1944, Gianfranco Contini went so far as to interpret Marino completely from this standpoint: «he is a poet of surfaces [...] for him, everything else is unessential.»[4] Contini's judgment appears too limiting, but Marino himself declared that, alongside the construction, he also took into maximum consideration the fabric of his sculptures: «The form, the structure, the architecture of my works are enlivened by a fanciful surface [...]. If the surface does not vibrate, the idea remains cold.»[5]
Claudio Zambianchi

1. See, for example, Pirovano, pp. 131-132, plates 120-121.
2. E. Trier, «Introduction» to H. Lederer, ed., *Marino Marini*, Milan, Garzanti, 1961, p. xx.
3. M. de Micheli, «Una scultura tra natura e storia» in Venice, Centro di Cultura di Palazzo Grassi, *Marino Marini: Sculture, Pitture, Disegni dal 1914 al 1977*, exh. cat., May 28-August 15, 1983 (Florence, Sansoni Editore Nuova S.p.A.), p. 19.
4. G. Contini, «Per Marino Marini,» quoted in L. Vitali, *Marini*, Florence, Edizioni U, 1946, p. 28.
5. Quoted in de Micheli 1983, p. 21.

Marino Marini,
Composizione: Monumento, The Hague,
1957-1958

Ceramic grès, 160 cm.
Exhibitions: Milan, *Quinta Triennale*, 1933; Milan, Palazzo Reale, *Manzù*, 1988-1989.
Bibliography: *Catalogo Quinta Triennale di Milano*, 1933, p. 463; *Manzù*, Milan, Electa, 1988, p. 73, b/w plates 35 and 36; L. Velani, *Giacomo Manzù*, Milan, Electa, b/w pl. p. 211.

Beginning at the end of the 1920s, in the Milanese environment that Manzù was a part of, an artistic movement was created which set itself up in opposition to 19th century tendencies, but without calling into question a return to figurative art. The point of reference for this movement was the art critic Persico who, in opposition to the celebratory monumentalism of the 20th century that had taken on fascist overtones, repeated the validity of returning to the old style which would stylistically manifest itself in an intellectual primitivism and simplified archaic forms, but not dissociated from the genuinely popular ideals of immediacy and communicativeness. Working within this setting were artists such as Sassu, Birolli, Grosso, Tomea, Oppi and Manzù himself who expressed exactly this sense of cultural ferment in works such as his *San Giovannino* from 1931, and these here, in which the result of his examination into the sculpture of the 15th century masters is evident.

These two sculptures were commissioned by the architect Muzio to place alongside the portal outside the Palazzo dell'Arte he had designed and which was built between 1931 and 1933. Again for Muzio, Manzù decorated, between 1931 and 1932, the chapel of the Università Cattolica in Milan with figures of Saints in high relief and with a statue in colored cement depicting the *Madonna with Child*.

Manzù sculpted the two figures in Mozzate at the workshop in which Piccinelli was experimenting with the use of klinker, also for the Palazzo dell'Arte. They represent Philemon and his bride, Baucis, the farmers who, in their barn, put up Zeus and Hermes, dressed as travelers, in their trip across Phrygia. The other villagers were not as hospitable to the two pilgrims, and so Philemon and Baucis were the only ones to survive the ter-rible flood sent by the gods. At the end of their lives they were transformed into two trees that rose up in front of their cottage which had become a temple. Manzù portrays them younger, at the height of the flood: they rise up isolated and mute with pain over the other human beings who are small and without hope. The elongated form, a purposely static sense, the birds and the other animals depicted as they search for refuge near them, foreshadow their transformation into vegetable life. Manzù synthesizes the various episodes of the story into a unified and symbolic representation in which it is the solitude that is portrayed.

In his treatment of the surfaces and elongation of the figures the inspiration he drew from Donatello emerges clearly, above all in *San Giovannino Martelli* and also, even if overall the similarities between Manzù and Arturo Martini are not that numerous, in the two pieces here, the influence of the latter's work, for example *Maternità* from 1927, is evident. Notwithstanding a different formal sensitivity, Manzù here approaches Martini's elementary dramatic sense, that world of popular and sad fairy tales typical of the poetic vein of this very great sculptor. It seems that Francesco Sassu, son of Aligi, posed for this sculpture.
Simona Pizzetti

Notes on the Restoration

Original technique
There are two statues, each 164 cm. in height with a circular base of 55 cm. and executed in klinker. The latter is a material made up of a mixture of limestone and clay fired at an extremely high temperature, reaching the beginnings of vitrification. The size of the sculptures, remarkable in ones having been fired, required that they be done as a single unfired piece. They were then cut in two so they could be hollowed out: starting from the feet, «Filemone» to a height of approx. 70 cm. and «Bauci» to approx. 60 cm., and then rejoined and fired. The different color taken on by the bases most probably also derives from problems in firing. Only on «Filemone,» on the inside of the base, does one find the inscription «1935/Mozzate/Manzù/Pasqua.» On the outside, on the

bottom of both the sculptures is stamped «Litoceramica Piccinelli Bergamo.» Very likely the sculptures originally had a patina. The darker area that perfectly delineates the neckline in «Filemone» seems intentional. Only on the «Bauci» are some traces of color found, and we do not know if this was accidental or intentional: green drops on the head, black on the thigh, yellow stripes on the guitar.

State of preservation
The state of preservation of the sculptures is good overall. The only evident damage are fractures caused by blows. In particular in the figure of «Bauci,» the dove on the head is broken in several places. It was reattached with a resin and further anchored with an iron pin. The missing pieces were integrated during a previous restoration with a material similar to papier-mâché or a type of modeling material like that used by children and amateurs, commercially sold as «Plasmolegno.» The same reintegrating materials and resin were also used on the toes of the central figure, on the animal's bottom on the right of the base, and on the left, the head of the lower figure. However, the whole head of the animal on the right of the base was missing as well as the head of the taller figure at the left of the base. Only the latter was probably reintegrated, as the presence of residue from the dripping of the resin demonstrates. Finally, in the area to the right of the base, there is a vertical fracture approx. 15 cm. high, most likely caused during the firing. The figure of «Filemone» had almost completely lost its toes that were reconstructed in papier-mâché or «Plasmolegno» or something similar. The head of the animal on the bottom left is missing. A large area at the front of the base is affected by a circular fracture with a diameter of approx. 25 cm., also most likely having occurred during firing. The fractured zone was reattached with a cement mortar during a previous restoration. On both statues there was also a deposit of atmospheric particles, primarily concentrated in the undercut zones. This weathering was also aided by the intentionally rough surfaces created by the artist for expressive reasons. Finally, present in some protruding areas are lighter-colored and smoothed out spots on the surface that may derive both from firing problems as well as a washing away by meteoric water.

Work carried out
There were two guiding principles for the work as indicated by Dr. Simona Tosini Pizzetti: substitute the previous repairs with more suitable materials but yet maintain the form, and effect a delicate cleaning.

Arturo Martini, *Maternità*, 1927

Giacomo Manzù, *Filemone*, 1932-1933, detail

Giacomo Manzù, *Bauci* at the Palazzo dell'Arte in Milan in 1933

Bronze, 59 cm.
Appearing on the bottom right is the circular stamp: «Manzù NFMM».

Aside from a previous academic *bas-relief* made during his youth in 1927, the subject of the dance step appears in Manzù's work in 1938 and 1941 following the famous precedents of Rodin and Degas, with the bozzetto for the *Ritratto di Francesca Blanc* and *Bambina che salta*, but becomes a recurring theme starting in the 1950s.

Manzù himself stated: «I created my first dance step portraying Francesca Blanc (in the 1940s). I remember that when she came to pose for me, she always brought ballet slippers. And so I had the idea of depicting her as a ballerina.» In addition to a series of small versions, there are some other very large ones, like the one in Middelheim Park in Antwerp from 1951, the one at the Zurich Kunsthaus from 1954, or the *Grande passo di danza* from 1955 in a private collection in London that is very similar to this one in the placement of the legs as well as the arms which hold up her long hair, in the slight twisting of her back and in the physiognomy which is unquestionably that of Inge, even if in this work less recognizable because of wanting to have the face smoothed out by the light.

It was in 1954, in Salzburg, that Manzù met Inge Schlabel, a ballerina called to pose for him at the Sommerakademie where the artist had agreed to give a sculpting course, an activity he continued until 1960. From that moment Inge, who became his companion in life, gave him new impetus to continue with this theme.

The most variable element, and at the same time central one in the different versions, is the position of the arms, often determinant in guaranteeing the formal balance of the composition, as in this version in which the arms counterbalance and bring into geometrical harmony the upper part of the figure with the lower part, and very effectively, inscribing it, focus attention on the face.

Simona Pizzetti

97
Giacomo Manzù. 1908-1991
Cardinale seduto
1939

Giacomo Manzù,
Grande passo di danza, 1955

Stone, 112 cm.
Bibliography: *Pittura e scultura del XX secolo, 1910-1980*, Parma, 1982, col. pl. p. 104.

Manzù wrote: «The first time I saw the Cardinals was in St. Peter's in 1934: they made an impression on me because of their rigid bodies, motionless yet vibrant with compound spirituality. I saw them as many statues, a series of lined-up cubes, and the impulse to create my version of that ineffable presence in sculpture was irresistible.»[1] The first result, that same year, was a drawing of a group of Cardinals, while the first bronze casting, later destroyed by the artist, was in 1936. Displayed at the Rome Quadriennale in 1939 was a *Cardinale* in bronze, rounded, and with a physiognomy which, while not identifiable with a particular subject, had features that were differentiated quite well and clothing with softly-defined folds. Overall, it was a figure quite removed from the increasingly simplified representations to follow with their pure and formal volumetric relationships that are, nonetheless, the prototype for the entire series of Cardinals which engaged the artist from the 1940s up to the last one done in 1960.

The artist repeated many times that this subject was singled out independently of any request or commission and bore no relation to religion, or even less, the Church. In the Cardinals, more than in any other of Manzù's works, the treatment of the surface is extremely important and significant and finds its first point of reference in the work of Medardo Rosso, in an unfolding that begins with the realization of the first works in wax and evolves until it reaches the point of breaking away, as is evident in the stylistic evolution of the Cardinals in which the effect of the light on the surfaces is completely reinterpreted, gradually distancing itself from Rosso's pragmatic Impressionism and increasingly subordinated to volumetric effects.

In the Cardinals from the 1950s, such as this one, the faces, which have become mummified, have lost any identifying features and have become increasingly closed up in themselves, solitary and solemn. Of the vestments, progressively simplified,

there remain only the cope that falls to earth in hard symmetry and the mitre, symbol of ritual authority that becomes a rigid, vertical stylization. What remains, as De Micheli wrote, is «the feeling of an irreparable absence in the most clear-cut seal of formal perfection.»
Simona Pizzetti

1. C. Brandi, *Giacomo Manzù, catalogo per le celebrazioni del suo settantesimo anno*, Florence, Giunti e Barbera, 1980, p. 156.

Giacomo Manzù, *Cardinali*, 1934

Giacomo Manzù, *Cardinale*, 1940

98
Giacomo Manzù. 1908-1991
Testa di Papa Giovanni XXIII
1963

99
Giacomo Manzù. 1908-1991
San Giorgio
1964

Gold-plated bronze, 29.5 cm.
Stamped on the back: «Manzù NFMM».

In 1958 Angelo Roncalli, from Bergamo, became pope with the name of John XXIII. The new pope had met Manzù when he was Patriarch of Venice and Manzù had been given the task of doing a portrait of the pope. As documented in the book by Curtis Bill Pepper, *Un artista e il Papa*, written on the basis of Manzù's personal reminiscences, there was a mutual sense of affinity, respect and understanding between the two. This allowed the subject for the project of the doors of San Peter's, for which Manzù had received the official commission in 1952 but which he finished only in 1964, to be changed from the original theme of «The Triumph of the Martyrs and Saints of the Church» to that of Death which the artist preferred. Here Manzù could express in the loftiest way his own feeling of admiration and affection for this pope, representing him absorbed in prayer, kneeling with his hands together and a large cope which completely covers him.

Manzù said about Pope John: «He was a man, finally a man, and this was enough for me. It is difficult to find a man! John was a man, and because of this he was also a rock of faith.» Between 1960 and the pope's death in 1963, Manzù produced seven busts, four of which he himself destroyed. Of the remaining three, two are found, respectively, in the Vatican Collection of Modern Religious Art and the San Marco Museum in Venice, and the third is the property of Mons. Loris Capovilla. Following the death of the pope, Manzù produced a number of variations of just the head, of which the one here is an example.

In this portrait, as in all Manzù's portrait work, we find the double aspect of a precise realism characterized by a skillful dismantling of the facial structure and a careful psychological investigation which here tends to depict the well-known good-naturedness and great humanity of this individual. Stylistically comparing this one with others of the artist's male portraits — for example, *Michael Park* or *Kokoschka*, also from the 1960s — here we note

surfaces which are more smoothed out done with a much softer manner and the complete absence of spatula marks. These characteristics insure that a great sense of peace and serenity emanate from the face.
Simona Pizzetti

1. C. B. Pepper, *Un artista e il Papa*, Milan, Mondadori, 1968.

Bronze, 112 cm.
Up top, level with the heart, is stamped: «Manzù NFMM».

All the warriors Manzù sculpted, including this St. George, are presented in such a way as to create a contrast between the figure positioned in a fairly monumental way and its battle dress which, instead of being rigid as it is normally, becomes soft and droops, for example the leggings and sleeves of the armor which are rolled up to the shoulder. This contrast is amplified upon until it becomes paradoxical with the hero presented half-naked who, instead of a sword, holds in his hand a strip of material (or perhaps a weapon that has dissolved like one of Dalì's timepieces?)

The expression is one of astonishment and, as always, the expressiveness of the figure is remarkable. In this case, in which the eyes are hinted at by just a very slight indentation, one has the sense of a complete defeat and, since St. George is a victorious hero, Manzù clearly wants to suggest the idea that in all battles, man, crushing underfoot his own humanity, is always the loser. In the sculptor's iconography always we find a greater sense of heroism in the figure of a farmer who works the earth with a spade, than in that of a soldier, so as to emphasize and reaffirm life as opposed to death and violence.

The appeal of Manzù's sculpture often arises from this poetic sense of his, from his belief, as De Micheli has written, in man: «Believing in man means speaking to man, finding the terminology of a non-heremetic and non-aristocratic language, lofty in the clearness of its plastic manifestations, but free of any formal rhetoric, even the best and most ingenious, that is difficult to elaborate just as it is always difficult to cope with the truth that the barest trifle can obscure and disturb. If there is something indescribable in Manzù's sculpture, it is this. How else can one explain his deep allure, seemingly in contradiction with the absolute and blinding clarity of the images removed from those motives which make the formal discoveries of such a large part of modern art exciting? There is no

100
Giacomo Manzù. 1908-1991
Amanti
1965

other explanation.»[1] In addition to this one, Manzù produced another *San Giorgio*, first commissioned by the Morandi sisters for the tomb of their brother, Giorgio, and which is now in the collection of the Fondazione Magnani Rocca. In this latter version, again from 1964, the saint is depicted as a young boy with drooping footgear, a sword purposely too big to be handled, and his stupefied, incredulous expression at having defeated the dragon.
Simona Pizzetti

1. M. De Micheli, *Manzù*, Milan, Fabbri Editori, 1988.

Giacomo Manzù,
San Giorgio, 1964

Bronze, 69 cm.
Stamped in back on the right: «Manzù NFMM».
Bibliography: *Manzù, Grafik 1970-72*, Staatsgalerie Moderner Kunst München, 1972, b/w pl. no. 13.

The themes of «Lovers» and «Striptease» entered into Manzù's works beginning in the mid-'60s and, in January 1967, an exhibition dedicated to the Lovers was held at the Galleria Galatea in Turin, while a noteworthy group of Stripteases was shown in March 1967 at the Galleria Marlborough in Rome. It is no accident that such vital and erotic themes appear at this moment in his life that for the artist was particularly gratifying both from the point of view of the extensive recognition and important commissions he received, such as the Rotterdam door, as well as that of his private life. Manzù himself wrote concerning these works: «Through the tight embrace in motion of the two lovers I wanted to portray the unity of two bodies which penetrate each other until they form a unified whole, exactly that image of rock which is not an inert mass but rather a concentration of power.»[1]

The *Amanti* unquestionably represents a very important stage, demonstrated by the fact that the artist produced a great number of versions in various formats and materials, including marble. As is also evident in this work, the structure is very complex and allows for, and even stimulates, the observation of extremely different points of view, and the union between the two figures is so intrinsically complete as to give way, as Brandi wrote, to a central nucleus from which spring the limbs of the man and woman as if in a new anatomical composition.[2] The man is always depicted naked, while the woman is dressed to allow the artist to so effectively use the draping of feminine clothing for formal and expressive purposes and also to enhance the eroticism of the scene.

Livia Velani wrote concerning this aspect: «The unfolding of the draping cloth becomes a fundamental compositional element in both subjects (also that of the Striptease); the interest created by

the relief of the folds which constitute a new mode of expressing himself in sculpture with strongly protruding elements, once again finds a parallel in Picasso's study of draping.»[3]
Simona Pizzetti

1. Giacomo Manzù, from the talk given in Bergamo on April 25, 1977 on the occasion of the opening of the hall at the Accademia Manzù which houses Manzù's gifts to the city of Bergamo.
2. C. Brandi, *Giacomo Manzù, esposizione per le celebrazioni del suo settantesimo anno*, Florence, 1979.
3. L. Velani, *Giacomo Manzù, Temas y Variaciones 1929-1985*, Milan, Electa, 1991.

101
Giacomo Manzù. 1908-1991
La sedia d'argento
1966

102
Giacomo Manzù. 1908-1991
Pittore con modella
1966

Gold- and silver-plated bronze, 43 x 22 cm.

The first drawing in which a straw-bottomed chair together with a human figure appears is dated 1930, while the first sculpture is from 1934. The chair no longer accompanied by the figure appears in the 1960s. There are various compositions with fruit and vegetables that are related to *Le Georgiche di Virgilio* illustrations and they were painted by Manzù in 1947. In one of these illustrations we find one of these chairs with branches, fruit and a draped cloth.

Manzù himself recalled that a Chiavari chair was part of a group of objects that had accompanied him since childhood and that a chair was the only thing inherited from his father. In the depictions of this object so dear to him, there always emerges with renewed freshness and poetry the love the artist had for daily objects worn by use. Thus the chair became the symbol of the past, of existence itself, almost taking on an archetypical meaning. With a refined randomness, the objects and still lifes reinforce with their presence this resurrection of the past: the fruit, which seems to have just been placed there, reacquires its true significance as fruit of the earth, the first nourishment. Gombrich, visiting one of Manzù's exhibits in London in the early 1960s, noticed one of these chairs with larger-than-life vegetables and wrote in the essay, «Tradizione ed espressione nella natura morta occidentale,» that what was surprising in this work was not, naturally, the attempt to render the fruit and vegetables through sculpture, but the abandoning of old modes of representing fruit belonging to the world of decoration and ornamentation that lacked a sense of permanence. Again in this case, the critic credited Manzù with a distancing from applied art in order to attain, and justly so, a true work of art.[1]
Simona Pizzetti

Giacomo Manzù, *La sedia* (*Le Georgiche di Virgilio*), 1948

1. E. H. Gombrich, *A cavallo di un manico di scopa*, Turin, Giulio Einaudi Editore, 1971.

Bronze, 68 x 100 x 65 cm.
Stamped on the right of the base: «Manzù NFMM».
Provenance: John Huston Collection, Ireland.
Exhibition: Milan, *Manzù*, Palazzo Reale, 1988-89.
Bibliography: Rewald, *Manzù*, London, Thames and Hudson, 1967, b/w pl. p. 152; *Pittura e scultura del XX secolo, 1910-1980*, 1982, col. pl. p. 105; *Manzù*, Electa, 1988, b/w pl. no. 100, p. 130.

This subject, for Manzù a kind of self-portrait, was taken on by the artist for the first time in the 1930s in some etchings and he revived it throughout his lifetime both in sculpture and paintings using various techniques: oil, tempera, charcoal, etchings, aquatints and lithographs.

In this series, in fact, we see a treatment which is more than ever connected to painting, not just from the standpoint of greater adhesion to human feelings about nature, but also from that of a choice directed towards a pictorially analytic descriptive style.

Manzù, taking advantage of this subject that allows for the creation of architectural spatiality in which the empty spaces and pauses play a fundamental role, also attains a sculpting style with decisive and clear linear interventions. If in his youthful works from the 1930s, referring fundamentally to Medardo Rosso, his painterly sense was predominantly linked to the treatment of the surfaces, in works such as this one it is primarily linked to spatial solutions.

In addition, as Livia Velani has written, « [...] the intensity of the interaction established between the artist and the woman is tied to Picasso's thematic manner and in the tension of a rapport also endlessly dwelled up and explored by the great Catalan artist.»[1] Argan also pointed out that « [...] it is this unfailing translation of the non-material image into a drawn figure that ties the knot between two artists with temperaments as dissimilar as Manzù's and Picasso's were.»[2]

Through the use of multiple variations on this theme, his compositional and technical experimentation was incessant, the latter characterized by great creative tension that manifested itself in a material molded with strong pressure from the fingertips and unexpected blows with a stick.

As for the iconography of the various realizations, Manzù sometimes represents himself fairly realistically with a solid form and often with a hat which, to tell the truth, he rarely parted with, while on other occasions, as here, he takes on completely different aspects that are idealized and almost classical. The model, on the other hand, unfailingly bears the facial traits of his wife, Inge, who played a major role in very many of his works.

The roles of the painter and model are not always as traditionally played as they are here. Sometimes the model is depicted on the painter's knee or alone, seen from behind or from the front, and other times she has at her side a chair which then takes on the importance of a real individual.
Simona Pizzetti

1. L. Velani, ed., *Giacomo Manzù, Temas y Variaciones 1929-1985*, Milan, Electa, 1991.
2. G. C. Argan, *Giacomo Manzù*, exh. cat., Florence, Contini, 1986.

103
Giacomo Manzù. 1908-1991
Grande chiave
1967

Bronze, 386 cm.
Bibliography: De Micheli, *Manzù*, 1971, b/w pl. no. 76; *Manzù*, Milan, Electa, 1988, p. 145.

The subject of the *Grande Chiave* appears for the first time at the end of the '50s in the bronze door of the Salzburg Cathedral in which the two Cardinals, St. Robert and St. Vigilio, patron saints of the city and portrayed near the bolt, act as the handle. Following the realization of the last Cardinals in the early '60s, almost always depicted standing up, tapered and extremely tall, this work represents an interpretation of the same subject at its extreme. Their reduction and loss of identity is definitive and complete and the decontextualization is so strong as to give the image an ironic connotation that is rare in Manzù's work. The subject, reduced to its minimum in the two small figures, stylized and in the distance, definitively clarifies the fact that the works in the Cardinals series never had a contextual aspect, even less so a religious one. At the most, since the Church with all its ritual had always been a part of Manzù's life right from infancy, they could have been images from his memory that underwent a rigorous examination and formal and volumetric synthesis.
Simona Pizzetti

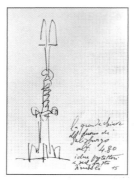

Giacomo Manzù,
Preparatory drawing of the
two patron saints for
Salzburg Cathedral, 1955

Giacomo Manzù,
Preparatory drawing,
1955

104
Giacomo Manzù. 1908-1991
Idea per un monumento
1968

Gold-plated bronze, 39 x 38 cm.
Stamped on the back of the base: «Manzù NFMM».

In 1971, the motif of drapery which had already appeared in the Rotterdam Door, took on its own formal autonomy with the completion of the giant sculpture, *Grandi pieghe*, for which this work was a *bozzetto*. In all of Manzù's work drapery was very important from a formal as well as an expressive point of view and, often very effectively portrayed the form's adherence to an emotional sensation or feeling, thus assuming symbolic connotations. One need only think of the two opposing functions of the drapery in the Cardinals in which it is depicted as a unified block with the figure and expresses separation and unreality, and in the Lovers in which it augments the dramatic and passionate potential of the work.

Compared to the final version in polyester resin eleven meters high found at the Fondazione Manzù in Ardea, this *bozzetto*, although very similar, is more twisted and tormented while the final monument, made of a more malleable and lighter material, seems to be truly inflated and pushed upwards by the wind.

The form, estranged from the countryside, takes on a metaphysical sense, a transcendental impulse, so much so that it has been seen as the fall of an angel plummeting towards earth with its long robes filled with the wind and its sumptuous and prodigious folds emitting an extraordinary allure, like something rare one sees for the last time.

This interpretation is effective, but perhaps too precise. I believe that the work strives to synthesize everything Manzù had intended expressing each time in his drapery, from the most vital energy to the funeral shrouds, and the sense of divine transcendence.
Simona Pizzetti

354

Giacomo Manzù, *Grandi pieghe*, 1971

Giacomo Manzù, *David*, 1938

Giacomo Manzù,
Porta della pace e della guerra,
bozzetto, 1965

105
Giacomo Manzù. 1908-1991
Fauno e Ninfa (bozzetto per fontana)
1968

106
Giacomo Manzù. 1908-1991
La Famiglia nel Risparmio (bozzetto)
1970

Bronze, 28 cm.
Stamped behind the figure of the faun on the left:
«Manzù NFMM».

In 1961 the artist went to the United States having received commissions for two fountains. One was realized in 1964 for the Detroit Gas Company with as its subject *Grande passo di danza*. The other, for which our work is a *bozzetto*, was done in 1968 for the McGregor Fund of the University of Detroit. Manzù introduced into this latter work motifs already amply treated in previous years: that of David crouching and the reclining female figure, uniting them into the group of the *Fauno e Ninfa*.

If David, portrayed by Manzù right from the 1930s, is one of the artist's oldest subjects, the subject of the recumbent woman is one of the ones dearest to him and was also used in monumental sculptures. The *Donna distesa* in ebony done in Gabon in 1967 was the prototype for the McGregor Fund nymph. The motif of the recumbent woman would also be the protagonist in *Guantanamera* which was copied twice in bronze, marble and again in ebony.

Our nymph here is extremely lovely, so slender and elongated, and made even more harmonious by the overall cadence of the spatial intervals created by the interstices of the three points of support. Under the faun is a stone Manzù had previously placed under his 1938 *David*. Manzù made a statement about this latter work which could also be ascribed to our faun here: «In the concentration of the entire figure in a point internal to itself, it expresses the centripetal force that has always attracted in the form and power of a stone. And he, crouched on it, is like a projection of the stone and from it receives the energy he needs and that completely pervades him.»[1]
Simona Pizzetti

1. C. Brandi, *Giacomo Manzù, esposizione per le celebrazioni del suo settantesimo anno*, Florence, 1979.

Gold-plated bronze, 34 x 92 cm.
Stamped on bottom right: «Manzù NFMM».

This is the preparatory *bozzetto* for the high relief *La Famiglia nel Risparmio* (270 x 800 cm.) Manzù was commissioned to do by the Cassa di Risparmio delle Province Lombarde in Milan.

This subject is handled emphasizing values that were very much alive for him such as familial ties and working the land, in order to have emerge the only concept of saving that was morally conceivable for him about which he stated: «I only try, in my own way, to fight against wealth and power which are the cancer of man. [...] Nonetheless, I am completely optimistic. I believe that man will soon succeed in making a new humanity [...].»

The motif of the mother lying down lifting up her child is found in two other preceding works: in a study for the Door of Salzburg Cathedral in 1956 on the subject of Love, and in the tympanum of the *Porta della Pace e della Guerra* of the church of St. Laurenz in Rotterdam. In all of the versions, in which the mother bears Inge's features, great emphasis is given on the left to the drapery, marked by deep folds, which rhythmically scans the space and confers on this section a great sense of movement in contrast with the contemplative stasis of the standing figure on the right. It has been noted by Cesare Brandi how in his high reliefs Manzù revived the Renaissance tradition of Donatello and Francesco di Giorgio, not through specific references but in their cadence, spatiality and rhythm. This *bozzetto*, while very similar to the final version in its spatial dynamic and definition of themes, stylistically presents a softer sculpting style compared to the jutting, dry and cutting plasticity of the final result. Overall, this piece demonstrates the great rigor and care with which the artist worked in all phases of the planning and elaboration of a work.
Simona Pizzetti

107
Giacomo Manzù. 1908-1991
Muro di Odissea
1985

Gold-plated bronze, 76 x 185, 29 cm.
Stamped behind on the right: «Manzù NFMM».
Bibliography: De Micheli, *Manzù*, Turin, Fabbri Editori, 1988, pp. 211 and 212, b/w ill.

Manzù offered once again in paratactical order some of the characters that recur most often in his work, presenting them as if lined up on stage at the end of a performance. The figures are reinterpreted through *The Odyssey*. We recognize the warrior with his drooping leggings very similar to the *San Giorgio* in the Magnani Collection, the Chiavari chair with draped cloth and the Striptease.

Part of the work's appeal lies precisely in the recognizability of these figures who seem to be reciting new and different roles. From this standpoint the extremely intelligent and measured study of the positioning of the characters is extraordinary and seems to suggest for each of them their stage entrances and exits at different moments. Note, from this standpoint, the lovely figure of the woman on the right who, with her knee bent and foot off the ground, indicates that she has just arrived, while the naked figure with its back turned, having recited its part, exits. And so, the immobility suggested at first glance by the parataxis, is masterfully and completely surmounted by the artist in a very refined and complex dynamic. The work is characterized by an extremely well-calculated rhythm in the spatial rapport between the figures which thus take on a truly musical lightness.

Two very similar versions of the *Muro di Odissea* exist, but in them the depiction of the warrior on the extreme left is completely different. In the version in the Barilla Collection it loses its resemblance to the Greek hero and takes on that of the young, lost warrior with the sagging leggings. We know that Manzù drew the inspiration for this figure from his son Mileto wearing his soccer shinguards.

In an essay dedicated to the other version of this work, Brandi wrote: «The figures are small, but not extremely small, of gold-plated bronze which dif-fuses a tender and pallid light as if invisible clouds interposed themselves between us and them: they are images which, at the same time, are precise and fleeting, ephemeral and corporeal, cast in light more than in bronze. They keep their distance, as close as we come we never see them up-close, and yet certain details clearly emerge as if, instead of being in relief, they were marked by a graver. [...] These are in fact Manzù's qualities, but of Manzù at his best, in this world of tragedy in which poetry does not seem to have a place, in which all the branches of art dry up like rivers that never reach the sea.»[1]
Simona Pizzetti

1. C. Brandi, *Scritti sull'arte contemporanea II*, Turin, Einaudi, 1979, p. 43.

Giacomo Manzù, *Il muro di Odissea*, the other version

108
Reg Butler. 1913-1981
Girl (Chrysanthemum)
1959

Bronze, 56 cm.
Casting of eight copies.
Signed and numbered on the back of the base: «RB 5/8»; written on the base: «F. Pace» (?).
Provenance: Galleria Toninelli, Milan.
Exhibitions: Rome, Galleria L'Obelisco, *Reg Butler*, inaug. March 11, 1961, no. 1 (b/w ill., erroneously as no. 3); New York, Pierre Matisse Gallery, *Reg Butler, Recent Sculpture (1959-1962)*, October 30-November 17, 1962, no. 14 (b/w ill. in cat.).

Responding to some questions posed to him by critic Addison Franklin Page about his work, Butler said that in the course of his life he had had in mind a very limited number of sculptures: «a girl figure — usually standing — a man [...], a kite figure — 'figure in space' — St. Catherine (associated very often with a wheel) and boxes.»[1] The girl figures in bronze done by Butler during the 1950s follow a limited number of typological schemata, one of which is exemplified by the *Girl (Chrysanthemum)*. It forms an upturned pyramid and is caught in a moment of muscular tension.[2] «There is a feeling of effort and closely-knit dynamism in all of Butler's figures and in this sense they are all prisoners; the spirit is prisoner to the body, the body is prisoner to the clothes. But they are escaping; they are escaping upwards, they are stretching on the slender legs that are reduced to simple points.»[3] The composition of these figures is not radically removed from that of Butler's sculpture before the 1950s: «the drive to make objects which are the opposite of pyramids remains constant,» Butler wrote. «It seems to me, looking back, that one very enduring formal arrangement is the one where the mass at the base is a minimum whereas at the top of the sculpture the mass is either greatest — or if not, is intensified in some other way by energy forms: faces, that look upwards vertically, arms and clothes that make dynamic configurations.»[4] If these are the elements of continuity, the change in the sculptor's output during the course of the '50s consists in the accentuation of the weight of the figures. This should be seen in relationship to the use of bronze, while previously he had favored

109
Andrea Cascella. 1920-1990
Aurora
1989

110
Pietro Cascella. 1921
Oracolo
1974

forged or soldered iron, with much more linear results. There is also an intensification of the intermittent luminousness of the surface which somewhat calls to mind the effects obtained by Giacometti, a sculptor Butler admired very much.[5] The subject of the female nude is also connected to Butler's passion for certain pre-historic Venuses, like the Willendorf and Lespugue Venuses. According to the artist: «These Venuses [...] describe the kind of sculpture which is most properly defined by the word 'sculpture': plastic forms which arise naturally from the act of shaping as opposed to the act of assemblage, or those forms which are involved in images which transmit their power through the direct imitation of nature.»[6]
Claudio Zambianchi

1. Butler in New York 1962.
2. R. Calvocoressi, «Reg Butler: The Man and The Work» in London, Tate Gallery, Reg Butler, exh. cat., November 16, 1983-January 15, 1984, p. 29.
3. A. Clarke in Rome 1961.
4. Butler in New York 1962.
5. Calvocoressi 1983-84, p. 19.
6. R. Butler, «The Venus of Lespugue and Other Naked Ladies» in London 1983-84, pp. 35-36.

Portuguese marble, 53 x 46 x 20 cm.
Provenance: the artist.
Exhibitions: Rome, Galleria l'Isola, Andrea Cascella: Sculture in pietra, December 1989-January 1990 (b/w ill. in cat.); Teramo, Nuovo Museo Archelogico, Scultori in Abruzzo: Andrea Cascella, Pietro Cascella, Mario Ceroli, Venanzo Crocetti, April 7-May 20, 1990, no. 3 (b/w ill. in cat.).

«One must work quite a bit before arriving at the conclusion,» Andrea Cascella stated.[1] From this comes the formal rigor that marks Aurora, based on «an interlocking form in which individual elements pursue and link up with each other in the harmony of an invented and contrived juncture.»[2] It is a sculpture based on thought, of a fundamentally «classical» inspiration. This classicism is based not only on the ancients, but also on some leading figures in modern sculpture. The influences on Cascella have been traced back by Luciano Caramel to a syncretism between a «geometric-constructionist heredity» and an «abstract organic unity,» with a special proclivity for Arp.[4] In the smoothness of the forms and the upward motion which distinguishes them, one can also see something of Brancusi. The refinement with which the surface is treated implies a particular love for the material: «In fact, the great secret of sculpture, other than inventing the forms, is that of making the material live, exploiting it with great respect.»[5] This respect, according to Piero Dorazio, drives Cascella to the point that his sculptures seem to be born from the «conglomeration of the molecules that [...] make up the material used.»[6]
Claudio Zambianchi

1. L. Sala Luraghi, «Il fascino discreto degli scalpellini» in Milan, Studio Reggiani, Andrea Cascella: Il corpo della scultura, Proposte e ipotesi, L. Caramel, ed., exh. cat., inaug. May 31, 1990.
2. G. Accame, «Vicino all'origine» in Rome 1989-1990.
3. L. Caramel, Andrea Cascella: Il corpo della scultura, Proposte e ipotesi in Milan 1990.
4. Ibid.
5. Sala Luraghi 1990.
6. Quoted in Caramel 1990.

Travertine, 220 x 450 x 650 cm.
Exhibition: Bologna, Galleria Forni, Comune di Bologna, Quartiere Galvani, Pietro Cascella, October 5-25, 1974 (b/w ill., full figure and 4 details).[1]
Bibliography: Pietro Cascella, (text by R. Sanesi), Vimercate, Vanessa Edizioni, col. pl. no. 10, b/w pl. no. 15; A. Del Guercio, Undici artisti italiani: L'apporto delle generazioni «di mezzo» all'arte italiana dal 1955 ad oggi nella ricerca di quattro scultori e sette pittori, Verona, Edizioni OGAM, 1976, full figure b/w ill. p. 103, color detail p. 105; La Vernice, year 23, no. 5, October-November 1984, cover ill.; «Della severa affettuosità: Dialogo di Pietro Cascella con Manuela Crescentini» in Siena, Palazzo Pubblico, Magazzini del Sale, La scultura di Pietro Cascella: i segni della memoria dell'uomo, exh. cat., June 27-September 16, p. 21; Forte dei Marmi, Galleria Comunale d'Arte Moderna, Pietro Cascella: Distesa Estate, exh. cat., August 2-31, 1986 (Fabbri Editori), b/w ill. p. 41; L. Quaroni, R. Sanesi, E. Crispolti, Pietro Cascella: Opere 1946-1986, Milan, Edizioni L'Agrifoglio, 1986, b/w ill. pp. 122-123; P. Zumerle, «L'autore che in marmo e travertino fa tornare in vita l'età megalitica,» L'informatore del marmista, year 30, no. 356, August 1991, p. 60, ill. p. 62; P. Cascella, Parole Pietre, S. Bondi, ed., Florence, Ponte alle Grazie, 1992, b/w ill. pp. 46-47.

«The real question is to involve people. I think the most important aspect of my sculpture, what truly is mine, is involving people in the work, having them become simultaneously actor-spectators inserted into the sculptural work as in the theater. For this reason I have done a work called Oracolo in which one participates by speaking, by consulting the sculpture itself.»[2] This is the way Pietro Cascella explained to critic Manuela Crescentini the reason for the creation of his large sculptures which the public is not only able to look at, but also experience. For Cascella, «architecture is closely tied to sculpture, they are two things that can complement each other.»[3] Cascella's art always aspires to a monumental scale and even when, as in Oracolo, «figures» can be recognized, they are «iden-

111
Arnaldo Pomodoro. 1926
Cubo IV
1965-1975

tifiable and at the same time buried in the silence of the architectural-monumental function.»[4] Starting with the Auschwitz monument (1960-67) Cascella's sculpture presents itself as a «practicable scene tending to establish the plastic conditions of an inviting space.»[5] In this Cascella makes a conscious reference to the forms of Megalithic art, «conceived of, or reinvented, as forms of a world and human society that build in the heart of nature the very first structures in stone.»[6] Del Guercio recognizes in Cascella's forms a search for contact between man and nature of an animist inspiration.[7] It has often been pointed out that the «primitivism» of Cascella's sculpture has nothing to do with a cultured revival of models from the remote past, as happened in the avantgarde movements at the beginning of the 20th century. It is, rather, the retrieval of a sense of art that would find its relation to nature not along the road of imitation, but through the rapport between sculpture and the earth and the use of humble materials. «There is no question but that the almost constant preference for a humble and living stone like travertine takes on an intentional reference to a raw material of telluric concretion, to geologic time; in short, to a sort of primary element as a vital means, as a basic element (stone/bread), in which a daily meditation takes place, exactly in that palpitation that is the hammering of the surface in order to activate it, bring it to life, render it vibrant and involved.»[8]
Claudio Zambianchi

1. *Oracolo* was exhibited outside in Piazza S. Stefano. For a list of reviews of the exhibit in the daily press see M. Crescentini ed., «Lavori, esposizioni, note biografiche e bibliografiche» in Quaroni, Sanesi, Crispolti 1986, p. 234.
2. *Della severa affettuosità* 1984, p. 21.
3. P. Cascella, quoted in L. Quaroni, «Pietro, come lo conosco» in Quaroni, Sanesi Crispolti 1986, p. 11.
4. F. Solmi in Bologna 1974.
5. E. Crispolti, «I segni della memoria dell'uomo» in Quaroni, Sanesi, Crispolti 1986, p. 36.
6. Del Guerico 1976, p. 20.
7. *Ibid.*
8. Crispolti 1986, p. 31.

Bronze, 130 cm.
Copy no. 2 of a two-copy edition.
Provenance: Art Program s.r.l., Milan.
Exhibitions: Paris, Musée d'Art Moderne de la Ville di Paris, *Arnaldo Pomodoro: Ecritures, perforations d'objets*, September 16-October 30, 1976 (ill. nos. 25 and 26 in cat.); Atlanta, Colony Square and Georgia State University Urban Life Center, *Arnaldo Pomodoro*, June 2-July 31, 1978 (ill. no. 5 in cat.); Caracas, Museo de Bellas Artes, *Arnaldo Pomodoro*, November 1978, (ill. in cat.); Florence, Forte di Belvedere, *Arnaldo Pomodoro: Luoghi fondamentali*, July 7-October 28, 1984, Italo Mussa, cat. ed., texts by Jacqueline Risset and Mark Rosenthal and two interviews by Sam Hunter and Francesco Leonetti (ill. pp. 110-111 in cat.).
Bibliography: Sam Hunter, «Intervista con Arnaldo Pomodoro,» cat. personal show, Milan, Rotonda della Besana, June-August 1974; Sam Hunter, *Arnaldo Pomodoro*, New York, Abbeville Press, 1982, ill. p. 73; Mark Rosenthal, «The Art of Arnaldo Pomodoro: Essence and Evolution,» cat. personal touring exhibition, *Arnaldo Pomodoro: A Quarter Century*, Columbus Museum of Art, Columbus, 1983-1984, pp. 5-11, republished in cat. *Luoghi fondamentali*, Florence, 1984, pp. 29-51 (trans. by Roberto Sanesi); *Arnaldo Pomodoro al Forte di Belvedere*, Rome, De Luca Editore, 1986, ill. p. 59.

Below we have put together commentary about Pomodoro's works with quotations about them taken from passages in his writings or remarks in interviews or conversations, along with some critical comments.
«Once again Brancusi with the never-ending column; the never-ending column is a beautiful theme that fascinates me. [...] For me, the column becomes the column of the traveller; at the beginning I hadn't yet understood that my mark could be inside a volume, a solid, and so the traveller's columns are slabs and are like cuts, slices of infinity. Then it occurred to me to use a cylindrical-shaped solid and intervene with corrosion; it is strange that this operation of intervening in a solid takes place in the column before it does in the sphere since the cylinder is in the column; and immediately I recognized that this was perhaps the right road. And so I immediately made use of all the geometrical solids, the cylinder, the sphere, the cube, the pyramid.» Arnaldo Pomodoro, 1982 «Then came *La Sfera* (1963), *Il Cubo* (1964-67) and *Il Disco* (1965). Together, these sculptures represent the beginning of his mature career. Utilizing easily-understandable and universally-recognizable forms that are contained or juxtaposed, are his first personal marks. The result is the creation of his personal metaphor in which, on a large scale, the dialogue between external and internal takes place.» Mark Rosenthal, 1983 «The comparison between Pomodoro's *Cubo* and Tony Smith's *Die* (1962) highlights the position of the former with respect to the unstable tendencies of art in the 1960s. Pomodoro vacillated between Abstract Expressionism and Minimalism. Using unitary forms typical of Minimalism, he nonetheless continued to maintain the expressive and personal content of the Expressionists. The comparison demonstrates that Pomodoro was not only interested in the formal presence of the object, but also in its life and story.» Mark Rosenthal, 1983 «In *Cubo* (1971) and *Frammento* (1972) is the realm of the partisans. As inevitable as it is that this work be likened to Brancusi's *Kiss*, here it is not the affection, but the danger, that is indicated. The internal areas become the clandestine hiding places, but threatened inside the walls of an omnipresent society-structure that is often intrusive and totalitarian. On the inner side of each half of the cube there appears a small block, and at the top of *Frammento* emerge sections of rectangles. Each of these elements echoes the form of the overall mass, a phenomenon also repeated in the spheres done at the same time, in which a smaller globe is sometimes visible within the larger one. These microcosms are, in effect, the embryos or skeletons of the larger forms.»
Mark Rosenthal, 1983

112
Arnaldo Pomodoro, 1926
Sfera con sfera
1979-1980

Bronze, 250 cm.
Copy no. 2 of a two-copy edition.
Provenance: Art Program s.r.l., Milan.
Exhibitions: Kanagawa-ken (Tokyo), The Hakone Open-Air Museum, *The 2nd Henry Moore Grand Prize Exhibition*, July 4-October 31, 1981, where he received the «Henry Moore Grand Prize»; Florence, Forte di Belvedere, *Arnaldo Pomodoro: Luoghi fondamentali*, July 7-October 28, 1984, Italo Mussa, cat. ed., texts by Jacqueline Risset and Mark Rosenthal and two interviews with Sam Hunter and Francesco Leonetti (ill. pp. 112-113 in cat.).
Bibliography: Arnaldo Pomodoro interviewed by Mila Pistoi, *Marcatrè*, Milan, nos. 8-10, July-September 1964, pp. 240-241; Sam Hunter, «Intervista con Arnaldo Pomodoro,» cat. personal show, Milan, Rotonda della Besana, June-August 1974; Gualtiero Schönenberger, «Sfera con sfera» in *Una sfera di Arnaldo Pomodoro*, Lugano, Interprogramme Holding S.A., 1981 (ill. on cover and inside, incl. photos of the various phases of work on the sphere and its installation in Lugano); Sam Hunter, *Arnaldo Pomodoro*, New York, Abbeville Press, 1982, ill. p. 135; Mark Rosenthal, «The Art of Arnaldo Pomodoro: Essence and Evolution,» cat. personal touring exhibition, *Arnaldo Pomodoro: A Quarter Century*, Columbus Museum of Art, Columbus, 1983-1984, pp. 5-11, repub. in cat. *Luoghi fondamentali*, Florence, 1984, pp. 29-51 (trans. by Roberto Sanesi); *Arnaldo Pomodoro al Forte di Belvedere*, Rome, De Luca Editore, 1986, ill. pp. 23, 24, 25, 26, 27, 28, 29, 30; Arnaldo Pomodoro and Francesco Leonetti, *L'arte lunga*, Milan, Feltrinelli, 1992, pp. 109 and 118; Philippe Nys, «Célébration d'une sphère,» *Le Débat*, Paris, Ed. Gallimard, May-August 1991, pp. 88-93.

«You are speaking about my spheres; you ask what it is that moves me to make them. First of all, they are perfect, magic, and I break them in order to discover (search for, find) the internal fermentation, mysterious and living, monstrous and pure; in this way, with the smooth shininess, I provoke a contrast, a discordant tension, a completeness made up of incompleteness. With the same act I liberate myself from an absolute form. I destroy it. But I also multiply it. The work can be interpreted continuously, from day to day; and in this way one has, I believe, the best of its continuity which does not just answer to a use, but rather answers to a need to discover we all have and which is unsatisfied by industrial mechanicalness. The fact that my spheres can move and turn is important: in this way they have a 'tactile' as well as visual, value of movement and involvement.»
Arnaldo Pomodoro, 1964

«I believe that light reflections are very important. During the day, with sunlight, or in the shade, the sculptures truly change. The mirroring effects take in what surrounds them, the spectator. One can be reflected in a sphere, having one's own image distorted. This makes the sculpture alive, a part of us, of nature, wherever it is found, whether in a park, a garden or in the city.»
Arnaldo Pomodoro, 1974

«The sphere is the universe, the world is in fact depicted in this way, by the sphere, in an experience I was able to create in the theater, the final representation in which the mother is killed, I portrayed it all not in an underground grave, but rather in a piece of this terrestrial surface and the result was that the characters walked on the spherical surface; the sphere is probably also this.»
Arnaldo Pomodoro, 1982

«I have always been fascinated by primordial designs, just as one is fascinated by some drawings done by children as they are just beginning to write. And this is, I believe, the same curiosity Paul Klee had.

«Cuttlebone was a revelation for me. I began my sculpture, without being aware of it, incising cuttlebone, leaving the pattern of cuttlebone. This organic unity, together with the mark, surprised me. I accepted cuttlebone in its human form, as if it were a kind of shell in which I myself could end up inside.

«Following the relief and thinking of Brancusi and, above all, the Constructivists, I thought of using the geometric solids: the column, the sphere, the cube, the pyramid and their variants. I am curious to corrode these elements, to enter into them, investigate them, go right inside and thus give life to this form, this solid.»
Arnaldo Pomodoro, 1990

113
Augusto Perez. 1929
Narciso (Grande Narciso)
1966

114
Mario Ceroli. 1938
Cavallo
1984-1985

Bronze, 185 x 147 x 96 cm.
Signed on the bottom of the oval: «Perez»; on the base is the mark of the foundary: «Chiurazzi Napoli».
Exhibitions: Venice, *33a Biennale Internazionale d'Arte*, June 18-October 16, 1966, no. 11 (Perez personal show; b/w ill. no. 92 in cat.); Rome, Galleria il Fante di Spade, *Augusto Perez*, March 18-April 7, 1967, no. III (b/w ill. no. 3 and before the text in cat.); Turin, Galleria Galatea, *Augusto Perez*, December 1-23, 1967, no. 4 (b/w ill. in cat.); Milan, Finarte, *Augusto Perez*, April 20-June 30, 1968, 1968, no. 13 (b/w ill. in cat.).
Bibliography: C. Brandi in Venice 1966, pp. 84-85; V. Corbi in Rome, 1967; V. Corbi, «Appunti per una lettura critica della Dafne» in Turin 1967; P. Bucarelli, *Scultori italiani contemporanei*, Milan, Aldo Martello, 1967, p. 12, ill no. 4, p. 202; M. Valsecchi in Milan 1968, p. 5; Carlo Volpe, «Che cosa dice lo specchio di Perez,» *Arte Illustrata*, nos. 3-4, March-April 1968, pp. 49-53, b/w ill. p. 50; V. Corbi in Rome, Galleria il Fante di Spade, *Augusto Perez: Bronzi 1973-1974*, exh. cat., inaug. November 28, 1974; G. di Genova, *Le realtà del fantastico: L'arte fantastica italiana del dopoguerra*, Rome, Editori Riuniti, 1975, b/w ill. no. 135; V. Corbi, *Perez*, Turin, Edizioni d'arte F.lli Pozzo, 1976, pp. 7-8, b/w ill. no.3, p. 21; M. de Micheli, «La scultura del Novecento,» *Storia dell'arte in Italia*, F. Bologna curator, Turin, UTET, 1981, p. 250; G. di Genova, *Storia dell'arte italiana del '900 per generazioni: Generazione anni Venti*, Bologna, Edizioni Bora, 1991, pp. 318-19, b/w ill. no. 459, p. 319.

This is one of Perez's most famous sculptures and was shown for the first time at the 33rd Venice Biennale in a personal show dedicated to the artist introduced by Cesare Brandi. At the time, the critic dwelled upon the novelty of the theme of mirrors in sculpture, interpreting this work as a «harsh dialectic against reality today, the hopes that cannot be raised and the trust in the world that has been disillusioned.»[1]
In reality — in the light of repeated statements by the artist — such a negative interpretation must be

corrected and expanded upon. In fact, according to Perez, sculpture is set in a state of constant tension between aspiring to the «ideal» form and the just as constant impossibility of achieving it. It is not the exploration of a point of synthesis between the absolute space of the geometrical volumes towards which sculpture, according to Perez, necessarily tends, and «contamination with reality,» also just as inevitable. It is, rather, «the aspiration towards an idea that does not tolerate compromises.»[2]
Perez continuously attests to the difficulty of taking on in modern sculpture the theme of the human figure which is understood plastically and this way of feeling is «explicitly made into a theme in the Narcissus in which [...] the image of man that the mirror sends back, mutilated and uncertain and yet so intense and pulsating with life, is, at the same time, the image of sculpture, or better, its present difficult condition.»[3]
Therefore, there exists in Perez a coexistence of opposing impulses, of «triumphs of death» and «triumphs of life,»[4] while the feeling of the simultaneous presence of time past and time present pushes him to make continuous reference to the mythological theme: «Perez's sculpture [...] chases after [...] its own horizon [...] of existential continuity at that level in which «history» is concurrent with existence, not so much in order to deny the present, but more to collapse the contingent and ephemeral present into a deeper and immemorial continuity which (and Perez said this mentioning Eliot's essay on tradition) is exactly this existential, and certainly not historical, simultaneity of the present and the past that is remote, very remote, mythical.»[5]
Claudio Zambianchi

1. C. Brandi in Venice 1966, pp. 84-85.
2. «Il mito nello spazio del presente,» conversation between V. Corbi and Augusto Perez in Rome, Galleria il Fante di Spade, *Augusto Perez*, exh. cat., inaug. February 6, 1969.
3. Corbi 1974.
4. G. Testori in Turin 1966.
5. E. Crispolti in Bologna, Galleria d'Arte Forni, *Augusto Perez*, exh. cat., March 13-26, 1971.

Bronze, 275 cm.
Casting of three copies from a model taken from the original in wood in the artist's possession.

«Full relief» appears in Ceroli's sculptures of the last decade alongside the silhouettes in wood. This new aspect does, in reality, have a precedent, as Fulvio Abbate has pointed out, in the «overlapping play» and «dislocation of planes» that appeared in the *Omaggio a Leonardo* or the *Collezionista* (1966), legacies of «Cubist analytical style.» «Of course,» Abbate notes, «the *Cavallo* (1985) marks the plastic and representative totality of the sculptural volume. But the analytical intent remains intact, one only need observe the detail in the head in which the physiognomical details are deduced from the scansion between empty and filled areas.»[1] Generally in silhouettes, one opts to synthesize the figures as if they were longitudinal sectional views, giving the maximum information while taking up the least amount of space. Here, on the other hand, the point of view turns and the horse takes on a third dimension through the depiction in space of the various planes which constitute it, almost as if it were the *écorché* of the «slices» of space that constitute the animal in movement. It is a process already used in the «'large heads' of the ancient heroes between metaphysical and classicism, layered, excavated and recomposed by a powerful plastic instinct which only has its equal in Moore [...] in terms of its articulation and compactness.»[2] In the translation of wood into bronze a monumental intent must be recognized. Nonetheless, there also seems to be present a subtle desire to practice, with an alchemic flavor, the transformation of one substance into another.
Claudio Zambianchi

1. F. Abate, «Traccia di lettera per Ceroli» in Viterbo, Palazzo degli Alessandri, *Ceroli*, exh. cat., January 18-February 18, 1986.
2. M. Calvesi, «Rileggere Mario Ceroli» in Florence, Forte di Belvedere, *Ceroli*, M. Calvesi, ed., exh. cat., July 14-October 16, 1983 [Usher], p. 17.

115
Giuliano Vangi. 1931
La campagna
1979

116
Giuliano Vangi. 1931
Donna vestita di azzurro
1991

Bronze, 40.5 x 84.5 x 79.5 cm.
Signed on the left side of the base: «Vangi 79».
Provenance: Galleria La Sanseverina, Parma.
Exhibitions: Rimini, Centro storico, *Giuliano Vangi*, July-September 1979 (b/w ill. in cat.); Florence, Giardino delle Oblate, *Giuliano Vangi: Sculture 1972-1980*, S. Salvi, curator, June 14-September 7, 1980 (b/w ill. pp. 52-53, details in cat.); Prato, Galleria Metastasio, *Giuliano Vangi*, April 1981 (b/w ill. no. 53, full view and no. 54, detail in cat.); Busto Arsizio, Galleria d'Arte Bambaia, *Giuliano Vangi: Sculture e disegni 1978-1982*, May 22-June 27, 1982 (b/w ill. in cat.); Parma, Consigli Arte, *Giuliano Vangi*, January 29-March 5, 1983 (b/w ill. p. 32, detail and p. 33, full view in cat.).

This work depicts the love between a man and woman, one in the arms of the other and both in nature's embrace. The «growing rapport with nature» is the characteristic that distinguishes Vangi's sculpture throughout the '70s, while previously the figure was seen «subjugated and imprisoned.»[1] *La campagna* is part of a group of works in which Vangi originally concentrated greatly on the relationship between figures and the base, transforming the support into countryside. This countryside becomes, as Pier Carlo Santini noted, the «habitat» of the figures, the «site of [their] life [...]. In it the figures not only find their place, but become concrete and, like trees, sink their roots into the earth.»[2] Figures and countryside exist in the same shining and smooth material, a bronze which differentiates itself in sinuous and organic volumes which reveal great mastery in the medium. Vangi is, in fact, a sculptor who converses familiarly with a great number of different materials.

    There is nothing anecdotal in this sculpture: as often happens in Vangi, it assumes, instead, a metaphorical value, «unquestionably a metaphor that refers to the substance of life, where the rapport between man and nature, nature and existence, existential truth and enigmas of our fate tend to reveal themselves instead of eluding the questions that surround us.»[3] Roberto Tassi, who has written about the *Campagna* on two different occasions,

insists on the necessity of not interpreting this work from a narrative standpoint. Rather, what must be recognized is its capacity to «assume the narrative within the plastic absolute, meld bodies and material, air and form, capture the sense of nature in the man-nature relationship [...]; in this work the cosmic nature of the love act is expressed, the union between man and woman, since the two lovers are flat on the earth, confused with it and emerging from it in a finite non-finite that makes them like the hills and rocks, and the fusion of the two bodies becomes a universal fusion.»[4]
Claudio Zambianchi

1. G. Testori, *Giuliano Vangi*, Milan, Fabbri Editori, 1989 (published on occasion of the exhibition: Turin, Palazzo del Valentino, *Giuliano Vangi*, December 2, 1989-January 28, 1990), p. 10.
2. P. C. Santini in Montecatini, Galleria l'Affresco, *Giuliano Vangi*, exh. cat., April-May 1982.
3. M. de Micheli, «I marmi di Vangi» in Milan, Appiani Arte Trentadue, *Giuliano Vangi: Sculture in marmo e disegni*, exh. cat., October 19-December 14, 1991.
4. Tassi in Busto Arsizio 1982.

White marble, volcanic stone from Vesuvius, blue Bahia granite, 174 x 50 x 42 cm.
Signed and dated on the back of the base: «Vangi 91».
Exhibition: Bologna, Galleria d'Arte Forni-Scultura, *Giuliano Vangi*, November 23, 1991-January 14, 1992 (b/w ill. p. 24, detail, p. 25, full view in cat.).

In recent years, the motif of the female figure, naked or clothed, has been developed by Vangi with constancy and richness of solutions.[1] The figure is a plastic block of extraordinary cohesion and synthesis, characteristics that Maurizio Calvesi has traced back to a «Giotto-esque» inspiration (Vangi, like Giotto, comes from Mugello): «As in some of Giotto's images, out of a block admirably sealed in its geometric turgidity of humanity powerfully internalized and solidified or built upon itself, only the head springs out.»[2] It is as if, in this very advanced process of formalization, the figure lost a bit of its human characteristics in order to get closer to the image of the earthly female deities and that, structurally, the «volumes [were] coordinated in a system of contrasts and juxtapositions that are more of telluric than an anthropic nature.»[3] A mass such as that of the *Donna vestita di azzurro* creates empty space around itself. The polish of the material does not capture the light, but rather reflects it off the clean and shining surfaces. The color is incorporated into the plastic block through the use of various types of stone which behave differently in the surrounding light. But the contrast between the materials is so strong that it is shocking and surprising to the observer, especially in the differentiation between the diaphanous face treated with the virtuosity of Wildt (a name that appears often among the critics of Vangi), and the masses of hair and the body. In this surprising effect, Erich Steingräber recognizes a Surrealistic ancestry: «The Surrealistic imagination would like to populate the world with shocking effects that take shape. The everydayness of an object is thus dramatized in the unusual.»[4] It is, nonetheless, an influence circumscribed with respect to the central theme which is

117
Giuliano Vangi. 1931
Il nodo (bozzetto)
1992

118
Giuliano Vangi. 1931
Il nodo
1993

exquisitely sculptoreal in the traditional sense of the term in this work: the creation of a statue with a solid «corporeal architecture, without waste.»[5]
Claudio Zambianchi

1. See E. Carli in Bergamo, Chiesa di Sant'Agostino, *Giuliano Vangi*, exh. cat., March 2-April 20, 1991.
2. M. Calvesi in Naples, Castel Sant'Elmo, *Vangi a Castel Sant'Elmo*, exh. cat., May 19-June 30, 1991, p. 15.
3. P. C. Santini in Bologna 1991-1992, p. 9.
4. E. Steingräber, introduction in G. Testori, *Giuliano Vangi*, Milan, Fabbri Editori, 1989 (published on occasion of the exhibition in Turin, Palazzo del Valentino, *Giuliano Vangi*, December 2, 1989-January 28, 1990).
5. Carli 1991.

Bronze and nickel alloy, 92.5 x 73.5 x 72.5 cm.
Signed on the back of the base: «Vangi 92».
Provenance: the artist.

This man and woman running are the *bozzetto* for a monument commissioned from Giuliano Vangi by Pietro Barilla in 1992 for the Pedrignano factory. The theme had previously been taken on by the sculptor in a bronze in 1988. While for the final monument a number of different materials were used, for the *bozzetto* the artist limited himself to two metals — nickel and bronze, one for the exposed areas and the other for the cloth — and developed the problem of the way the light reacts through a fabric of extremely rich surfaces. It is a radical change from the closed plastic block of the *Donna vestita di azzurro* and it is Vangi's preferred modality for his «dramatic images of life [...], rendered with the thick and encrusted irregularity of the shaping in a sort of centrifugation of the spatial lines.»[1] With respect to the sculptures in which the figure takes on a fixed, architectural and immobile aspect, here there is the search for greater naturalism that finds its confirmation in the glorification of the mutability of the light and the movement of the figures, a movement that is particularly evident in the female figure with her long scarf in the wind and just one foot on the base.
Claudio Zambianchi

1. M. Calvesi in Naples, Castel Sant'Elmo, *Vangi a Castel Sant'Elmo*, exh. cat., May 19-June 30, 1991, p. 19.

Stainless steel, 180 x 146 cm.
Provenance: the artist.

Technical data and materials: Casting in stainless steel 316 L carried out in the Fonderia Artistica Verrés in Verrés (Aosta). Inserts in pure gold and alloy. Eyes in semi-precious stone: for the woman, pupil in pyrolusite, iris in Afghan lapislazuli, cornea in Brazilian shell; in the man, pupil in pyrolusite, iris in Chinese jade, cornea in Brazilian shell.

Since during the preparation of the catalogue the work was still being cast, the illustration here is of the plaster model.

Giuliano Vangi,
Il nodo, 1993 (plaster model)

Index of artists

Printed in June 1993
by Artegrafica Silva, Parma
Printed in Italy